H TO SYST P9-AFT-443

1992

01

DATE DUE

JE 2 8 '93			
JA 7 '95			
AR 1 0 '95			

DEMCO 38-296

A STRUCTURED APPROACH
TO SYSTEMS DEVELOPMENT

THE McGRAW-HILL INTERNATIONAL SERIES IN SOFTWARE ENGINEERING

Consulting Editor

Professor D Ince
The Open University

Other titles in this series

Portable Modula-2 Programming
Woodman, Griffiths, Souter and Davies
SSADM: A Practical Approach
Ashworth and Goodland
Software Engineering: Analysis and Design
Easteal and Davies
Introduction To Compiling Techniques
Bennett
An Introduction to Program Design
Sargent
Object Oriented Databases
Brown
Object Oriented Software Engineering with C++
Ince
Expert Database Systems
Beynon-Davies
Practical Formal Methods with VDM
Andrews and Ince
SSADM Version 4: A Users Guide
Eva

Forthcoming titles

Introduction to VDM
Woodman and Heal
Rapid Information Systems Development
Bell and Wood-Harper
Software Engineering Environments
Brown, Earl and McDermid
Introduction to Software Project Management
Ince, Sharp and Woodman
Systems Construction and Analysis
Fenton and Hill

A STRUCTURED APPROACH TO SYSTEMS DEVELOPMENT

Gary Heap

John Stanway and

Alfie Windsor

McGRAW-HILL BOOK COMPANY

London · New York · St Louis · San Francisco · Auckland · Bogotá · Caracas · Hamburg
Lisbon · Madrid · Mexico · Milan · Montreal · New Delhi · Panama · Paris
San Juan · São Paulo · Singapore · Sydney · Tokyo · Toronto

Riverside Community College
Library
4800 Magnolia Avenue
Riverside, California 92506

APR '93

Published by
McGRAW-HILL Book Company Europe
Shoppenhangers Road, Maidenhead, Berkshire, SL6 2QL, England
Tel 0628 23432; Fax 0628 770224

British Library Cataloguing in Publication Data

Heap, Gary S., *1957–*
    A structured approach to systems development.
    I. Title   II. Stanway, John, *1942–*
    III. Windsor, A. T.
    004

    ISBN 0–07–707483–1

Library of Congress Cataloging-in-Publication Data

Heap, Gary, 1957–
    A structured approach to systems development / Gary Heap, John
Stanway, and Alfie Windsor.
        p. cm.
    Includes bibliographical references and index.
    ISBN 0–07–707483–1 : £35.00
    1. System design.   2. Electronic data processing–Structured
techniques. I. Stanway, John, 1942–   II. Windsor, Alfie, 1949–
. III. Title.
    QA76.9.S88H42   1992
    005.1–dc20   91–40020
                                                            CIP

Copyright © 1992 McGraw-Hill International (UK) Limited. All rights reserved. No part of this
publication may be reproduced, stored in a retrieval system, or transmitted, in any form or by any
means, electronic, mechanical, photocopying, recording, or otherwise, without the prior permission
of McGraw-Hill International (UK) Limited.

1234 HWV 9432

Typeset by TecSet Ltd, Wallington, Surrey

Printed and bound in Great Britain by
BPCC Hazells Ltd
Member of BPCC Ltd

CONTENTS

Contents xi

TRADEMARKS

SSADM: is the copyright of the Crown.

LSDM: is the copyright of LBMS plc.

PRISM: is the copyright of Hoskyns plc and LBNS plc.

IE: is the copyright of JMA plc.

PREFACE

And in the beginning there was chaos . . .

The computer industry evolves at a tremendous pace, and some areas evolve more rapidly than others: hardware obsolescence for example should become part and parcel of the Oxford English Dictionary! However, amid the emergence of standards, the divergence of standards, the enabling technologies and, unfortunately, the disabling technologies, one factor remains constant — people.

People are complex and no two are exactly the same. The same may be said of a business; when the two need to work together there are problems. When this also requires the use of business aids, such as machines, it further compounds the problem.

The authors have offered a solution to the problems of people, business and machines. They have a natural empathy with their problems because they too have faced similar problems. The method contained in this publication is a framework to offer practical assistance in the complexities of people, business and machines within the context of information technology (IT).

The very nature of this book should ensure that it addresses the needs of all types of people involved in information technology. This covers 'What do I really need for the business?' to 'How can I possibly achieve it?' It will be a practical guide for managing directors, chief executive officers, directors, business managers, data processing people and also the education sector, universities, polytechnics and colleges of further education.

PART 1

THE BOOK

Part 1 contains a description of the Winway method. It describes why a comprehensive method is needed.

1

INTRODUCTION

This chapter provides an overview of the book's contents. It covers all aspects of information systems development, from strategic information systems planning to system evolution and replacement policy. It introduces and discusses the concept of total quality in relation to the scope of, and investigates why there is a need for a fully integrated approach to, the software life cycle. The final section outlines the answer to the need. It outlines the Winway method for a fully integrated approach to strategic planning and systems construction through to production.

1.1 OBJECTIVES OF THE BOOK

This section contains a brief summary of the structure and scope of this book. The objectives are as follows.

- To offer a procedural and structural framework which integrates all phases of the information systems development life cycle. This begins with strategic information systems planning and ends with individual system evolution and replacement policy.
- To build a definitive framework around existing approaches to structured systems analysis and design. This provides a complementary rather than a competing approach to established analysis and design methods.
- To provide the total quality management system (TQMS) to support the method. A critical goal is the provision of a quality and documentation continuum for monitoring, tracing and controlling project quality and documentation.

1.2 BOOK STRUCTURE

The book is divided into three parts. These are: Part 1: Principles; Part 2: Reference; Part 3: Techniques and documentation.

Part 1: Principles explains the fundamental concepts of a total life cycle approach to software engineering. It addresses specific issues such as the origins and need for an engineered product. It also provides a lucid insight into the origins and traceability of structured analysis and design methods and the constant demand for quality systems.

Part 2: Reference is the main body of the work and provides a comprehensive reference guide to the whole method. This includes strategic planning (i.e. what information systems does the business really need), analysis and design (of the information systems) through to construction and ultimately production of those systems. There is also a detailed chapter on the quality and documentation continuum, i.e. not just a system but the right system, right every time.

Part 3: Techniques and documentation provides an outline of the commonly used techniques recommended in Winway; techniques specific to Winway; outline contents lists for all the major documents recommended by Winway.

There is a clear relationship between Parts 1, 2 and 3 of the book. Each major area of the work has an interlinking thread from principles through to the detailed reference, and supporting techniques and documentation. As an illustration of this link, the principles of strategic planning are explained in Part 1, Chapter 2, the detailed reference work is contained in Part 2, Chapter 6 and the supporting techniques and documentation are in Chapters 10, 11 and 12 of Part 3.

The major areas, their links and chapters are defined in Fig. 1.1.

Major area	Principles, Part 1	Reference, Part 2	Techniques and documentation, Part 3
Strategic planning	2	6	10, 11, 12
Analysis and design	3	7	10, 11, 12
Construction to production	4	8	10, 11, 12
Quality and documentation	5	9	10, 11, 12

Figure 1.1 Structure of the book.

1.2.1 Physical structure of the contents

Each of the chapters contains one major topic, and as an *aide-memoire* the methods logo is printed at the beginning of each chapter. The part of the method being addressed by that chapter is shaded, for example in Chapter 2 the strategic planning portion of the logo is shaded (see Fig. 1.2).

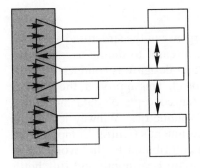

Figure 1.2 Logo 'Strategic planning

1.3 THE EVOLUTION OF STRUCTURED METHODS

The major historic events in computing have focused on attempts (with varying degrees of success) to further understand the problem of building systems. Often the answers were elegant, and offered solutions to the perceived problem as understood *at that time*. However, in most instances the 'problem' was not actually a problem but rather a symptom of the real underlying problem. Gradually, over a period of some 20 years, better solutions have evolved but the problem has not yet been solved, nor has it gone away!

The need for a fully integrated approach can be demonstrated by examining the history of the problem.

1.3.1 Structured programming

The image many people outside the computing industry have of computing ranges from 'people with white coats' to 'very mathematical'. The stereotype image is of course quite different from reality. The origins of computing were of scientific staff, often in physics or mathematics disciplines, programming in machine code or even the luxury of an assembler language. As organizations realized the potential of computing, things had to change. Higher level languages such as Cobol, Pascal and Fortran began to dissolve the 'white coats and mathematics' images, but brought along their own problems. More was expected from computing, which failed to deliver.

At this time, structured programming began to evolve as a technique, the most influential being Jackson's structured programming approach[1]. The premise was simple: there are problems with programs, so the way we program must be wrong, therefore we will adopt a more rigorous approach. The result was good, well structured and documented programs, but although the programmers had produced an elegant design and implementation they had only a poor perception of what the requirement really was. There was no mechanism for communication. Users spoke userease, computer people computerease. There was no foundation, no starting point, no mutual understanding of the problem and no end point. There was no common ground to provide the firm foundation upon which to build systems and hence fulfil requirements.

1.3.2 Structured methods

The late seventies and early eighties witnessed the emergence of the structured approach to systems analysis and design. One, if not the first, attempt to define a systematic, objectively based and controlled approach to analysis and design was conducted by the authors in 1973, on a very large Ministry of Defence project. This approach, the Winway Methodology as it later became known, introduced the concepts of data modelling, process profiles, access path analysis and the use of volumetrics. Winway led to the creation of the Data Analysis Working Party in the government's Central Computer and Telecommunications Agency (CCTA), which in turn contributed to the evolution of SSADM. Other methods which evolved from this time are Learmonth and Burchett's LSDM and the CACI method developed by CACI Ltd. In parallel, in the US, Gane and Sarson, De Marco, Constantine and Yourdon were evolving their ideas, with a particular emphasis on process modelling. These included entity modelling and structure charts to represent function and process logic, together with data flow diagramming to represent information processing.

The approach concentrated on building models of the system. The models were either static, i.e. descriptive or expressive, or they were dynamic, i.e. how the system reacted to the real world. To summarize:

- Static models
  - Functional decomposition
  - Entity models
  - Structure charts
- Dynamic models
  - Event, state diagrams
  - Entity life history
  - State transition diagrams

Like structured programming, they provide elegant solutions based on a technical understanding of the requirement. They provide a good framework for understanding and modelling the technical issues of the system. They provide a common ground between system users and system developers with easy to understand, diagrammatic techniques.

The problem has still not gone away. Systems are still delivered late or not at all, over budget and not to the required level of quality. There are a number of criticisms levelled at structured methods approach:

- It does not clearly address business needs.
- It tends to concentrate simply on the project under development.
- The logical progression from the design to the finished product is ambiguous or non-existent.
- It is difficult to quantify and measure quality.

Understanding the totality of the requirements of the business is the problem. Businesses need to be pro-active to constant business and technological change. As the business evolves, so must the infrastructure that supports it. The application of information technology is only one (albeit important) part of that infrastructure.

In summary, there have been three major stages in information systems developments to date:

1. Injection of rigour and discipline in program definition and construction by using structured programming.
2. Recognition that, although programs were now well defined, they failed to meet the real user requirement, giving rise to structured approaches to the discharge of the analysis and design functions.
3. Individual projects were still being developed in isolation from overall corporate requirements, resulting in the identification of the need for, and development of, corporate strategy methods.

1.4 THE FUTURE FOR INFORMATION SYSTEMS DEVELOPMENT

Firstly, let us not detract from the major successes. The effective use of structured programming has brought many benefits. Coupling this with the structured approach to systems analysis and design has dramatically improved the probability of a successful system. The challenge now is to develop the all-embracing infrastructure which can evolve with the business and become as flexible as the business requires it to be. The computer industries' role is to make information technology the servant of the business, responding quickly and effectively to its master's requirements—to provide, in essence, a total quality service for the business in which everyone plays their part. This book describes such a service: Winway Software Engineering (WISE).

Winway has been built on previous successes and learnt from past failures. Its key strengths are:

- Driven through strategy to satisfy business needs
- An integrated approach from strategy through realization to phase-out and re-placement
- Loose coupling for maximum flexibility
- Cohesion within each phase for consistency of approach
- Clearly defined deliverables
- Well tried and tested techniques
- An opportunity for prototyping and evolutionary delivery of systems
- A total quality management structure to ensure requirements are met first time by ensuring zero defects.

The method contains a procedural framework with structural standards and is supported by documentation standards, all encapsulated within a total quality approach. The method is driven by the business for the business.

Why has it not happened sooner? There are two reasons:

1. Firstly it has taken this long to begin to understand the real problem, rather than the symptoms of the problem. The industry has tried various approaches and had some

notable successes, i.e. structured programming and structured analysis and design. Winway has its origins circa 1974!
2. Secondly, perhaps, a failure to think laterally. There is an analogy that will serve to illustrate this, called the enigma variations.

1.4.1 Enigma variations

The reason it took so long for the invention of the automobile was not so much the lack of technology, but that the *requirement* to move from A to B was satisfied by the horse! Here are some examples of not thinking profoundly about the real problem, and offering solutions to the symptom rather than the problem itself:

- *Requirement A:* I need to deliver something quickly from A to B.
  – *Solution:* Pony express (fast horses).
- *Requirement B:* I need to move more than one person, and possibly, at times their belongings.
  – *Solution:* Stage coach, wagon train (more than one horse).
- *Requirement C:* I need to cultivate large areas of land to grow food for myself and others.
  – *Solution:* Horse and plough (strong horse).

When all solutions are based on a predetermined conception of what the solution could/should be or contain, the result will only be variations on a theme. At best a horse, at worst a donkey!

1.4.2 Extending structured methodologies to encompass the full system development life cycle

The method in this book addresses some fundamental problems:

- There is inadequate integration between corporate strategic studies and the implementation of individual projects. Even though the need for strategic plans are increasingly accepted, we still tend to assume that individual projects exist in isolation rather than as part of a cohesive strategic framework. Passing attention might be paid to interfaces with other applications, and corporate entity models often shape an individual system's data requirements, but there is still inadequate interaction between the strategic and the individual project views.
- Insufficient thought has been given to systems design and subsequent stages of systems development. There is still no common 'structured' framework defining development activities beyond the design stage, although a number of attempts have been made. We need to extend the systems model beyond the design stage to provide a clearer definition of these activities.
- Existing methodologies and techniques are too fragmented and do not integrate well together to give a comprehensive and coordinated approach to the whole life cycle. This should include comprehensive deliverables, a management and control framework, and effective quality assurance procedures.

The term 'engineering' has been adopted to represent the trend towards a more disciplined and professional approach. This, as we have already seen, has been developing for some time. The nineties are being called the decade of information engineering, in which the information technology system will be seen much more as an integral part of corporate activities. This is a major change and it will need a fundamental reappraisal of our approach for it to succeed. We must move to a second generation of methodologies, which must, inevitably, be highly automated and will extend into far more aspects of our work than is possible at present. This is not simply 'variations on a theme'. Automation in this context means *automating* the process, because we must break out of the current mould where our workbenches and other related products simply provide automated *support* for the process.

One thing is certain: unless we achieve further understanding and rationalization of our environment, the very real prospect of evolving highly automated and coordinated systems generation and maintenance tools from the best of our current workbenches, data dictionaries and other products, will be significantly delayed, or worse still, implemented in a fragmented way. This problem is already manifesting itself with data dictionaries, where a lack of internationally agreed standards is a critical logjam inhibiting progress.

1.4.3 Structured methodologies for development and beyond

The principle underpinning the definition of structured methodologies is that of functional decomposition, used so successfully by the CACI methodology. In this, any activity can be broken down into its composite parts or steps and each of these can be similarly subdivided. Each task produces a set of results or deliverables, all of which are used as input to one or more subsequent tasks. The whole framework builds into the methodology. This is a sound approach, so why should it stop at the initial design stages? It should cover the whole life cycle from start to finish. This means adding new activities to the ends of the existing models.

When the Winway methodology was first defined in 1974 it covered the whole life cycle, and it has influenced the development of many other methodologies since, although the leading methodologies inexplicably restricted their view to only early life-cycle activities. Winway continues to evolve, and has now rationalized existing models and produced a generic structured systems analysis and design model, on to which existing models can be mapped, and extended it to embody a two-part construction stage, a two-part delivery stage, a one-part post-implementation stage, and a special stage which underpins the whole life cycle. This special stage covers such things as procurement and installation of equipment, and the provision and support of the development, testing and operational environments, including such things as configuration and capacity management.

At the end of each stage, a comprehensive set of deliverables is defined. The recipients of the various deliverables may vary, but they will always involve representatives of the user, customer or client community. In each case the deliverable will comprise the fully documented product of that stage of activity, recommendations and plans for the next stage of the activity, and the necessary input for the commencement of the next activity itself. The deliverable is constructed so as to provide continuity through each stage of the life cycle, to provide a comprehensive audit trail of the project, and the input for any future enhancement or further additional projects.

The whole of the life-cycle process is subject to comprehensive extended quality assurance (QA) and quality control procedures. These have three components:

1. A series of inspections, using informal walkthroughs and more formal reviews, such as those developed by Michael Fagan of IBM in the 1970s. These take place throughout the development, but specifically for inspection of critical elements such as the database design, sample program specifications and/or code, etc.
2. A rigorous review of the documentation and content of each stage's deliverables.
3. Provision for an independent series of reviews by a body external to the project, such as internal audit and/or QA. The information technology industry has realized the need for a formal quality management system (QMS) only in the last few years. Initiatives by the British Standards Institute (BSI)[2] and the Department of Trade and Industry[3] have set out QMS standards which are now being adopted. Winway includes highly sophisticated and well proven procedures for implementing a QMS.

The whole of this extended structured life-cycle approach is represented diagrammatically in Fig. 1.3. Having established this framework at an individual project level, we now need to consider how this might be integrated into corporate strategy procedures.

1.4.4 Integration with strategic analysis

A corporate approach to information technology (IT) recognizes the strategic business importance of information systems. Projects are not viewed in isolation, but as a cohesive unit to support the business. The main strengths of this approach are:

- It is carried out in conjunction with other business planning cycles, such as marketing, sales and production.
- It removes sub-optimization at a project level, where decisions are made on business and technology policy.

There are five areas within strategic planning procedures which provide the links and guidance at the project level. The following provides a brief synopsis of these links and their importance (the five areas) together with an explanation of how they are monitored (feedback loops).

Corporate information Strategic planning sees information as a corporate asset. Information can be used to competitive advantage. Planning information requirements at the strategic level concentrate on defining the information needs of each of an organization's business areas. This is then centrally coordinated, with the information being made available to the business in information systems. The provision of an information centre to disseminate corporate information is often a strategic service provided for managers to make use of the information in their business.

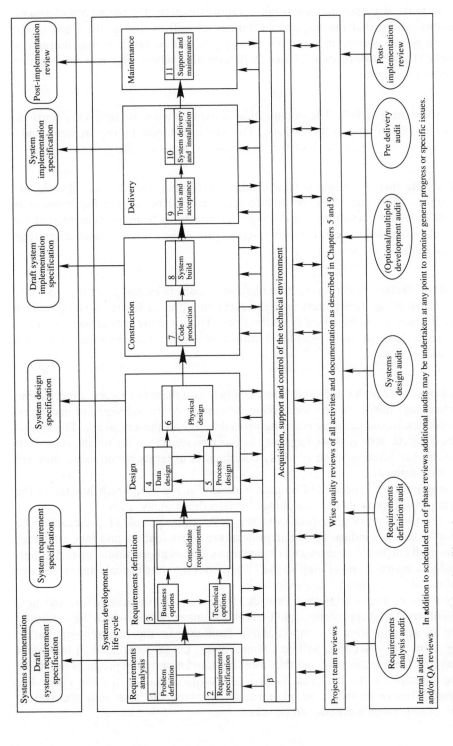

Figure 1.3 The extended project life cycle.

Business functions   A corporate view is taken on the functions the business undertakes. The functions are carried out to achieve defined objectives and goals. Each of the functions can be categorized in a number of ways, depending on their contributions to the business. This categorization assists in determining where and how information systems should be deployed.

Information systems portfolio   The organization derives, at a corporate level, a portfolio of systems required to support the business. This provides a focus on requirements and a clear direction at the project level of the real business needs for the system.

Technical architecture   A corporate view is taken on computer hardware, software and communications. This quantifies the architecture required to support the business in search of its objectives, and prevents disparate architectures being implemented at the project level and provides control over architecture issues on business rather than technical grounds.

Critical success factors   A corporate investigation of objectives and goals reveals those few areas where things really must go right every time; areas where, if things did go wrong, the business could be seriously undermined. These are the critical success factors and are carried down to the project-level information systems as clear indicators of a project's success criteria.

Feedback loops   Since policy decisions have been taken on these key issues, a mechanism is needed to ensure that these decisions are implemented. At the individual project level, there is feedback to the strategic planning procedure on all the key areas. This allows each of the projects to be reviewed against the business objectives set for the project. It also allows all the projects to be centrally coordinated in terms of the value they are adding to the business.

These proposals are represented diagrammatically in Fig 1.4, which has taken the Winway project life-cycle model and plugged it into the strategy study.

Finally, the total corporate approach to the development of all IT projects can be represented by Fig. 1.5, indicating that all projects are dependent on, and have interfaces with, the overall corporate strategy and objectives as well as interaction with each other.

The final task is that of integrating all the IT activities into one logical, comprehensive and coordinated framework for the industry.

Winway software engineering then provides the means of progressing into the next generation of structured approaches, and thereby a framework from which the automatic generation of systems from a comprehensive definition of the requirements within overriding corporate objectives, will be commonplace. CASE tools have an important part to play in achieving this goal, but they must be transformed from products providing automated support for the life cycle to products which automate the life cycle. We believe that Winway provides the platform from which the leap into the second generation of structured methods can be taken.

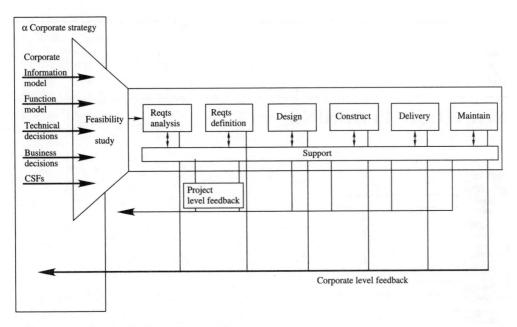

Figure 1.4 Corporate/project strategies interface.

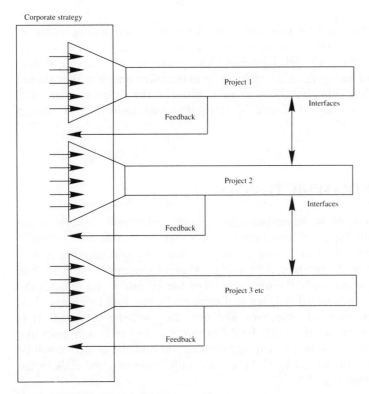

Figure 1.5 Integrating the IT environment.

2

STRATEGIC PLANNING

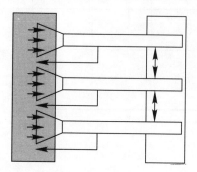

This chapter establishes the need for strategic information systems planning within all organizations. It examines how the definition of business goals and targets should be the key determining factor driving IT developments. The principles of strategic system planning are examined to identify the main tasks to be undertaken and how they should be planned and controlled. Finally, there is an outline of the Winway structured approach to this activity and how it should be integrated with individual IT project developments.

2.1 THE NEED FOR STRATEGIC PLANNING

The need for and purpose of strategic planning is well understood at very senior management levels in all types of organization, whether in commerce, industry, government or the military. Indeed, it can be argued that strategic thinking is best understood and practised in the military. The military view of strategy is the easiest to comprehend: the winner is generally the one who takes the initiative and dictates the pace, who keeps the enemy both off balance and continually reacting to events. This demands a clear strategic view of objectives and how they will be achieved. It is essentially a top-down activity, starting with the definition of an objective and cascading down through various levels of more detailed plans setting out how the objective will be achieved over time, until at the lowest level there are detailed operating procedures for each component activity (see Fig. 2.1).

14

Figure 2.1 Corporate planning.

At each level there are certain key activities or features on which success depends. These are the critical success factors (CSF) and they may vary from level to level. CSFs were first defined by Rockart[4] and subsequently elaborated by Bullen and Rockart.[5] Each level sets the one below it quantifiable and measurable parameters for controlling progress and monitoring achievements. These vital feedback loops ensure that plans can evolve and adapt to changing circumstances. The responsibilities for achieving these are as shown in Fig. 2.2.

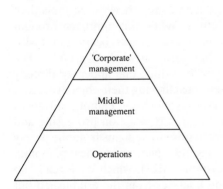

Figure 2.2 Corporate activities.

The nature of work undertaken at each level is also very different. Corporate management has extremely varied and individual duties, and they could be seen primarily as decision makers, monitoring and interpreting information from within and without the organization, evaluating options, and from these assessments issuing clear directives to middle management. Corporate management is primarily concerned with management in its 'classic' sense:

- *Planning* — what is to be done, where, when and how?
- *Organizing* — who is to do what, with how much authority and under what physical environment?

- *Directing* — communicating instructions to organizational components and motivating them to do their work.
- *Controlling* — evaluating whether the planned work is being carried out, and applying remedial measures.

A key feature of middle management work is the analysis and review of management information — summaries of operational data, volumes, frequencies, and costs in both finite and exception terms against targets. The lowest level, arguably where all the real work is done, is that of operations. This is where the products or services of the organization are created and provided to the external marketplace, and where the internal supporting or administrative services (personnel, accounts, etc.) needed to facilitate day-to-day operations are performed. This is where most staff are employed. Activities at this level are generally well defined, routine, repetitive and frequent.

The operational level of any organization, is usually its revenue generator, but, potentially, it is also its main consumer of resources and therefore costs.

With this corporate framework in mind, it is appropriate to evaluate how computing technology has been applied over the years to support it. Until very recently, our industry was primarily about installing computer hardware and software systems to support individual business applications at the operations level, such as accounting, payroll and stock control. These areas were addressed because, as people-intensive tasks, they represented major cost centres for most businesses. They involved repetitive, well defined processes, so they were capable of automated support with the tools then available, and gave clear immediate cost-benefit return. While this approach brought significant benefits, it was very fragmented. It also tended to address 'backroom' tasks, not directly related to revenue generation, and, therefore, survival or growth. The application of computing at the strategic level was not something that appeared directly relevant or helpful to corporate or senior management in achieving their objectives, so it played little part in corporate planning. During the late seventies and eighties, advances in technological capabilities, particularly the move towards transaction processing and online database systems, allowed computer managers to raise their sights from the purely operational support level into middle management and the sphere of tactical planning. They began to develop management information systems (MIS), which were really no more than the provision of statistics, summaries and analyses from the established but evolving operational support systems. The experience was not a happy one for recipients of the information. Many of these systems, dating from the sixties and early seventies, were freestanding batch systems based on flat files, frequently with extensive duplication of data. The information provided to managers was often out of date, inaccurate and inconsistent. Tozer[6] represents the extent of existing computerization as shown in Fig. 2.3.

More recently a number of technological changes have altered the balance. These include increased processor power, reduced size and costs of hardware, more sophisticated development facilities, the growth of structured methods and the growing automation of development work. Very importantly there has also been a coming together of three technologies:

- Computing
- Communications
- Office automation

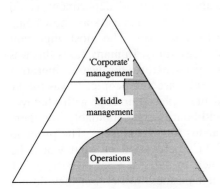

Figure 2.3 Current IT systems support © E E Tozer.

to form information technology or IT: Once again, technological advances allowed IT managers to raise their sights to the highest level of organization management and to examine how systems might be provided at that level. The use of decision support, artificial intelligence, expert systems and executive information systems has hardly begun. The pace of business has changed fundamentally in the last decade. Change continues and, indeed, appears to be speeding up; the driving force of this revolution is IT. Machinery made the industrial revolution; technology is driving us into a new revolution that will make the industrial revolution seem like a skirmish. IT should now be firmly established in the 'front office' of all businesses. It no longer simply supports business operations, it is the means of providing business services, the means of production. More and more frequently, IT is the competitive edge that allows a company to compete, survive and grow. Businesses are demanding new, more sophisticated systems, that can grow and adapt to business needs and that can keep pace with the tempo of modern commerce, industry and government. Figure 2.4 indicates Tozer's conception of growth.

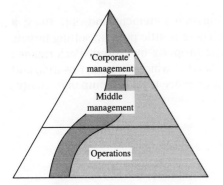

Figure 2.4 Potential for new systems © E E Tozer.

The result has been controlled chaos in IT departments, longer and longer backlogs, spiralling staff costs as demand outstripped supply, and ill-considered purchasing of equipment, software and services in order to stem the tide. The advent of desktop personal computing added a new threat and complication: because IT departments could not deliver, users started to build their own solutions, and IT managers are now being forced to reassess the way in which they provide their services. The most important change was the move towards the concept of the strategy study. In many cases this was no more than a technical review of the existing IT infrastructure, hardware, operating and systems software, communications, applications software and people. It was the IT department's view of how these should be expanded and replaced, to cope with whatever demands were made on them. Finance directors and boards understandably saw them primarily as empire building and unjustifiable demands for expenditure. The problem with this form of review was that it represented IT's perception of what would be required in the future, based on what had happened to date. It was, at best, an IT strategy. IT managers understand very well how their business works, but they do not often understand what it is trying to achieve. Businesses exist to achieve corporate objectives, not to advance the aspirations of their IT staff. A corporate strategy should be:

- A fundamental appraisal of business objectives, plans and priorities.
- A determination of the best organizational and systems timetable to achieve a structure to support these goals.
- An assessment of current positioning, strengths and weaknesses.

The first priority therefore is to focus on business objectives and priorities. This should be a familiar concept for business managers. If there are no corporate objectives expanded into marketing, sales, production, personnel etc. strategies, then the organization can have little sense of purpose or direction. Departments will vie for limited resources and budgets. They will find themselves reacting to competitive forces, continually wrong-footed and therefore having little chance of survival. 'At some point in the life of every organization, its ability to succeed in spite of itself runs out' (R. H. O'Brien[7]).

The corporate strategy incorporates a business mission statement and objectives; a business plan; business priorities; business policies. There is little point in setting targets or goals of any sort unless their achievement can be properly measured. Performance measures (PM) are primarily objective, quantifiable ways in which progress towards, and achievement of, goals can be monitored. PMs exist at every level of company activity. Types of PM are:

- Objective
  - Financial
  - Volumetric performance
  - Qualitative
  - Personnel (turnover, percentage, promotion)
  - Standards and compliance

- Subjective
  - Stuffy attitudes
  - Customer care
  - Ethos

This highest level of strategy is then expanded by different parts of the organization into a number of other studies. The first of these, shown in Fig. 2.5 is the corporate marketing strategy.

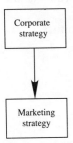

Figure 2.5 The marketing strategy.

This is arguably the key review which expands the 'ideals' of the corporate strategy into a set of tangible products and services derived from the market, i.e. supplying products and services to markets. This is followed by a number of other reviews conducted by various parts of the organization. These are shown in Fig. 2.6, and can generally be conducted in parallel.

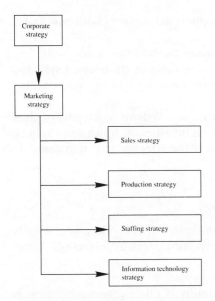

Figure 2.6 Components of a marketing strategy.

There is therefore a hierarchy of activities to be completed. If a business is to survive in an increasingly competitive future, it is vital that business people understand the role IT can play in each stage of this activity, and that IT specialists understand the wider business arena in which they are competing. This book focuses on the information systems and technology aspects of corporate strategic planning:

- A definition of the technology systems and services needed to support the realization of business plans and priorities.
- A determination of market positioning and the selection of the mix of products and services to be offered in the future to achieve this.
- The migration strategy for moving from the status quo to the required future.

2.2 THE PRINCIPLES

2.2.1 Objectives of information systems planning

Information systems planning (ISP) cannot take place without a clear indication of the business objectives and goals. This often materializes as the business plan, and coordinates all the planning cycles, i.e. marketing, sales, production and information technology. It is important to have a clear understanding of the objectives of ISP. In summary, these are:

- Understanding the business's objectives, goals, priorities and direction (aims).
- Interpreting the business's aims and establishing the information architecture required to support the business.
- Determining the information systems needed to support the business both now and in the medium term.
- Identifying how well information systems are meeting the business need.
- Managing changes in business aims and implementing them in information systems.
- Defining the technical architecture required to implement the information systems.

The planned, prioritized and targeted use of information systems in support of clear business objectives can provide a tremendous return on investment, which can easily be quantified using the measures implemented to monitor the effectiveness of systems.

2.2.2 Principles of information systems planning

There are a number of principles which underpin the ethos of ISP. They were clearly defined by Martin[8] and have their origins in marketing strategy planning. These principles are as follows:

- Strategic planning is a top management responsibility. Collectively management is charged with executing this responsibility by defining, clearly and succinctly, the business objectives, goals, priorities and direction.

STRATEGIC PLANNING

- Strategic planning needs a clear, concise and enduring mission statement. This defines the business(es) the organization is in, and may refer to customers, customer needs, products and services.
- The organization's mission is customer and market-driven, and not defined as products and services offered.
- The statement focuses the organization's direction in order that objectives and goals may be set.
- Information is a corporate asset.
- Mission, objectives, goals, information and functions allow the organization to make difficult business decisions more easily.
- Information systems are built to support the organization in the pursuit of its mission through its objectives and goals.
- Information systems can be manual or computer-based.

2.2.3 Ground rules of information systems planning

There are a number of ground rules which formulate the approach to ISP. These are that:

- ISP must have top management commitment and active participation to develop the ground rules.
- ISP is developed for long-term enduring objectives, not short-term transient measures, although information systems can be deployed at a tactical level to either bridge or fill a gap in the business that requires urgent, remedial work.
- Confidentiality is never compromised.

Some facts have to remain company secrets. This has no effect on the ISP, nor does it need this information. For example, if it is to be secret that company X is to be purchased, this does not have any effect on the ISP. The objective the ISP needs to establish may be something similar to:

- Sustain a 20 per cent growth rate in selected business areas by judicious acquisition of companies with a compatible business.
- Migrate the business from light haulage to heavy haulage, warehousing and distribution by judicious acquisition of a company compatible with the business requirement.

The objective (whatever it is) can then be translated into goals. Goal attainment can then be achieved by examining the information (data) and functions (process) needed to support the organization. Information systems deployment has the capacity to change the way in which business is conducted. This change is a key feature of the ISP process. The management of this change, together with the synchronization of ISP cycles with other business planning cycles such as marketing and sales, are the key to ISP success.

A number of information planning methods make no provision for other planning cycles which have an effect on the initial scoping exercise, i.e. what do we need to do first? What is already under way, or has already been completed? The fact that planning in other areas is not in the same format as the ISP does not mean that it is not important. The essential components *will* be there although their expression may be different and may only concentrate on short-term measures for one aspect of the business, e.g. a product launch, a recruitment campaign, or new market research.

2.2.4 Managing information systems planning

It may come as a surprise to find that the ISP manager in many organizations is the marketing manager or the sales director or the accountant. The role of the ISP manager is to understand the business the organization is in, or wants to be in, to understand the business planning cycles and to derive the portfolio of systems needed to support that business. The technology to support the information systems is more specialized. The planning manager will require an understanding of the underlying trends of the computer industry, in terms of open standards, together with their applicability to the organization, e.g. the emergence of open standards tells us something that is so important it is often missed — the suppliers have made a financial commitment to a standard: they have a vested interest in making it work and making it last. The open standard will evolve with advances in technology, ensuring that it at least keeps pace with change, although typically it will be pioneering the state of the art.

The standards issue is central to the information system portfolio, as systems are derived to meet the enduring objectives of the organization. From a business viewpoint they will have an expected life of at least the length of the business planning cycle, usually 5 years, but sometimes longer. The technical implementation of the systems will be subject to obsolescence; this is something that the computer industry has to live with. However, this is not a negative issue: it must be seen as a positive way of keeping the business at the front of technology while still retaining the integrity of the information systems which are independent of their actual implementation.

2.2.5 Information systems planning in practice

This section provides an overview of the procedures involved in the ISP process. The process is summarized in Fig. 2.7.

The ISP process is a top-down approach, in terms of both procedural approach and management participation. Only the top level of management can determine what business they are in or want to be in. Top management determines the factors that are absolutely critical to the organization's wellbeing.

To achieve the organization's mission, objectives are set, each in isolation of the existing situation, since this often influences the objectives. For each objective, goals are set and means of *achieving* those goals are defined. In parallel to this, the current business organization is analysed. This gives an indication of what is currently happening and can often contrast sharply with the objectives and goals set. The objectives are matched against information and function models, to determine the changes necessary to support the objectives and achieve the goals set. Having established this, the organization must be realistic in terms of what it can implement and when. Resources are a key issue: time, people and money are the elements that will dictate what is implemented and when. The emerging organization model is revisited to determine the organization's priorities — the priorities and practicalities will shape the portfolio of information systems.

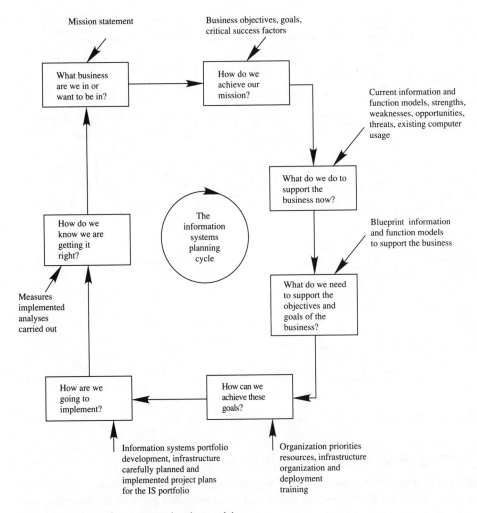

Mission statement

Business objectives, goals, critical success factors

What business are we in or want to be in?

How do we achieve our mission?

Current information and function models, strengths, weaknesses, opportunities, threats, existing computer usage

What do we do to support the business now?

How do we know we are getting it right?

The information systems planning cycle

Blueprint information and function models to support the business

Measures implemented analyses carried out

What do we need to support the objectives and goals of the business?

How are we going to implement?

How can we achieve these goals?

Information systems portfolio development, infrastructure carefully planned and implemented project plans for the IS portfolio

Organization priorities resources, infrastructure organization and deployment training

Figure 2.7 Information systems planning model.

Implementation of information systems requires a clearly defined interface to the procedures used for system development. This will affect the feasibility study and the way systems analysis is carried out. It is now not simply a question of requirements analysis. Information systems planning closely aligns the use of information technology resources to the business needs.

2.3 THE METHOD

The strategy and information systems planning method has five core components of activity, which are depicted in Fig. 2.8.

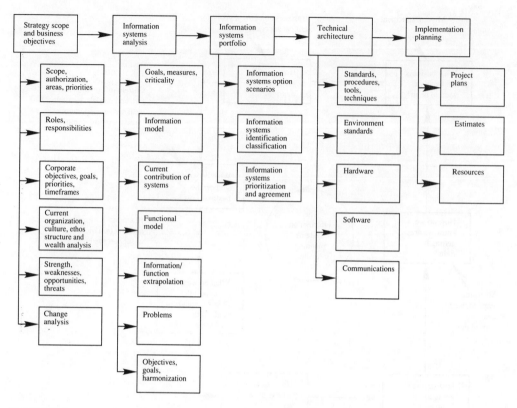

Figure 2.8 Core components of strategy and information systems planning.

2.3.1 Strategy, scope and business objectives

The *raison d'être* for information systems is to add value to the business the organization is in, or wants to be in, by supporting the stated objectives and goals of the business. For this to happen, a clear understanding of those objectives must be documented and agreed.

The first, and perhaps the most important, unit of work is to define the scope of the study. It may be that the organization wants to concentrate its efforts on one division (or department or subsidiary), or maybe on a recent acquisition. An understanding of the scope and the business reasons for the scope being defined will provide a valuable starting comparison when the objectives and goals are elicited.

Similarly, a clear identification of the roles and responsibilities is required. This should always, without exception, be done top-down. The people who will make a telling contribution to the study should be identified by top management, depending on the scope of the study. These people will be responsible for defining their goals, information needs, measures, problems, etc. Their commitment and cooperation are fundamental to the success of the study.

There needs to be a clear statement of the business objectives. Often these will be general statements of direction and are usually limited to perhaps 10–15 enduring statements. This again is an important point. The statements must be carefully worded and must endure both the test of time and different interpretations. When they become repeatable by different people, and are actively repeated by peer groups at differing levels, they can then be classed as enduring statements of direction — in essence, true business objectives.

Sometimes, and particularly if the study is aligned with other current planning cycles, e.g. because of a new product launch, objectives and goals may already exist. A goal is a target which is set to achieve a specific objective. People call them by many different names, depending on the organization, and even the job they perform, but some typical synonyms are 'brief', 'target', 'responsibility', 'delegation' and 'scope'. Examples of an objective and goals may be as follows:

- Objective — reduce fuel costs
  - Goal — by 1992 replace all 2000 cc and above motor vehicles with 1600 cc vehicles
  - Goal — by 3rd quarter 1991 convert all motor vehicles capable of running on unleaded petrol to unleaded
  - Goal — by 2nd quarter 1991 introduce route planning training and tools for all sales representatives.

Notice that the three goals all contribute to the enduring statement of direction, but with differing time frames.

The current organization is examined to determine quantifiable elements such as its functional organization into departments, divisions, subsidiaries, etc., and the contributions they make to the overall wealth of the organization.

Some things, however, are not easily quantifiable, such as the organization's culture and ethos, but they need to be recorded as they play a key part in determining the shape and overall success of the strategy.

During the strategy, an assessment is made of any changes that may occur during the life of the strategy planning. There is little point in building a strategy that has made no provision for the possibility of change. Some changes are predictable, such as forthcoming government legislation or change instigated in direct response to an opportunity or problem presented. If the changes are brought into the strategy planning, then they can be quantified in terms of overall impact on the strategy, i.e. where, when and at what level.

This core activity has little to do with information technology. It is a strategic business analysis that will be used by the IT specialists and the business managers as a clear statement of direction. It becomes the central focal point of communication of the organization's aims and objectives within the scope of the study.

2.3.2 Information systems analysis

Having defined the business objectives, the strategic analysis is carried out to expand on the business objectives. This is achieved in this core activity by a series of interviews to determine CSFs, cascading down the organization's structure.

There is an argument worth considering, that it is best to start at the bottom of the structure and work upwards, comparing and harmonizing goals and objectives along the way. The reason for this is that the business knowledge gained on the 'shop floor', i.e. at the operational level, will be invaluable as you ascend the levels. The counter argument is that it is possible to become too involved in what happens now, and thereby lose sight of the objectives. Also, the lowest level tends to become accepted in the organization as the peer group. This presents all kinds of communication problems higher up. From past experience, we have found that the most productive way was top-down. This:

- Establishes peer-group status in the hierarchical levels
- Provides a clear insight into the business, its objectives and how it is to achieve them
- Assists in providing a clear insight into why functions are performed
- Allows levelling of goals and information to be directed
- Allows information to be successively refined in detail.

Another useful way of determining who to interview has been to stick to the guideline of interviewing only people who make, interpret or implement policy decisions. This usually starts with the managing director and ends with the line manager or operational level supervisor.

During the interviews, two streams of modelling are conducted. These are the information model and the function model. The interaction between the two, i.e. which functions use which data, are determined by cluster analysis, using create and update information as the clustering algorithm.

An evaluation of the existing systems is conducted to determine how well they currently support the organization's objectives and goals. This can happen in one of two ways:

1. Independently of CSF interviews — this is a good way of comparing and contrasting what people believe the business goals are, i.e. what they state in the interviews and then what they perceive as success or failure in the systems.
2. As an additional component of CSF.

It may well be that, in order to get the complete picture, both have to be used. The existing systems analysis is a good way of 'pointing the finger' at reasons why goals cannot be achieved — and in so doing you have elicited the goal!

2.3.3 Information systems portfolio

The previous core activity is highly visible to the people in the organization. The deliverables are either used to back up the levels such as the goals and problems, or to present a negative picture such as how well the existing systems support the organization. There appears to be a hiatus after the fact finding. One quote from the fact-finding exercise was 'Don't give me the labour pains, just give me the baby'. The information systems portfolio is the baby, the fact finding the labour pains for all concerned.

This core activity brings all the fact finding together, presents a range of options, and identifies and prioritizes the options chosen for information systems.

These options can be presented either as 'blue skies', i.e. no constraints are imposed by the existing systems, or as 'pragmatic reality', i.e. building on the existing systems. It is better to take a blue skies approach to strategic information systems because anything else could prejudice their success. It may be possible to adapt pragmatic reality for tactical and operational systems.

Each of the options is derived from the objectives, goals and/or problems it supports, and each option must add value to the business. In demonstrating the added value, the measures incorporated into the option are explained.

For example, a system to support route planning may have measures that record the individual vehicles' current average mileage, miles per gallon and service costs. It then measures and reports on general average mileage, miles per gallon and service costs. This, from the previous example, contributes to the goal of: 'By second quarter 1991 introduce route planning, training and tools for all sales representatives'. This goal in turn contributes to the objective of: 'Reduce fuel costs'.

From the information supplied by the measure, the business manager can clearly see if the goal is being achieved. Collectively, all the related goals can be judged against the objective.

The strength of presenting options in this way is that decisions are made on business, not technical, grounds. Therefore the business community can and does make a valued contribution to the decision-making process.

This process allows information systems to be defined from the options, and the impact is judged from the results of the cluster analysis of functions to information.

Once the information systems have been identified they are prioritized. Priorities are drawn not from a single person or personality, but from the objectives and goals set for the business and prioritized by top management.

2.3.4 Technical architecture

The information system portfolio is derived in isolation from the technical architecture, which is the enabling mechanism that makes the business information systems happen. The architecture is influenced by:

- Communication between consumers – organization – suppliers
- Geographic dispersal of business functionality
- Current investment in hardware, software and communications
- The size, complexity and number of information systems
- National and international standards
- Technology trends and obsolescence

Architecture divides into two streams, the infrastructure and the environment. The infrastructure, in this context, consists of the standards, procedures, tools and techniques that will be required to develop and evolve the business information systems. The environment is the hardware, software and communications required to implement the systems. The two streams support each other and collectively provide the technical architecture to support the business.

2.3.5 Implementation planning

This core activity prepares the way for implementation of the complete strategy, i.e. the information systems and the technical architecture. Project plans are produced for each

information system and infrastructure project (e.g. training). Estimates are also produced both of resources and timescales, from which resources are procured to carry out
the subsequent life cycle phases.

2.4 INTEGRATION

2.4.1 The integration of milestones and deliverables

The integration of the strategic planning process with the system development process
focuses on the deliverables produced. Each produces deliverables and executes a number
of tasks to produce them. The strategic planning deliverables have an impact on both the
tasks and deliverables of some of the phases in the systems development process.
Historically the two approaches have been incompatible. The strategic development and
tactical implementation of information systems contrasts with the system-by-system
approach of systems development.

The information system portfolio needs to drive the system-level development, and in
order to do this it must interface with the key decision-making processes in system
development. The structured methods approaches all have generic equivalents of:

- A feasibility decision
- A business functions decision
- A hardware and software strategy decision

For example, in SSADM and James Martin Information Engineering, these are
described, respectively, as:

- Feasibility project skeletons (business area analysis)
- Business system options (business system design)
- Technical options (technical design)

The first generation of the integration of strategic planning and systems development
shows the integration by deliverables and milestones. Winway shows the restructuring of
the feasibility study and the analysis phase to streamline the delivery of business systems
in line with business evolution. Figure 2.9 summarizes the main components in terms of
milestones, and notes the checking and feedback mechanisms.

2.4.2 The impact of integration

The impact of strategic planning has two distinct effects on the subsequent development
phases: the viability of the feasibility study, and the provision and use of Stage β
feedback loops to strategy. From a practical viewpoint, it is recognized that not all
organizations will become involved with full strategic planning procedures. Often the
starting point for such organizations is either the feasibility study or the analysis phase.
The following quantifies the effect of the strategic planning function on the development
procedure.

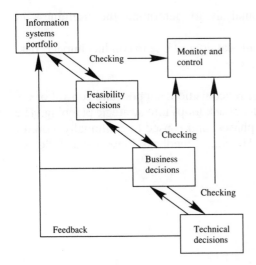

Figure 2.9 Information systems feedback mechanisms.

Viability of feasibility study If strategic planning is implemented, the need for a feasibility study is in doubt. The feasibility studies objective is to determine the feasibility or otherwise of the project at a system level. Since traditionally systems were developed system-by-system, the feasibility study was a logical starting point. However, the development of ISP portfolio systems has changed the emphasis from 'Is it feasible?', to 'How are we going to achieve it?' The premise is, 'the system is needed, how are we going to implement it?'

If strategic planning is implemented, it is recommended that the feasibility study is made redundant. The link is between the individual ISP portfolio system definition (and its deliverables) and the initiation tasks of the requirements analysis phase. The impact of the ISP portfolio deliverables on the requirements analysis phase are summarized below:

- Initial data flow diagram (information model). Use business units affected and the function model to provide initial scope. The system boundary must be drawn in terms of objectives and goals to be satisfied.
- Initial data structure. Use the data model per business unit affected. Cross-reference any corporate data used but not owned by the system.
- Initial requirements. Cross-reference to the objectives and goals, cross-reference to the goal-attainment measures. Demonstrate how they will be achieved in the information model and the data model.
- Feasibility plans. Superseded or subsumed by implementation plans for the information system.
- Constraints. These are business constraints identified in the information systems planning process.
- Interview plans. Use the business units affected and the function model to scope the plans.

- Current system. Use the organization analysis to determine the usefulness of conducting a current system investigation.
- Information model, data model, requirements catalogue. Use to conduct impact, risk, complexity and resource implication analysis.

Stage β feedback loops The provision of Stage β acquisition, support and control of the environment handles a number of important feedback loops into strategic planning. The feedback is provided by all the post-strategy phases, and is used to continually monitor and refine the strategic planning procedure. The major feedback loops are as follows:

- Business decisions
- Technical decisions
- Environment procurement
  - Test environment
  - Live environment
- Operational procedures
- Capacity planning
- Configuration management
- Change control procedures
- Project administration procedures
- Standards usage
- User acceptance testing
- Sign-off and acceptance
- System post-implementation review
- System enhancement process
- Major enhancement proposals
- New project proposals

The feedback loops are controlled by a project administrator, who is responsible for the day-to-day operational supervision of the procedure, preparing and passing over to the strategic planning manager the updates on the items being controlled.

The strategic planning manager is responsible for the continual monitoring and tuning of the implementation of the strategic planning procedure.

While strategic plans may be initiated periodically, e.g. in response to an opportunity, the monitoring procedure is continuous, and is provided as a specific step in the strategic planning procedures.

3

STRUCTURED SYSTEMS ANALYSIS AND DESIGN

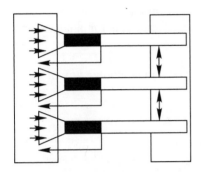

This chapter covers the principles of systems analysis and design. It explores why and how formal methods have evolved since the mid-1970s. It examines this by building a generic model of structured systems analysis and design which can be used as a means of validating all the available methods.

3.1 WHY STRUCTURED ANALYSIS AND DESIGN?

Some questions beg an answer:

- What are we really doing in analysis and design?
- What is it we are investigating?
- Why are we doing it?
- How can we do it?

The answer is information. Without information no organization can survive. It is an organization's lifeblood, running through the corporate veins, supplying the corporate organs so that they may function individually for the mutual benefit of the organization.

Information, and not data, is the key to corporate success. Data can be seen as a vast lake, while information can be seen as the water that runs when you turn on a specific tap. From the vast quantity of data available, the refined, purified information the organization needs to survive can be extracted. Analysis and design can be viewed as a catalytic filter converting data into information. If we now view analysis and design as an information processor, let us consider again what it is we are doing, and provide answers to the questions posed above.

What are we really doing in analysis and design? We are processing data into information. What is it we are investigating? We are investigating information in its many forms. Why are we doing it? We are doing it for the wellbeing of the corporate body and its organs, i.e. its business functional areas. How do we do it? We do it using a structured approach to information processing called structured systems analysis and design (SSAD).

From the objectives of the individual stages of our generic model we can now determine that we need:

- Procedural standards to transform and/or manipulate information
- Documentation standards to capture and express the information for analysis and checking deliverables

The information is captured in a variety of processes which may involve any or all of the following:

- Collation
- Validation and verification
- Sorting
- Merging
- Extraction

The information is then expressed using the documentation standards and may involve the following:

- Selection of information
- Structuring of information
- Documenting of information in single-source form
- Cross-referencing information by way of matrices, indexes, keys, etc.

Information is analysed for completeness, consistency and correctness. This involves analysis of:

- Problems, requirements and solutions
- Impact (analysis of decisions)
- Cost
- Benefit
- Risk
- Organization

Information is transformed from one model to another to reflect the above. Information has transitional states within the generic model until its final status is determined. The transition model of information relies on a simple feedback loop (utilizing the above), where input is processed to produce output and the output is scrutinized against the input to determine its acceptability. The generic model in Fig. 3.1 illustrates this principle.

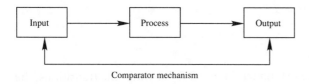

Figure 3.1 Information transition model.

Is it really valid only to transform information? This gives a one-dimensional (albeit consistent) view of the information. What it does not give is a three-dimensional view. These added dimensions are required to model information's static and dynamic characteristics. At a lower level, i.e. procedural standards level, this translates directly into *functions, data* and *events*. *Functions* and *data* provide a static analysis and consequently design of the information requirement. *Event* analysis and design provides the much-needed dynamic analysis of the information requirements. Event modelling is an opportunity to model real-world significance representing in the models the dynamic aspects of the systems data and processes. Hence the procedural standards for this type of modelling are a key requirement in our generic model. They model the effects that real-world events have on information. Figure 3.2 provides a useful summary of information transition and dimensions.

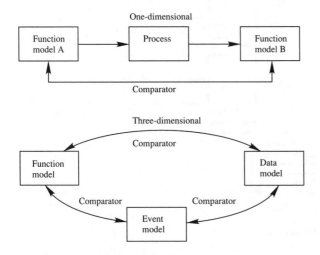

Figure 3.2 Information transition and dimensions.

An example of transition is SSADM's (Version 3's) use of the data flow diagramming (DFD) technique which models the following:

- Current existing system(s)
- Current logical system
- Business option(s)
- Chosen business option

- Technical option(s)
- Chosen technical option
- Required system

Each is a discrete transition to the next model. Figure 3.3 illustrates the transitions, the numbers in brackets showing the logical sequence, i.e. 1–9. The comparator mechanism compares the input against the output. The exact definition of the comparator mechanism will determine which inputs are compared with which outputs. For example, the business model options in SSADM (Version 3) are compared against the logical model, and also against the physical model. The precise objectives of the structural standards, i.e. the tasks, determine the requirement for comparisons to be drawn.

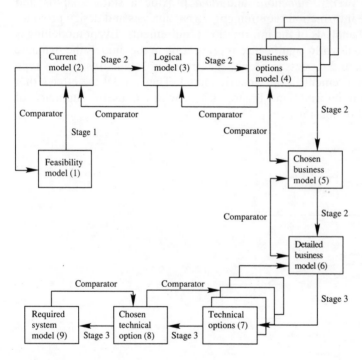

Figure 3.3 One-dimensional transition (DFD) models.

There is a dimension that underpins all the other dimensions — the fourth dimension.

The fourth dimension The building of various models and transforming them, either in isolation (one dimension) or collectively (three-dimensional), will not in itself guarantee the required system. The fourth dimension is 'conformance to requirement' and is modelled by the quality dimension. This uses the other dimensions to guarantee the sponsors' definition of quality.

3.2 THE PRINCIPLES OF STRUCTURED SYSTEMS ANALYSIS AND DESIGN

Structured systems analysis and design (SSAD) is one facet of software engineering. The approach in this section will be to build a generic model of this structured approach to analysis and design. The model is based on best current practice in the computing industry, and uses the software engineering approach to problem solving. Early developments in software engineering were described by Boehm.[9]

First the concepts of software engineering need to be identified, since the model is built from these concepts. The software engineering approach includes:

- An ability to separate concerns into wholly contained logical units
- A clearly identifiable start and end point
- Clear milestones of achievement marked by baselines
- A structured approach where activities at a number of levels can be broken down into their constituent parts
- Each activity has a clearly defined relationship with other activities
- Each activity has one or more deliverables
- Procedures for quality assurance

  SSAD in particular:

- Can be taught
- Can be used and reused
- Can be managed
- Can be researched and developed

3.3 WHY IS A GOOD SYSTEMS DEVELOPMENT METHODOLOGY NECESSARY?

A good systems development methodology lessens the risk of wasting resources — and thus money — on systems development. A proven methodology means that the most effective way of doing things is defined in advance of the project, so there is at all times a framework for development staff to follow. It also increases the productivity of development staff, and does this in a number of ways:

1. By providing a standard framework so that the developer does not have to 'reinvent the wheel' for each project.
2. Like a good tool kit, it provides the right tools to enable each development task to be successfully completed.
3. It allows effective review procedures so that errors and inconsistencies can be identified early.
4. It acts as a productivity aid by reducing the amount and content of development documentation.

5. It should be flexible (rather than prescriptive) in terms of components and techniques used, which should be determined by the circumstances prevailing for the project.

The methodology also improves the quality of the systems finally developed. How good are your current systems? Are changes easy to accomplish? Are the users convinced that they are getting exactly what is required? A good methodology forces the developer to produce flexible systems that are adequately documented as they are developed. In addition, a good method allows the analyst to identify user needs accurately, and allows the user to verify easily that his needs have been catered for. It provides a communication base between all those concerned with system development:

- User and analyst
- Analyst and programmer
- Analyst and database administrator (DBA)
- User and system administrator
- Staff and management
- Operations and the development team

Communications are improved because as far as possible, long and complex narratives are replaced with pictorial methods and structured English.

It makes planning easier. If you cannot plan it, you cannot do it. A good methodology allows you to plan, monitor, correct and replan as the project progresses.

3.4 UNDERLYING PRINCIPLES OF SSAD

3.4.1 Data-driven

Many structured methods are based on the analysis and functional decomposition of the processing of a system. These methods tend to begin the development process by analysing the required system in terms of information flows. Data flows, processes that manipulate data and data stores, are identified at a high level and progressively decomposed into more detail. The resulting systems tend to be very 'process'-oriented, with the processing needs being the paramount consideration. The data stores tend to be secondary, simply providing convenient repositories for accessed and stored information.

SSAD approaches the creation of systems from a different standpoint. Using SSAD, the developer is encouraged to build 'data'-oriented systems. Justification for this approach is based on a number of factors:

1. All application systems have an underlying, generic data structure.
2. In general terms this generic data structure tends to change very little over time. Although there may be extensions and minor changes, given that the application remains in the same business area, the data structure remains broadly the same.
3. Processing requirements may vary considerably over time, in terms of what is required and how it is to be accomplished. Typically, systems may move from batch to online, to real-time, to distributed, back to centralized, etc.

4. Much of what we think of as conventional computer processing (executing programs), is essentially concerned with building temporary data structures, processing those structures, discarding them and building similar structures for the next transaction. In a conventional order-processing system, for instance, the program that prices orders, checks stock availability and creates consignment notes may have to extract data from many sources to create the right information structure to process an order.

In fact, for each order the program is extracting data from the database, building a data structure, updating the content of the structure, returning the updated parts of the structure to the originals, and then discarding the structure and repeating the process for the next order. If we build the structure as part of the system's architecture, then programming should be easier because much of the complex logic in conventional systems' programs will already have been built into the system. Coupled with the above, we should be able to keep the same basic data structure and write simpler processes which we know are likely to be subject to more frequent change.

3.4.2 Separates logical and physical design

Structured methods separate logical and physical design. While the conceptual stages of analysis and design are being undertaken, the developer and users should not be concerned with any aspect of physical systems, such as files, data organizations, indexing, program flows, operating schedules or hardware.

3.4.3 Allows accurate logical views

Given the separation of logical and physical development, the developer must be provided with the tools and techniques that allow the creation of totally accurate and unambiguous logical models. All too often the term 'logical' is a euphemism for 'ambiguous', 'general', 'vague' or 'meaningless'. Structured methods provide a range of techniques which the developer and user can use to create completely meaningful logical models.

3.4.4 Verifiable/provable system logic

A major problem in the analysis and design phases of development is the lack of a systematic way of proving that all the necessary systems logic has been adequately defined. Another problem is proving that unusual sequences of events or error conditions will be identified and appropriately dealt with by the system. Structured methods provide a method of producing and checking system logic during the analysis and design phase. Special techniques provide a systematic approach to:

- Identifying the events that cause changes to the system's data
- Identifying the correct sequence(s) of those events
- Specifying the processing required to handle each event
- Forcing the analyst and user to consider the system implications and actions required if notifications of events are presented out of sequence

- Producing a simple-to-use description of processing, error handling and validation requirements for each event

SSAD uses a number of principles which together make it a unique and particularly effective way of developing systems, and with significant advantages over traditional methods of systems analysis and design. They are:

1. System structures should be determined by data structures. It is a data-driven method and not a function-driven one.
2. Logical and physical concepts are separated. A detailed logical design is developed before hardware, software and implementation constraints are taken into account.
3. Development should be iterative, in that an eventual cost-effective solution is arrived at by the development of partial views, based on the parallel development of the three crucial system views — data flows, data structures and time cycles. Reliance is not placed on one single 'pet' technique. Validation and consistency checking between the different definitions lead to an objectively accurate total system model.
4. The conversion of logical to physical design is covered in a prescriptive way. Rules and guidelines are provided for the definition of files/databases, and programs and runflows.
5. Detailed performance, estimation and optimization tests should be carried out on the physical design before committing to implementation.
6. The user should be actively involved throughout all levels of the development process. By contributing to the achievement of a system which meets his needs, he will become committed to its success.
7. A top-down approach is taken; a start is made at a high level, initially showing the broad picture and then allowing gradual and controlled decomposition into increased levels of detail.
8. Regular and formalized reviews are incorporated, which ensure that all work done is critically received for quality, completeness and applicability.

3.5 THE COMPONENTS OF SSAD

3.5.1 The generic model

The separation of concerns is represented by the simple generic model in Fig. 3.4. This separates analysis from design, and also distinguishes between logical and physical design. Each of the areas — analysis, logical design and physical design — represents a phase which can be split into subdivisions such as requirements specification, called stages. Within each stage will be a series of steps requiring the execution of one or more tasks. The net result from a step will be one or more deliverables which can be quality assured. The following sections provide a definition of the objectives of each of the stages.

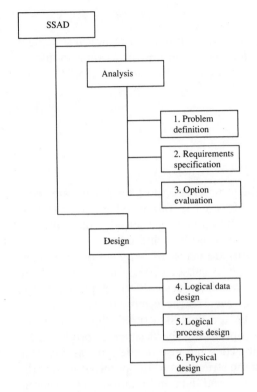

Figure 3.4 SSAD: the separation of concerns.

3.5.2 Problem definition

This is the identification and quantification of one or more problem in an organization which may be susceptible to resolution, or acceptable containment, by an information technology-based solution. Evaluation of the identified problem(s) could identify requirements meriting further investigation. Where an information system strategy exists, this task may be greatly simplified.

3.5.3 Requirements specification

This is the definition of requirements in precise detail as a result of discussions with end users. As they are defined they should be carefully reviewed, to ensure that they are a complete, correct and consistent reflection of the users' needs. Once complete, various option evaluations can be drawn up to show how the requirements could be implemented. IT and business staff should work together to select the most appropriate option based on factors such as cost, benefit, feasibility, practicality, resources, constraints, business priorities, risk and impact analysis.

3.5.4 Logical design

This translates the requirements for data and processing into a non-technical statement of how data should be organized and cross-referenced, and how processing should be grouped to provide units of functionality which are logical to the user and avoid the need for duplication of work.

3.5.5 Physical design

Physical design implements those simple logical structures on to a technical framework which makes effective use of the hardware and software (operating system, programming language, database management system etc.) to be applied, and ensures that performance standards and other service-level requirements can be achieved.

At critical stages of the design process decisions are made based on certain characteristics of the processes to be computerized. Only a subset of transactions is used to determine the overall pattern of transactions for which the design is to be optimized. The selection is made based on certain criteria, but even so there must be an element of subjectivity involved. In the development of the original structured approach by the authors,[10] a very precise objective method for optimizing the design was produced for various DBMS and file structures. This was objective because the design was based on the totality of all processes using the data, and the structures were optimized to give the most efficient access paths to the most frequently used data and relationships ('transaction volumetrics'). Special rules were introduced to cater for online transactions.

This approach has been successfully used to design many databases using different DBMS, which included, among others, the largest database in Europe at the time. This was done entirely manually by a very small team over a reasonable time (2–3 months), and had no adverse impact on the project delivery times.

Any online system is, by its nature, volatile in the profile of transaction mixes it will experience. The mix will inevitably change over time as new transactions are introduced and old ones fall into disuse. Therefore, the subjective nature of the selection of any subset of transactions is likely to be compounded by the nature of online systems usage and development. The conclusion is that any design based on such concepts must be high-risk and extremely suspect. This has direct parallels with early experiences of database design, in that, even if the original design was sound, performance very often deteriorated rapidly, leading to massive database reorganization/restructuring costs.

What is the solution? It is to use the algorithms derived in the original methodology, based on the totality of processing volumetrics. These will be used to produce optimum data structure and transaction process (TP) designs for various extremes of transaction mixes and growth patterns. A compromise design would then be produced based on the analysis of the various 'optimum' designs, which would not be optimum for any specific mix but which would ensure acceptable performance for all mixes, and would ensure some longevity of design. Careful performance monitoring of actual transaction volumes and access paths will allow cost-effective restructuring decisions to be taken.

3.6 SSAD THEORY INTO PRACTICE

In 1976 the authors published a paper '*A Methodology for Data Analysis Leading to Database Design*'.[10] This summarized their experiences of conducting one of the largest such activities in Europe, if not the largest, and contained proposals for a more formal and controlled approach to analysis and design activities. This influential paper defined, for the first time, many of the techniques, approaches and terminology now in common use. At the same time, individuals such as Chris Gane and Trish Sarson[11] were defining new techniques based around data flow diagrams. Over the years since then, a number of SSAD methodologies have been adopted, the most successful of which has been the structured systems analysis and design method — SSADM, also known as Sadism by its aficionados! First introduced in 1983, it is now at Version 4. Its success is primarily due to its being adopted as the recommended standard for use on all public sector IT developments. This forced its wide take-up in the IT service industry, which in turn has led to its adoption in the private sector as well. SSADM was developed by LBMS Plc, and was very similar to their own Learmonth and Burchett System Development Method (LSDM) in the 1980s, although LSDM and Version 4 are somewhat different. In effect, SSADM is the de facto standard for SSAD in the United Kingdom, and initiatives to define it as a British Standard will consolidate its position. Figure 7.1 is an illustration of the framework of SSADM (Version 3). It is reproduced from the National Computing Centre's SSADM (Version 3) Reference Manual,[12] and shows how SSADM implements the generic model in Fig. 3.4.

A number of other methods were influential in the 1980s, especially the CACI method for its data modelling techniques, many of which have been adopted in Version 4 of SSADM.[13] Arthur Anderson's Method 1, Hoskyns' PRISM (actually based on an early version of LSDM) and James Martin Associates' Information Engineering (IE) have also achieved widespread use. The market continues to grow, with new methods such as Ernst and Young's Navigator. All these methods have much in common, including a number of shared techniques. Chapter 7 examines each of the established, commercially available methods to see how they can be used within the Winway framework. This evaluation contains only an outline of these other methods; there are many publications and training courses dedicated to each of them, to which the reader is directed for more practical detail.

4

CONSTRUCTION TO PRODUCTION

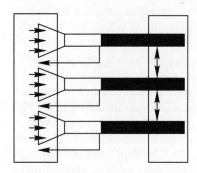

This chapter identifies the stages of the project life cycle necessary for successful completion of a project, beyond those covered by current structured systems analysis and design approaches, i.e. program construction, testing, delivery and production activities. Also described is a special activity relating to the acquisition and control of the project environment. It provides an overview of how they might be integrated to form a cohesive structured approach to the total life cycle.

4.1 INTRODUCTION

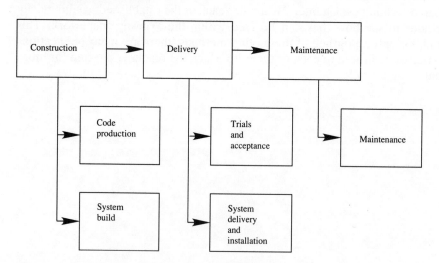

Figure 4.1 Core components, construction to production.

The justification for adopting a structured approach to the whole project life cycle was fully detailed in Chapter 1. The proposed extended 'stages' are represented in the extended life-cycle diagram in Fig. 4.1 and further expanded in the following text. The major activities considered are construction, delivery, each consisting of two stages, a single maintenance stage, and Stage β, which underpins and supports all of the activities.

4.2 SUPPORT PHASE

As Stage β is so central to the support of the other stages, it is perhaps sensible to consider its function first. It provides for:

- Procurement and installation of all hardware, software and networking elements of the total configuration.
- The definition and maintenance of all live systems environments.

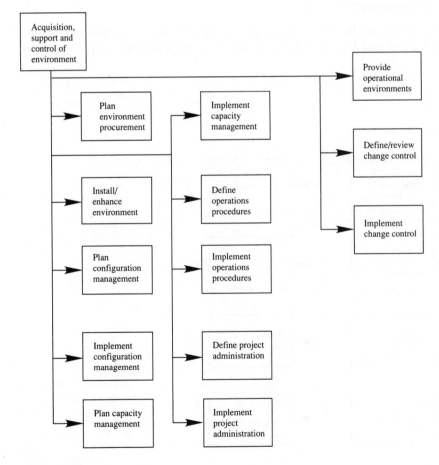

Figure 4.2 Stage β: acquisition.

- The establishment of configuration and capacity management.
- The definition of management and change control procedures, as shown in Fig. 4.2.

In many organizations, elements of all the above will exist; where this is the case, Stage β allows for a rationalization of all the procedures at a corporate level, while also allowing the assessment of the implications within specific projects. Where these facilities do not exist, then Stage β clearly quantifies what is required and this should be addressed at the earliest opportunity in the life cycle. Certainly in most current projects, it is likely that some support features described in Stage β will be required during design — perhaps even before. This will be necessary because tools, workbenches and dictionaries may need to interface with any mainframe configuration and may well be an integral part of it, particularly where prototyping techniques are being considered.

4.3 CONSTRUCTION PHASE

4.3.1 Stage 7: construction

The construction phase of the extended model consists of Stage 7: code production, and Stage 8: system build (see Fig. 4.3). Stage 7 addresses the generation of the necessary

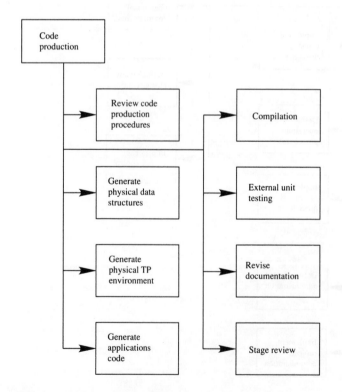

Figure 4.3 Stage 7: code production.

development environment(s) to support whatever code generation facility is being used, be it 3GL, 4GL or application generators. It deals with the actual production of the code components, the production of comprehensive documentation, and the independent (external) testing of the units, preferably by the analyst who produced the specification, rather than those who produced the code.

At Stage 7, and thereafter throughout the whole production phases of the project, the very powerful Winway QA/QC mechanism underlining the quality and documentation continuum philosophy, as described in Chapter 9, is applied.

4.3.2 Stage 8: system build

Stage 8: system build, as shown in Fig. 4.4 covers what is perhaps more conventionally called link and integration testing, leading to full system testing where the system as a cohesive integrated whole is built for the first time. This again is conducted by teams (preferably the analyst involved) completely independent of the production teams and subject to Winway QA. During this stage, plans are drawn up for tests necessary to prove the integrity of the system beyond its pure functionality. These include user acceptance, recovery/fallback and infrastructure-proving trials. Draft manuals are produced and initial training of the system trainers conducted.

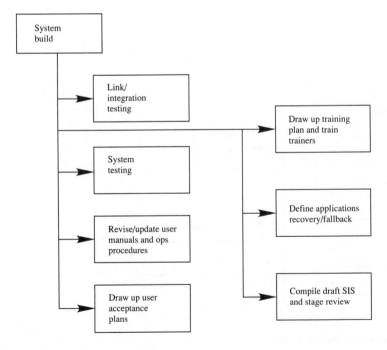

Figure 4.4 Stage 8: system build.

4.4 DELIVERY PHASE

The delivery phase consists of Stage 9: trials and first-phase acceptance, and Stage 10: system delivery and installation. This comprises of a two-phase trial stage, with the second phase culminating in the delivery of the system for operational running.

4.4.1 Stage 9: trials and first-phase acceptance

Stage 9, as shown in Fig. 4.5, provides the bridge between pure functional testing, although this is the major activity of the first phase of user acceptance testing (UAT), and the wider administrative and support systems. This includes initial infrastructure testing, which will prove the resilience and recovery capabilities of the hardware, software and networking facilities and establish some basic performance parameters. It will also provide for the proving of any data conversion and/or cleansing requirements, and any user training programmes.

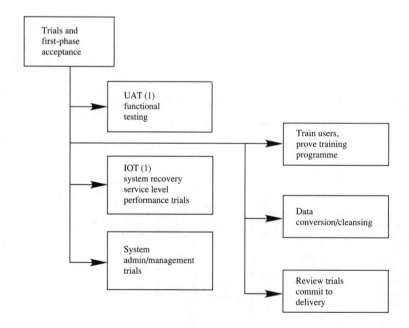

Figure 4.5 Stage 9: trials and first-phase acceptance.

4.4.2 Stage 10: system delivery and installation

Stage 10 allows for the final phase of testing, the delivery of the system and its installation, including:

- Parallel running and/or system simulation
- Final configuration tuning and performance proving of all operations procedures and standby/fallback provision
- Completing the build of the operational 'database'
- The sign-off of any service level and maintenance agreements
- The delivery of the operational software and all attendant 'accepted' documentation. These are shown in Fig. 4.6.

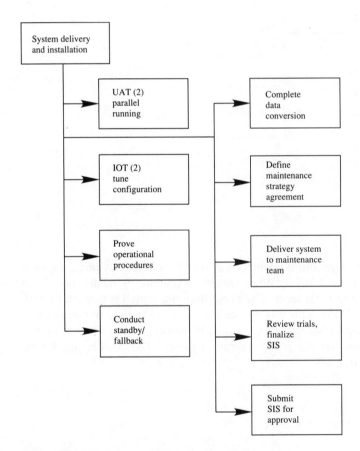

Figure 4.6 Stage 10: system delivery and installation.

4.5 MAINTENANCE PHASE

Maintenance provides for ensuring that the system is adequately monitored, policed and maintained post delivery. Stage 11 provides facilities for bug detection reporting and correction, with attendant software restriction and release notification; and for system enhancement requests and upgrades. It also provides for periodic reviews of system performance, expansion, revision, etc., and for the specific one-off post-implementation review. This is shown in Fig. 4.7.

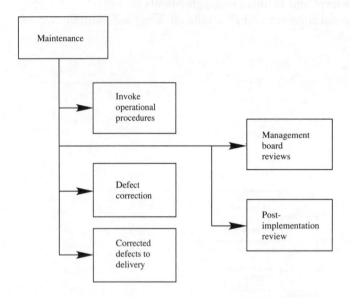

4.6 THE NOTATION

The full details of the precise steps and tasks involved, how they generally integrate with the analysis and design phase, and any strategic capability together with the associated feedback paths are contained in Chapter 8. The presentation adopted is consistent with that used for Version 3 of SSADM. This was adopted because at the time of compilation this was the de facto standard for structured methods. However, the way this book has been constructed would allow for the ready migration to an SSADM Version 4-type presentation if this was felt desirable.

5

TOTAL QUALITY MANAGEMENT

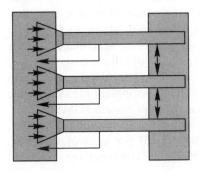

This chapter provides the outline of the Winway approach to total quality management. Firstly, the principles of the generic requirement for quality systems are explored to provide an insight into the infrastructure of the system. The next section considers what must be done to achieve an effective quality ethos in an organization. The remaining sections provide the practical detail of the Winway approach to total quality management, with its special focus on achieving quality through careful integration and control of documentation. The approach is intended to be compatible with British, European and international quality standards. Finally, the role of audit in IT QA is considered.

5.1 THE REQUIREMENT FOR TOTAL QUALITY MANAGEMENT

There are two fundamental questions to be asked by everyone involved in business. Ask these questions now of your colleagues and then ask them again after reading this section.

- Do we really need quality?
- What do we really mean by quality?

In considering 'do we really need quality?', consider what is currently happening in information technology, as shown in a Department of Trade and Industry survey:[14]

- 66% of projects stated a timescale overrun
- 55% of projects stated that effort was over budget
- 58% of projects were affected by an unexpected major problem
- 45% of projects saw their development task as difficult or complex

There has been a long history of failure of software projects, including late deliveries and excessively high maintenance costs. Indeed, most IT departments will have experienced at least one runaway project. Another study for the DTI[15] identified an annual wastage for traded software of at least £500m in the UK alone. This results in lost profit, dissatisfied customers and increased costs. There is concern that software contains too many errors, which become difficult to correct as a project reaches maturity. Studies, e.g. DeMarco,[16] have consistently shown that defects discovered late in an IT project cost a great deal more to fix than defects discovered early. Rework and spoilage typically account for 30 per cent of development costs and 50–60 per cent of full life costs. The way forward is to devise a system of controls which make software and development activities visible, and hence manageable, at all stages throughout the development life cycle. Such a system of controls may be combined as a quality management system (QMS).

DTI surveys[15] have shown that, for a company with only a £3m annual turnover, software failure costs can be in the order of £600 000 or 20 per cent of turnover. Implementing a QMS would, conservatively, save £150 000–£300 000 per year. We can draw some conclusions from these figures:

- Companies' business needs are, at worst, not being met; at best they are only partly met.
- Companies are losing competitive edge because their information technology cannot deliver what is needed when it is required, or at an acceptable cost.
- Companies are wasting money because of poor software quality.

At this point we need to understand what we really mean by quality, and how it can be measured. How is quality achieved? The crudest yardstick is the number of times the product is rejected by the customer for whatever reason. Unfortunately, this measure can only be applied retrospectively. A much more effective criterion would be the number of times a quality product is accepted first time, i.e. it has zero defects.

5.2 THE INFRASTRUCTURE AND COMMITMENT FOR QUALITY TO HAPPEN

'Quality is conformance to customer requirement'; so suggests Crosby,[17] one of the 'fathers' of quality management systems. This is not a complete definition — that will follow later — but it is adequate to serve the purpose at this point. What happens when companies fail to meet customer requirements is almost always negative. To clarify what happens, consider the following: when quality does not feature in the boardroom, there comes a point in a company's life where attracting new customers or repeat business becomes a low probability, and there is a high probability that existing customers cease to be customers. In a nutshell, the customer takes his business elsewhere because the company fails to deliver what he requires when he requires it, and to his definition of quality.

So how is quality achieved? There are national standards for QMS: the British Standards Institute's (BSI) BS5750 and BS5882, and international ones — European Norm (EN) 29000, International Standards Organisation (ISO) 9000 — which are intended to provide a measure of the adequacy of an organization's QMS. While a growing number of IT services organizations have been certified under BS5750, the DTI has recently launched its TickIT initiative in collaboration with the British Computer Society. It will take some time for one of these standards to establish itself as the most widely used. BS5750 has been used as the example in this book, as it is currently the most common. The BS5750 Quality Vocabulary defines QMS as: 'The totality of features and characteristics of a product or service that bear on its ability to satisfy stated or implied needs'. This is interpreted within the systems development process as: 'Conformance to specified requirements is to be assured by the supplier during several stages which may include design/development, production, installation and servicing'.

Total quality is achieving the definition of quality at the lowest cost applicable to deliver, on time, the level of quality the customer requires. The customer's — not the supplier's — definition of what quality is and should be, is the single deciding factor in determining conformance to requirement. Total quality management is how the quality objective is to be achieved, and includes:

- What infrastructure is needed to support total quality?
- Who needs to be involved?
- Why are they involved?
- When are they involved: phases, stages, steps, tasks and deliverables?
- What are their roles, i.e. what is required of them?

In essence, what commitment is required by the organization to deliver total quality?

5.2.1 Total quality in practice

It is prudent to examine the impact that companies have made by adopting a total quality approach to their customer requirements. The origins stem from the post-second world war depression. Countries were realizing that simply delivering quantity that was poor or substandard was not good enough.

The total quality movement began in earnest when the Japanese realized that the 'Made in Japan' sticker of the late fifties and early sixties was synonymous with poor quality. In the mid-sixties they began to take quality very seriously,[18] such that today Japan is the single biggest threat to the American and European markets. All Japanese products have quality underpinning them, from the car industry to cameras. Europe entered the total quality market only recently, after the Americans. How has this manifested itself? For example, German car manufacture has been synonymous with a total quality product, from the small hatchback models to the specialist turbocharged sports cars. The customer's definition of quality is the single deciding factor, hence quality hatchbacks for some and quality sports cars for others.

The developing countries are also entering the total quality market. In Great Britain alone, low cost, quality cars are being bought from developing countries, to the detriment of the indigenous car suppliers. In other words, total quality is something which applies equally at both ends of the market spectrum, not just the luxury/high price end. The Citroen 2CV and the Rolls Royce are both quality products.

To emphasize the need for quality and to demonstrate what happens if it is not a boardroom consideration, consider the following:

- If you do not take your customers' quality requirement very seriously, serious quality companies will.
- Whatever happened to the British motorcycle industry?

5.2.2 A sound basis for agreement

When systems are being developed which feature software as a significant component, agreements at varying levels need to be reached. These agreements in traditional systems development would vary from organization to organization and from project to project. Often, the only criterion that determined a successful project completion was that all parties agreed that it was finished — why, and for what reasons did not really matter — the project was 'finished' and there were always more pressing matters to attend to.

This is not a condemnation of the people involved, but rather of the tools and materials they had to work with. If you have little concept of what the product will be, how can you select the right tools and materials to make it? How do you know when to substitute materials and when should you sharpen the tools, or even replace them? Who should be involved in the product development, at what points, and with what contribution?

Before attempting any project, a policy decision needs to be made. This is an enduring corporate statement of purpose that expresses the policy agreed by everyone. In the BS5750 quality vocabulary, the following is that sound basis for agreement: conformance to specified requirements is to be assured by the supplier during several stages, which may include design/development, production, installation and servicing. Three questions immediately arise from this:

- Who are the suppliers?
- Who can specify requirements?
- How do supplier and specifier achieve conformance?

These questions point to the requirement for an infrastructure to assist both the supplier and the specifier achieve conformance to requirement.

5.2.3 The infrastructure to support supplier and specifier

Let us not reinvent the wheel: the generic quality standard BS5750 satisfies this requirement. It is also compatible with the EN 29000 and ISO 9000 international quality standards, and it provides the generic structure required for the software industry.

Companies can be assessed against the BSI quality assessment schedules through a third-party quality assessment scheme. This leads to certification to BS5750 Part 1 for software quality management systems.

So what is being assessed and what are the elements of the quality system? The key elements from BS5750 Part 1 are:

- Management responsibility
  - Quality policy
  - Organization
  - Management review
- Quality system
  - Procedures
  - Instructions
  - Quality plans
  - Quality manual
  - Controls
  - Processes
  - Inspection equipment
  - Acceptability of requirement
  - Quality records
- Contract review
  - Requirements definition
  - Requirements resolution
  - Contract review records
- Design control
  - Design and development planning
  - Design input requirements
  - Design outputs
  - Design verification procedures
  - Design changes procedures
- Document control
  - Document approval and issue
  - Document changes/modifications
- Purchasing
  - Assessment of subcontractors
  - Purchasing documentation
  - Verification of purchased product
- Purchaser-supplied product
  - Verification, storage and maintenance
- Product identification and traceability
  - All stages
- Process control
  - Production and installation processes
- Inspection and testing
  - Procedures and records

- Inspection, measuring and test equipment
  - Verification procedures
- Inspection and test status
  - Conformance/nonconformance of product
- Control of nonconforming product control procedures
- Nonconformity review and disposition
  - Rework, reiteration and rejection procedures
- Corrective action
  - Cause, effect and control procedures
- Handling, storage, packaging and delivery
  - Procedures
- Quality records
  - Achievement and operation
- Quality system audits
- Training
  - Training needs
- Servicing
  - Servicing maintenance
- Statistics
  - Procedure capability
  - Product acceptability

Company quality manual This is a reference document setting out the policy on the quality standards, procedures and practice within the system operation.

Company detailed procedures A document that provides the detail of the procedural, structural, documentation and quality assurance standards adopted for each of the specific quality elements. Each element is grouped into its constituent group headings, i.e. design/specification, development, production, installation and servicing. For software quality systems this effectively covers the whole of the software life cycle, from strategy to system replacement policy.

Quality plan A plan produced for each project or contract that sets out how quality is to be achieved. As no two projects are the same, the tools and materials used to achieve quality may differ. This sets out the policy for use.

Project plan A plan produced and refined for each project, that defines the projects' deliverables, schedule, estimates, constraints and the tools and materials to be used. This is decomposed into discrete phases, each consisting of a number of stages and each stage consisting of a number of steps. In the execution of a step, a number of tasks will be completed resulting in one or more deliverables to be quality assured.

The elements of a quality system together with the infrastructure provide the foundation for developing quality systems. However, simply following procedures will not deliver quality irrespective of what the product or service is. It is the totality of the approach together with effective management that makes the system deliver total quality systems. The next section provides an insight into some of the management techniques inherent in the Winway TQMS, which has been constructed to be BS5750-compliant.

5.2.4 Total quality needs effective management

There are three critical success factors applicable to all projects or contracts which determine the success or failure of the project. These factors are depicted in Fig. 5.1. Time, cost and quality are all interrelated. If they are not planned, controlled and monitored then the project is not under control.

Time Time is defined as time available, and is qualified as time spent and time left. There is little you can do about time spent — it has gone! However, it is analysed as either achievement or non-achievement time. Achievement time is where the time spent directly contributed to the successful completion of a deliverable. Non-achievement time is overhead time, such as configuration management or project control, or it is non-productive time spent on tasks such as uncontrolled iteration and/or rework. Time left is subdivided as fixed or definable. The definable element provides for earliest and latest date-mapping of milestones and deliverables.

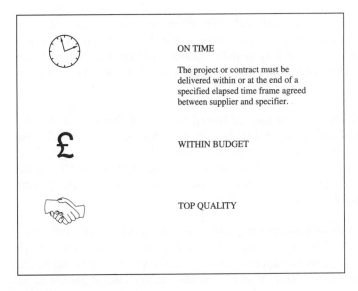

Figure 5.1 Project critical success factors.

Metrics information should be gathered on this, relating it to the entity attribute or relationship that caused the non-achievement. The fault logging and metrics associated with this are known as software engineering defect notes. These are equally applicable to development and maintenance.

Cost Cost is expressed in two ways: the cost of the deliverable(s) production, and the cost of not producing. This is particularly important when making business decisions in the strategy, feasibility or analysis phases. The cost should be expressed in business terms, i.e. business objectives met or goals attained, and where possible depicted as return on investment. The return on investment may not necessarily be simply cost recovery. Many benefits are not quantifiable in monetary terms. These usually concern the people elements of systems, and include such things as job satisfaction, motivation, commitment, etc. They do show some unexpected benefits, such as fewer absences, higher throughput of work and lower staff turnover.

Quality Quality is expressed as requirement. Requirements cover business objectives and goal attainment. They therefore cover management, supervisory and operational levels. Each requirement is qualified in terms of how well that requirement must be met — we need a measure of success, which should demonstrate the value-added benefits to the business, mapped out and measured.

Do not be afraid of accepting an imposed deadline for delivery. Often the deadlines coincide with some major event in the company's calendar, such as a new financial year, new product launch, etc. What really needs to be done is a short-duration design study to show the options available within and beyond the timescale suggested. This shows categorically *what* can be achieved, given the time available, the quality expected and the budget constraints.

Helm management Never be afraid to admit that your assumptions were wrong, before it is too late. The project manager should be at the helm of the ship. The rudder can turn the project on time, cost and quality as long as the consequential effect is known. There is no point in changing direction unless you know why you are doing it, and where you are going now.

No surprise, no compromise Projects are steered to expect a sea of change. Change is a fact of life. If you expect and anticipate change, then no unexpected problems will arise to surprise and compromise the project. Forward planning and a clear definition of the deliverables and what they are used for both now and later will allow all project contributors to anticipate change, predict its effect and collectively steer the project within the time, cost and quality factors.

I've started so I'll finish — knowing when to stop All steps have a deliverable, otherwise why are you doing it? Each deliverable must contribute to the project goals. Each deliverable must be derivable from the application of a technique. The contents of the deliverable should be derivable from more than one technique. Techniques are refinable or replaceable.

For each deliverable, a level of detail should be defined for its contents. Once this level is achieved the following activities can be commenced.

When deriving a deliverable, a number of transformations, iterations and rework will take place. The control of this is critical to the success of the time, cost and quality factors. As a starting point, the number of transformations, iterations and rework should be calculated as minimum, average and maximum. This can be part of the software metrics regime or per project or project phase of a live project. The maximum is the worst case and is the baseline for improvement e.g. if it currently takes 10 iterations an improvement would be 9 iterations and so on.

The causes of failure should be noted and changes implemented to remove them. Typical causes are:

- Technique: wrong techniques, not rigorous, wrongly applied.
- Input: ill-defined, not available, incomplete, not quality assured.
- Comparator: ineffective comparator mechanism.
- Inspection: static or dynamic sampling, prediction or inspection inappropriate, ineffective or incomplete.
- Output: ill-defined, not required, incomplete, not quality assured.
- Skill: wrong skills.
- Training: no training, inadequate, wrong level.
- Experience: none, some, wrong.
- Resource: people mix is wrong, personality.

The human element The human element introduces a degree of uncertainty into the time, cost and quality equation. Good quality people are in short supply and high demand, irrespective of their profession. Good people always succeed and always do a good job. The options available are:

- Chase this short-supply high-demand commodity and then try to retain its services.
- Attract the commodity.
- Implement the total quality management system that includes procedures for individual encouragement and improvement.

The companies that set and deliver total quality attract the attention of good quality people who want to work in a professional environment. Implementing a total quality approach will attract and retain such people. The prospects of a peer group of quality will give the company the critical mass it needs to deliver on time, to quality and within budget.

Individuals alone cannot deliver to a consistent level of quality without the peer group and the quality procedures to support them. Almost invariably they move to pastures new. One of the acid tests to apply is simply:

- Are you attracting and retaining good quality staff?
- Are you attracting them from competitors?
- Are your good staff leaving for competitors?

5.3 THE WINWAY APPROACH TO QUALITY

The Winway approach to TQMS is designed to operate within the framework of the formal international standards. While these identify the types of documents and checks that are needed, Winway identifies precise, well proven procedures for the most critical areas. A unique feature of the Winway approach is the very precise focus on the flow and transition of information from one activity to another, as it is recorded in the project documentation, and the concept of quality gates. These procedures are described in Chapter 9.

5.4 PROJECT MANAGEMENT

Very few structured analysis and design methods adequately address the management issues surrounding most technology projects. They give a veneer of project management by including planning and review activities, but this is not really sufficient. By its very nature, management is not something which can be completely regimented and prescribed. While there are many techniques and tools to help the manager, a great deal of the skill of the successful manager is down to personal characteristics and experience of dealing with people. However, a lot can be done to ensure that the environment exists for effective project management. We recommend the use of the PRINCE project management method.[19]

5.5 QUALITY AND DOCUMENTATION CONTINUUM STANDARDS

An important building block in the definition of a quality management system is the definition of documentation standards. The purpose, content, usage and quality control of each document should be defined. Equally importantly, the definition of preceding and succeeding documents should be defined. This is important in implementing quality control techniques, and provides a complete continuum audit and traceability of documents. Figure 5.2 demonstrates the documentation continuum at the highest level in the documentation production. Each document represented in the figure has sample contents defined in Chapter 12.

The standard is carried down to the individual deliverables of each of the major documents. For example, the Program Specifications of the System Design Specification is defined to an agreed standard. The quality element of the continuum relates to the application of the quality assurance (QA) and quality control (QC) procedures. Both the document's usefulness and the standards are proven continuously by the QA/QC procedures. The application of the QC procedure is met, in part, by the Winway inspection technique (Chapter 11).

The net result of the quality and documentation continuum is that:

- All documents are defined to a standard and have preceding/succeeding links
- All projects operate the same standards and documentation
- Feedback through quality control helps to refine the quality and documentation standards

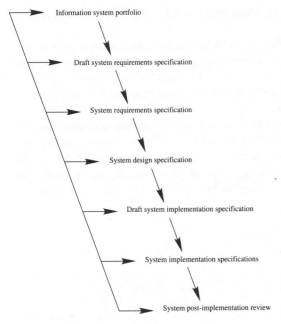

Information system portfolio

Draft system requirements specification

System requirements specification

System design specification

Draft system implementation specification

System implementation specifications

System post-implementation review

Figure 5.2 The document quality continuum.

5.6 CORPORATE STANDARDS

Some of the documents produced at a project level are defined at a corporate level. These are the ones where external consistency of a standard is required on an interproject basis. Such documents include:

- User manuals
- Training manuals
- Operational procedures
- Human–computer interface style guides

This provides interproject consistency and prevents the project teams from reinventing the wheel on each subsequent project.

5.7 THE ROLE OF INTERNAL AND EXTERNAL AUDIT

Many organizations have their own internal audit departments, and it is increasingly common for these to include computer audit specialists. The role of internal audit is to advise senior management on the effectiveness, efficiency and economy with which the organization conducts its business. This means evaluating controls and systems across the organization. Good internal audit teams work to professional standards such as those published by the Institute of Internal Auditors and the Chartered Institute of Public Finance and Administration.

While it is vital for internal audit to maintain its independence within the organization, there is a great deal which can be done to forge mutually beneficial working relationships. The internal auditor utilizes many techniques of benefit to the IT manager.[20] It is strongly recommended that the internal audit branch be encouraged to review proposed audit standards and their operation.

External auditors are more concerned with the statutory company accounts and are particularly interested in the internal controls exercised over financial systems. This has led to an increased use of computer-assisted audit techniques, which can also help the project manager to better understand what he or she is trying to achieve and how this might be done. Stronger and closer working links between IT and audit staff are recommended.

PART 2

WINWAY REFERENCE MANUAL

This part describes the Winway method in technical detail. It describes the procedures, standards and documentation to be used as well as the main techniques used.

6
STRATEGIC PLANNING

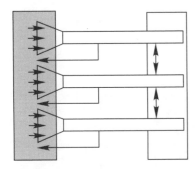

This chapter provides the detailed Winway method for strategic planning. It itemizes the tasks involved and the documents to be produced. The planning process consists of one complete stage, Stage α, a number of steps and the individual tasks of each step. References are made throughout to goals, objectives and specific techniques. Therefore, please read Secs 10.1, 10.2, 10.3 and 11.4 before beginning.

6.1 STAGE α: BUSINESS STRATEGY AND INFORMATION SYSTEMS PLANNING (Fig. 6.1)

6.1.1 Objectives

These are to create a business blueprint for the successful deployment of both information systems and technology. They must support the business objectives and goals of the organization, and provide a comparator to ensure that the business objectives set for the information systems are being met.

6.1.2 Description

This stage is primarily concerned with the business infrastructure, its aims and ambitions. The successful deployment of IT is achieved by aligning the strengths of IT to the business, for business and not technological reasons. The information systems derived from this stage will support demonstrable business objectives and goals.

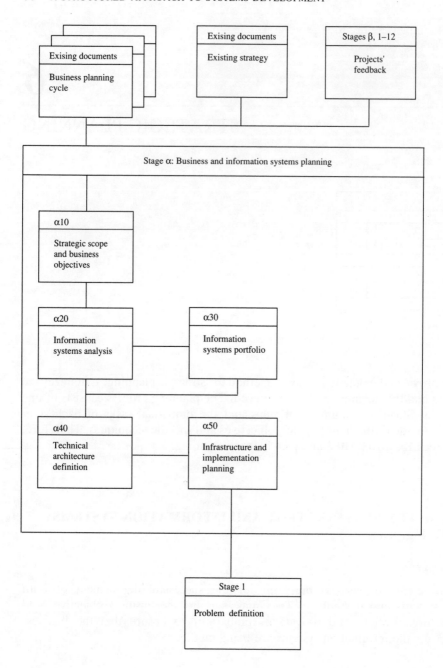

Figure 6.1 Stage α.

Strategic planning is an iterative exercise with feedback from individual projects being used to tune and refine the ISP.

STEPS

α10 Strategic scope and business objectives

.10 Determine the scope of the study
.20 Establish roles and responsibilities
.30 Define the corporate objectives within the scope
.40 Define the current organization structure and its contribution within the scope.
.50 Define the strengths, weaknesses, opportunities and threats presented at the organization level
.60 Conduct change analysis on current scope
.70 Produce scope of study definition

α20 Information systems analysis

.10 Prepare interview strategy
.20 Conduct critical success factor interviews
.30 Construct information model
.40 Construct functional model
.50 Construct information/function matrix
.60 Construct problem analysis
.70 Review current systems contribution
.80 Rationalize results
.90 Document results

α30 Information systems portfolio

.10 Develop the information systems options
.20 Identify, prioritize and agree information system requirements
.30 Produce information systems portfolio

α40 Technical architecture

.10 Classification of information systems
.20 Definition of technical environment
.30 Definition of infrastructure
.40 Capacity planning
.50 Production and agreement of technical architecture

α50 Infrastructure and implementation planning

.10 Define and procure infrastructure to support IT strategy
.20 Produce individual project plans for infrastructure and IS projects
.30 Prepare briefing and handover documentation for individual projects

Stage α inputs

1. Business planning cycles, e.g. sales, production, finance, marketing
2. Existing strategy

Stage α outputs

1. Scope of study definition (Step α10)
2. CSF results (Step α20)
3. Information systems portfolio (Step α30)
4. Technical architecture definition (Step α40)
5. Implementation plans (Step α50)

STEP α10: STRATEGIC SCOPE AND BUSINESS OBJECTIVES (Fig. 6.2)

Tasks

α10.10 When defining the scope of the study a number of avenues must be investigated, to document the perceived problem, business need or opportunity that the study needs to address. When doing this, review any existing initiatives from the current business planning cycles. It may well be that the study and some terms of reference have been originated as a direct result of a business need in one or a number of business areas.

Terms of reference should include a list of objectives and, where possible, goals and timescales. This will assist in pointing towards the business areas affected and in scoping what should/should not be included, and what is/is not possible given time and resource constraints. During this task the key sponsors of the study need to be identified. These may not be the people who originated the study. It is the key people who influence or make decisions and policy in the business area(s) within the scope of the study.

α10.20 During the study there are a number of roles and associated responsibilities. These are sponsor, project manager and team leader. The sponsor will be expected to devote time to the study, understand the principal techniques and make key decisions on findings. The sponsor will also be responsible for organizing interviews with the people who will make a telling contribution to the study. The sponsor should be made aware that these people may have to be given some training in the study's procedures and techniques, in order to maximize their contribution.

α10.30 Defining the corporate objectives within the scope of the study is either very easy or very difficult. If they already exist in one form or another, then the task will be easy. If they do not exist, they may have to be evolved by interviews, discussions

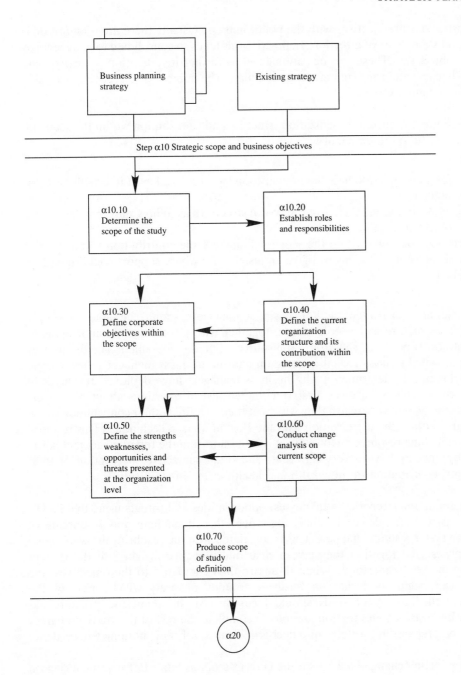

Figure 6.2 Step α10.

or demonstrations of objectives with the policy makers. Usually there are no more than 15 high-level statements of direction. In practice this tends to consolidate to between five and eight objectives. These can be rationalized as further investigation is carried out, until they become enduring statements of direction. The number of objectives covered is part of the scoping exercise.

α**10.40** Defining the current organization structure and contribution within the scope of the study is useful on three counts:

1. It provides an insight into how the organization has organized itself internally to carry out the objectives.
2. It is useful in comparing the current physical structures as to how they may best carry out the objectives.
3. The organization units within the scope will make some contribution to the overall wealth of the company. This will give an insight into where support could/should be channelled.

The personnel department and/or business managers should be able to supply departmental structure and people charts, together with job titles and major areas of responsibilities. If possible, sets from both sources should be obtained. The differences between personnel's view of what is going on and the business manager's view can be quite enlightening in determining why business managers have deployed resources in particular ways. This often gives a 'starter for ten' list of questions about objectives, goals, etc., and how they perceive they will meet them. Defining their contribution to the wealth and health of the organization uses the Boston Matrix Technique. This is useful again in channelling resources. However, it is best built from the top management layer. Individual managers have a very different, and often subjective, perception of their departments' contribution to the wealth and health of the organization.

α**10.50** Defining the strengths, weaknesses, opportunities and threats using the SWOT technique, is a useful device in analysing where the channelling and resourcing of information systems should happen. This is correlated with the results of the wealth and health analysis, and together they give a clear and objective insight into the current positioning of the organization. When these are then compared to the objectives, the managers can begin to decide on business grounds precisely which areas of the organization the rest of the study should focus on. At this point the structure has effectively been scoped and the foundations to complete the rest of the study prepared. However, be prepared for a status quo decision. That is, for now, nothing will be done.

α**10.60** Conducting change analysis on the current scope is vital. Before embarking on the rest of the study, and even into information systems development, it is pertinent to judge the future. It may be that as a result of the earlier tasks a number of factors were listed that were known to be imminent, such as reorganization, new management style, government legislation, etc. These should all be examined for potential impact on the study's scope. Another useful technique is to use the critical success factor (CSF). This could be used selectively for determining factors that will or could change, and are either inside the control of the organization, and so can be controlled, or, outside the control of the organization and so can be planned.

α**10.70** Producing a scope-of-study definition is used for a number of purposes:

* To demonstrate the results, conclusions and decisions.
* To confirm the way ahead.
* To obtain clear authorization from top management to proceed.

The document should be selectively targeted at its participants, and should not be bulky. For example, the key decision-maker who will authorize continuation may only want to see the overall scope, and each of the business managers may only need to see their contribution; the boardroom may only wish to see the objectives, wealth and SWOT analysis.

Also the deliverable should be released as soon as confirmed results of the study are available. At the end there will be no surprises to encounter and the document will get read: people will read it because it is properly targeted, and because they made a contribution.

One last point is worth bearing in mind: by using an accurately scoped study it is estimated that something in the region of 30–40 per cent of time and effort could be saved, compared to using one which is not accurately scoped.

STEP α20: INFORMATION SYSTEMS ANALYSIS (Fig. 6.3)

Tasks

α**20.10** A carefully prepared interview strategy is one of the best investments made during the course of the study. It is quite possible to simply prepare a list of names and then conduct interviews to obtain the information required, but this is unproductive. Firstly, check the organization structure charts obtained in Step α10. From these, check which organization units carry out the objectives within the scope of the study. Within each of the units, establish which functions are carried out in support of the objectives. From this prepare a tentative list of the people charged with achieving those objectives. Often one objective crosses functional boundaries, and equally often there is a large peer group associated with achieving the same objective, for example a sales manager for each region, or a production manager for each site or product.

Given the organization's culture and ethos, decide on the interviewing strategy. Remember that facilitated meetings, as described in Chapter 10, are excellent for rationalizing group input. The objective of the interviews is to define the goals, measures, etc., and the information model and functional model.

As a valuable alternative, much of the work, with some preparation, of Steps α20 and α30 can be achieved using the facilitated meetings described in Chapter 11. This has the added value of creating the critical mass of both people and commitment needed to see the strategy through to a successful conclusion.

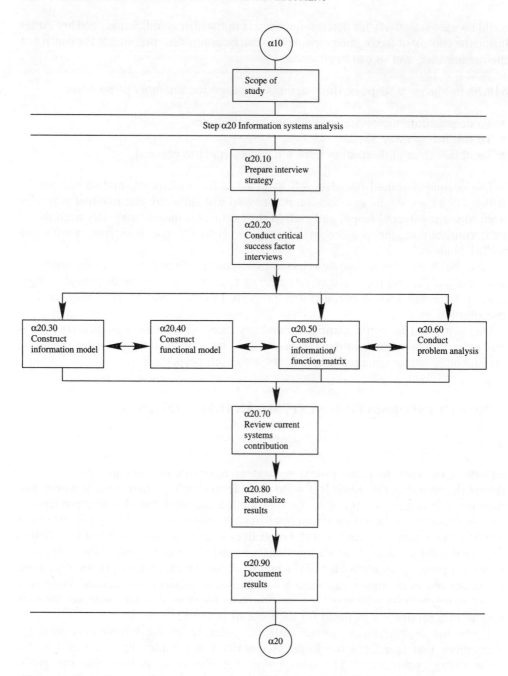

Figure 6.3 Step α20.

α20.20 Before conducting the critical success factor interviews, some preparation must take place. As a minimum, the participants need to understand the technique, and this is best achieved by working from the output backwards to the components of the output, and the use and benefits of the participants' contribution. It is useful to develop some relevant examples from the organization with which they can identify. Bear in mind that if they are not prepared, or have not given any serious thought or deliberation to the interview session, you will waste your time and effort. Using peer groups as a catalyst to obtain results is very useful in these circumstances. From experience, people tend either to make very good contributions because they have prepared, or a poor contribution because they cannot grasp why it is being done, or because they have not received any rudimentary training in the technique.

During the CSF interview there must be a plan of what is to be achieved, for example, concentrating only on certain functions during this interview. Also, when deciding on what information is required to support the goals and CSFs, it is worthwhile extending the interview into a mini session to establish the model for such information.

This makes it easier to establish the measures of achievement, as invariably the measures involve the information. Another useful point is to investigate the problems associated with achieving the goals. These often give an insight into CSFs and breakdowns in communication and information.

In a number of sessions previously conducted, the interviewees have actually produced their own information flow diagrams. This has proved to be a good investment.

α20.30 The information model should be constructed as a by-product of the CSF interviews. During the interviews, mini information models are constructed, which should be rationalized into an overall information model within the scope of the study. During this exercise there will be problems with completeness and consistency, and so the business jargon or language used by the interviewees should be standardized, not turned into a technical description: otherwise the users cannot immediately relate what they said with what has been recorded. Some of the sources, usage and sinks of information will be outside the scope of the study, but are now the first indications that either they may have to be included or that interfaces may have to be provided. That is, the information systems will change the way in which information is currently prepared and used. This will affect both the areas within the scope and those outside the boundary who supply or use information within the scope of the study.

α20.40 The functional model is a further refinement of the information already available about the organization, its units, its functions, job titles and people. In this task the information is rationalized by relating the present physical structures to the objectives and goals they carry out. From this there is often an incomplete mapping, suboptimization of organization or resources, duplication and redundancy of information, procedures and practices. It is a good investment to logicalize the functional model in terms of what is trying to be achieved, i.e. the objectives and goals themselves, rather than how they currently operate to achieve them.

α20.50 The information/function matrix is developed as a clustering device to determine what use is currently made of information within the organization. The clustering algorithm should use the creation and update of information as the clustering criterion. This will be used later when information systems options and information ownership are determined. It will provide an insight into information dependencies within the organization.

α20.60 A review of the current systems is conducted in terms of how well they support the stated goals and objectives. This is usually elicited during the CSF interviews, though it may be carried out separately to give a different perspective. This should be done by asking how well, on a scale of 1–10, do the systems support the objectives and goals? Poor scores should require reasons to be supplied, whereas high scores indicate success. This should be capitalized upon: successes and strengths should be built on. This may influence what are presented as options later.

α20.70 Problem analysis takes the results of the CSF interviews and analyses the problems presented, at an individual or even a group level. It looks for overall problems, symptoms of a further problem or underlying trends.

α20.80 The objectives and goals need to be rationalized from the top down, so that they are consistent with each other. A clear hierarchy needs to be seen, where lower levels reflect the higher levels.

α20.90 The results of Step α20 should be documented; however, the target audience will dictate what should be included/excluded. The rationalized objectives and goals should be included prominently in all the documents, and consideration should be given to a presentation of the objectives and goals.

  Much of the work in tasks .30 to .60 can be done in parallel. The results should be fed back immediately to the people involved for quality control. By the end of the step, all the people involved will have seen the results, and a walkthrough followed by a presentation of the objectives and goals is a useful technique in maintaining the momentum and profile of the study.

STEP α30: INFORMATION SYSTEMS PORTFOLIO (Fig. 6.4)

Tasks

α30.10 Developing the information systems options involves pulling together many of the individual threads of the earlier tasks. The information system requirement must be based on business needs. When deriving this requirement, the following should be considered:

● How well do the current systems support the business goals? What, if any, is the shortfall? Does this point to an information system or to additional work?
● What can be done immediately for major problem areas?
● What information requirements exist for which there is no current, planned or developing system?

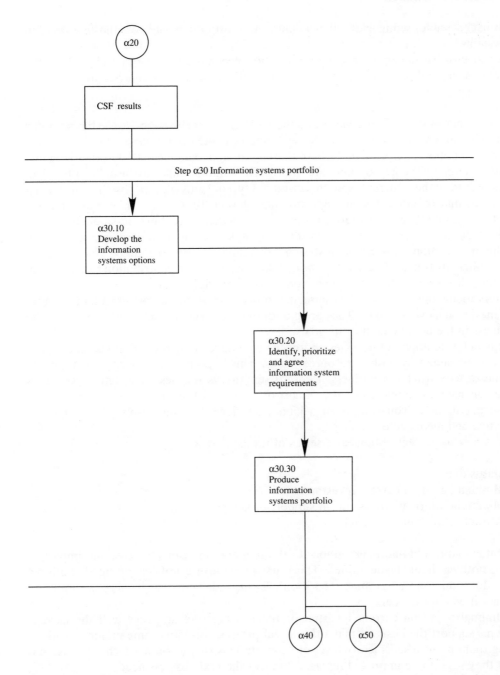

Figure 6.4 Step α30.

- What possible sequencing, dependency and priority exists for the information systems?
- What business dependencies and information dependencies exist that may affect the sequencing and priority? The functional model and the cluster analysis are useful for investigating this aspect.

The results of the CSF interviews and the resulting rationalization are the basis for this task. The options are presented as tactical, strategic and operational.

Tactical options are presented where there is an immediate need to do something in a short timespan. Tactical options are short-term solutions and are usually offered in response to either current system unsuitability, or pressing, persistent underlying problems that require a fast and appropriate solution. By the very nature of a tactical solution it can only be short term; however it does deliver real business benefits.

Strategic options are presented for information needs that are of strategic importance to the organization. This can be in strategy, planning or even operational systems. They are defined as strategic because they will make a value-added contribution to the overall business direction, or to the organization's most important goals.

Operational options cover the transaction processing and infrastructure administration required to achieve the goals. They are part of the infrastructure necessary to support the business in the achievement of its goals.

It is better to adopt a blue skies approach when developing these options, that is, not to be constrained by cost or resource issues. This is perhaps the only opportunity to define exactly what the business needs to support its policies. If in later tasks hard decisions have to be made because of cost or resource issues, it will be easier to make those decisions. If you start from a jaundiced viewpoint, the result will tend to be negative and incomplete.

It is best to present options as a series of levels; that is:

- Status quo
- Minimal based on current investment
- Minimum information systems in support of key goals
- Attractive information systems

Status quo is a 'do-nothing' option. In the preparation of this the cost and impact of doing nothing should be quantified. This usually has the effect of converting 'do nothing' into 'do nothing now but must start soon'. Realism dictates that if there is simply no budget it will not happen.

Minimal based on current investment: the investigation into how well the current systems support the business may offer a real prospect of doing some minimal work to bring them up to a satisfactory level of support. This should show which systems, and how they need to be improved/replaced to meet the real business needs.

Minimum information systems in support of key goals: this is primarily a subset of the 'attractive' information systems. This derives the minimum information systems requirement in support of the key objectives and goals. This is also useful later in determining sequencing, dependency and priorities.

Attractive information systems: this is the information systems that have carefully balanced the two extremes of 'no risk strategy' and 'entrepreneur strategy'. The 'no risk' strategy has a low degree of failure but an equally low business return, whereas the entrepreneur strategy has a high degree of failure but an equally high business return. The middle ground is termed the 'attractive area'. In essence, a carefully researched 'blue skies' approach. The positioning of the information systems in the attractive area will depend on the organization's policy on investment and risk taking. Invariably, if no risks are taken the organization is stagnating; taking the right risks and minimizing the possibility of failure while maximizing the chances of success are part of a dynamic business.

α**30.20** This task takes the options that have been prepared and consolidates them into the chosen option. This can be a combination of the options presented; for example, an interim measure may be selected to deploy tactical solutions to pressing needs, while the attractive information systems are pursued in parallel. At this point the user population will almost certainly require details of the possible costs, benefits and return on investment to assist them in deciding which route is suitable.

When developing a cost-benefit appraisal, due cognizance must be taken of the audience for which it is being developed. Since the entire study has been concerned with developing a business case for information systems, this is the point where business decisions are made. It is easier to make even difficult business decisions if the facts are clearly presented. The people who will make those decisions need time and space to absorb the options and associated cost benefits. These should be circulated and then a facilitated meeting or meeting(s) arranged as a 'decision think tank', so that decisions can be made.

Clearly, when the options and cost benefits are presented, nothing will be gained by producing detailed spreadsheets of projected benefits — they will almost certainly change as more detail emerges. The type of audience in this session will be looking for the effect on the business and the bottom line re profit or loss. They will be looking for solutions. It is the team's responsibility to guide them successfully through the options, and this can only be done by presenting, succinctly, solutions to known business needs and problems. The following represents a useful starting point to guide and shape the work involved in this task to a successful conclusion. However, it must be borne in mind that a company's culture and ethos influence the approach to be taken with the following checklist:

1. Start with immediate results, what can be done now and what business benefits or prooblems will it solve.
2. Benefits should be demonstrably linked back to the objectives or goals, and should be quantified — cost, timescales, return on investment.
3. Benefits which achieve business goals, for example cost reduction, customer service, new opportunities, improved margins or market share, quality supplier, inventory control, production and/or distribution chain benefits, carry more weight than other benefits such as technical ones.
4. Outputs using graphs or pie charts are easier to comprehend than pages of costings.

5. Summarize the total options on one or two (at the most) A4 sheets of paper. This will become a focal point from which extra levels of detail can be discussed as and when needed.

Overall, the task depends heavily on the business knowledge and skills of the presentation team. Success will be attributable primarily to understanding the business rather than to understanding IT issues.

α30.30 This task is concerned with producing the information systems portfolio using the contents in Chapter 12. This is the business blueprint and is the basis for resourcing and funding of the finalized strategy. The portfolio presentation and layout must be considered: it is a quality document and should be professionally produced to reflect its importance. If the document is not seen as important, either the strategy is wrong, or the company's time has been wasted, or both!

The individual information systems and their constituent components will be used at the project level. Thought must be given to the presentation and layout of these documents so that they may be utilized at the project level. If a computer-aided software engineering (CASE) tool has been used for the data and function modelling, this should be forward-compatible with the subsequent phases.

STEP α40: TECHNICAL ARCHITECTURE DEFINITION (Fig. 6.5)

Tasks

α40.10 The purpose of classifying the information systems is to assist in the definition of the technical environment required to support such systems. The classification is based on the characteristics rather than the purpose (tactical, strategic, operational) of the system. The characteristics allow decisions to be made that will shape the technical environment. The characteristics assessed are:

- Data volumetrics
- Data distribution requirements
- Data presentation standards — graphics, textual
- Number and location of users
- Speciality or uniqueness of application
- Commonality of application
- Static or dynamic nature of application components

The decisions that can be made will include:

- Platform(s)
- Workstation(s) suitability
- Networking requirements

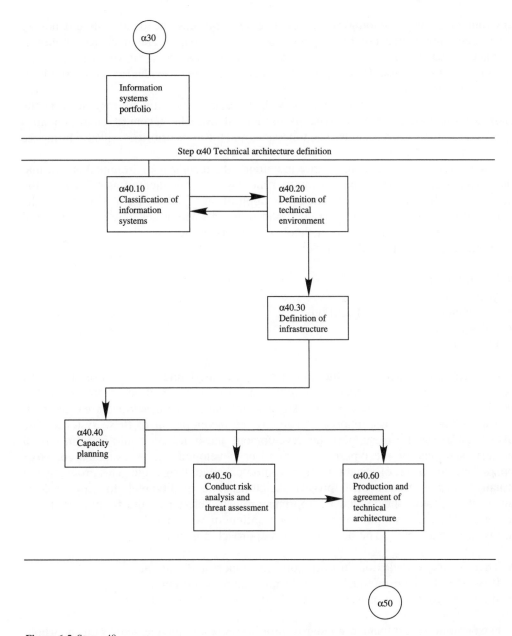

Figure 6.5 Step α40.

α**40.20** The technical environment is best defined in terms of discrete units, but it may not be possible to define one environment that supports all the information systems requirement. A reasonable guideline is that technology becomes obsolete quickly, therefore individual units of technology should be planned within an overall technical environment. The technology is there to serve a business need, and should not be 'upgraded' simply because the supplier has a new version. The need for change is planned proactively in strategy reviews. If there is a need to change it will be for business reasons and not because, for example, the programming team leader says postscript laser printers are needed.

The definition of each system, i.e. tactical, strategic or operational, together with the classification by characteristic type, is used to define the technical environment(s) required to support the systems. The timescales and business priorities will also influence the technical environment.

One point of paramount importance in defining the technical environment is information independence. When the information models are implemented as databases, the information should be independent of its application. That is, an ability to use the information independent of its current application. This will be severely compromised if the technical environment places technology barriers in the way.

The final definition should include:

- Hardware platforms
- Workstations
- Communications and distribution
- Software languages
- Database

α**40.30** The infrastructure, in the strategic context, is defined in terms of standards, procedures, tools and techniques required to support the information systems within the technical environment. The types of systems which have to be developed are examined, and an infrastructure is proposed to support the development of these systems. The overall infrastructure to support the development and build takes into account typical project skeletons for the type of projects to be developed, e.g. package-based, large operational multisite, office automation, computer-aided design, etc. This grouping will usually result in four or five project skeletons. The quality plan for any projects undertaken should specify the appropriate project skeleton as the framework to be adopted. The quality and documentation continuum will then be used to prove the infrastructure adopted. The benefits of this approach are that:

- There is only one flexible infrastructure to support and maintain.
- It is easier to build the quality and documentation continuum.
- It allows progressive proving of the infrastructure standards adopted.

The definition must include standards, procedures, tools and techniques for the whole of the software life cycle. The definition will be influenced by the type of projects developed (project skeletons), and the physical environment selected to support the technical environment definition.

α**40.40** This task requires the estimation of the total capacity required to support the strategy. Capacity planning is undertaken using the volumetrics collected during the information model production, system characteristics, technical environment definition and the infrastructure definition. This information is then fed into the infrastructure and implementation planning.

α40.50 A risk analysis and threat assessment study should determine the need for:

- Disaster planning
- Security of information
- Physical security

α40.60 After the volumetric information supplied by the capacity planning step has been considered, the final definition of the technical architecture is produced. This is a formal document-producing task, and brings together the outputs from tasks 10, 20, 30 and 40. The output is the Technical Architecture Definition.

STEP α50: INFRASTRUCTURE AND IMPLEMENTATION PLANNING
(Fig. 6.6 see page 80)

Tasks

α50.10 This task utilizes the definition of the infrastructure needed and expands it into a set of definitive standards and procedures. The components of the infrastructure that are not already in place are procured, together with the associated support and, where necessary, training.

α50.20 Individual project plans for both the infrastructure and the information systems projects are prepared in conjunction with the business users. Equally important in the drawing up of these plans is the identification of sponsors. A sponsor is a business user who will champion the cause; a project without a sponsor is in for an extremely rough ride, whatever extra time is needed to obtain a sponsor must be taken.

α50.30 Individual project teams need to be briefed on the projects, and the handover documentation prepared for release to the project manager and team leader: they should have been involved in the previous task, so the building of business relationships between IT project manager and business sponsor may proceed. It is also not unusual, as the result of a business approach to systems, for a business user to be the project director overseeing developments and interpreting results through the project manager.

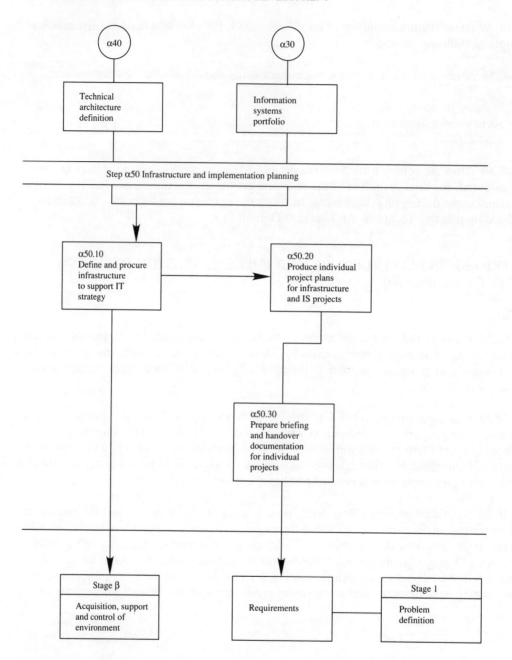

Figure 6.6 Step α50.

7

STRUCTURED SYSTEMS ANALYSIS AND DESIGN

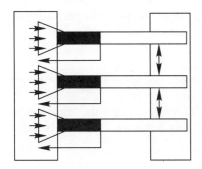

This chapter provides a description of the major analysis and design methods in terms of structure, the major techniques used and the documentation provided. The methods covered in chronological order are: SSADM (Version 3), SSADM (Version 4), LSDM, PRISM and Information Engineering. Comparisons are made to show how each method maps on to the generic Winway model for SSAD as shown in Chapter 3. Similarly, Winway documentation from Chapter 12 is mapped on to each method.

7.1 WINWAY AND SSADM VERSION 3

7.1.1 Background

The structured systems analysis and design method, SSADM, has already been referred to earlier in this book. It is the standard adopted by the government's Central Computer and Telecommunications Agency and recommended for use on public sector IT projects. It was first published in 1983 and has evolved through a number of Versions. Version 3[12] is probably the most widely used method in the UK, and is now gaining wider adherence in the private sector. Version 4 was published in 1990 and will inevitably take some time to become established, even though it contains many important advances over Version 3 (V3). Section 7.1 considers V3, and Section 7.2, Version 4. There are various textbooks describing the use of Version 3, the most notable being *SSADM, A Practical Approach* by Ashworth and Goodland.[21]

7.1.2 Stage structure

SSADM V3 consists of six stages, each broken down into a number of steps. Each step is further broken down into tasks, i.e. the activities which are necessary to create the finished products of the step. A diagram of SSADM V3 is in Fig. 7.1. The three major phases of SSADM V3 are feasibility study, systems analysis, defining what has to be done, and system design, defining how it is to be done. These phases map very clearly on to the generic model for SSAD shown in Fig. 3.1. The individual steps in the method are explained in detail in the following paragraphs.

Analysis phase The objective of the analysis study is to create a detailed specification of the user's requirements, and to agree with them what levels of service and performance are required. The stages in this phase are:

Stage 1: analysis of current operations and problems.
Stage 2: specification of requirements, in terms of what the system must provide rather than how it will work.
Stage 3: selection of user options, in which the user selects a system for implementation from a menu of possibilities, each having differing service levels, cost benefits and development implications.

Design phase The objective of systems design is to define the structure and content of the system: how it is to provide the required services and how it is to be implemented. The stages in this phase are:

Stage 4: data design, in which the detailed logical structure and the content of each component are defined.
Stage 5: process design, in which individual processes are specified in detail.
Stage 6: physical design, which involves the conversion of the logical design to one for implementation on a particular hardware/software environment, refined to meet performance requirements to within fine tuning limits, and specified in detail.

Stage 1: analysis of system operations and current problems

In the first stage there are three major activities:

1. The analysis phase is set up. This involves the initial scoping of the system, some preliminary high-level analysis to provide a sound estimating base and a start point for subsequent steps, and, finally, detailed planning of the analysis phase.
2. A detailed representation of the physical system that currently serves the users, together with its problems and shortcomings, is built up. This is done by creating three products in parallel, the current physical data flow diagrams (DFDs), the logical data structure (LDS), and the problem/requirement list (PRL), the production of each interacting on the others.

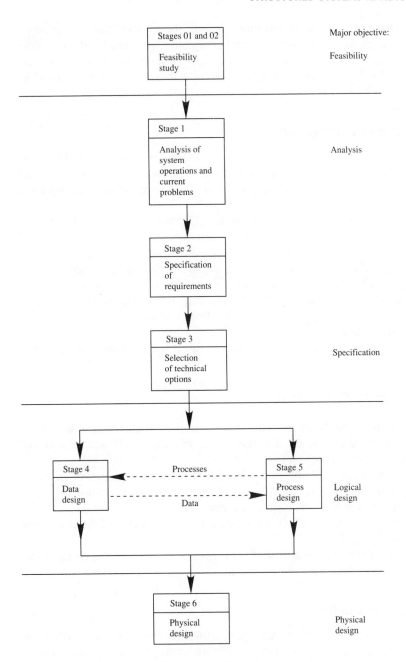

Figure 7.1 SSADM Version 3 © NCC.

3. The products of the stage are reviewed formally with the user(s). This represents a formal QA checkpoint to ensure accuracy and completeness of the products before continuing to the next stage. It also provides an opportunity to agree the system boundaries, since the detailed analysis of the current system may well show that the initial scoping of the project was inappropriate.

Stage 2: specification of requirements

1. The representation of the current physical system, mainly in terms of the DFDs, is converted to a logical view. In this manner constraints imposed by the way the current system is organized, which may otherwise be taken into consideration unnecessarily, are eliminated.
2. The requirements for audit, control and security (ACS) in the system are examined. This ensures that facilities to meet these requirements, vital to the successful operation of a sophisticated information system, are incorporated in the design from the earliest stages, and therefore form an integral part of the implemented system.
3. The PRL is extended by the inclusion of requirements from a user requirement (if it has been produced as a separate document), and ACS requirements already mentioned. Entries are expanded to give a clear understanding of the point addressed, and duplication eliminated.
4. Different business options are presented to the user for selection of the most appropriate.

A model of the chosen system is produced:

- Firstly by application of the problems/requirements to the existing logical model, to produce a required model, in terms of DFDs and LDS, which is in accord with the user's wishes for the required solution.
- Secondly by creation of entity life histories (ELHs), which at this stage serve a useful validation function in that they tie together the LDS and DFDs; by taking this third view any inconsistencies in the other views are revealed.
- The creation of ELHs also allows a start to be made on the definition of the processing logic of the system.
- Finally the products of this stage are formally reviewed to ensure that the requirement specification is in accordance with the user(s) needs.

Stage 3: selection of user option

There will always be a number of ways of implementing the requirement specification produced from Stage 2. Each way will provide differing levels of service, and will have differing costs and benefits associated with it. The people who should make the decision as to which option will be implemented should be the user(s), since they will have to pay for the system and live with it. This stage services that decision-making process by:

1. Creating a specification of each option in a limited menu, in sufficient detail for the user(s) to understand the implementation implications.
2. Presenting the options to the user(s), and clarifying the various implications.

3. Creating a system specification for the selected option, in sufficient detail for the work in the design phase to be carried out.

Stages 4 and 5: data and process design

These two stages represent the first part of the design phase, which is concerned with the production of the detailed logical design. The conversion of the logical design to a physical design is the province of Stage 6. The break between logical and physical design is made to cater in a flexible way for the wide range of project circumstance. The two stages interact, and are carried out in parallel. The activities involved are:

1. Data design. The data within the system, in the form of I/O descriptions, data flows, and, perhaps, existing documents or file structures, are analysed in detail using the relational data analysis (RDA) technique, also called third normal form (TNF) analysis and (Codd's) normalization, to ensure an objective complete view. The results of this analysis are merged with the business view of the data, provided by the LDS, in order to produce the composite logical data design (CLDD), which reflects both views.
2. Process design. The processes identified in the updated requirement specification are to satisfy the processing requirements of the CLDD and extended to show the detail of processing required.
3. Validation, in which the functions — logical groups of processes in the function catalogues — are mapped against the CLDD to prove the integrity of the complete logical model.

Stage 6: physical design

This stage involves the conversion of the logical design, produced from Stages 4 and 5, into a specification of the physical design sufficiently detailed for subsequent development phases to be carried out. The activities are:

1. Production of a 'first cut' physical design for the target hardware/software environment, by the application of 'first cut' rules to the CLDD, and the conversion of logical functions to physical programs by similar prescriptive techniques.
2. Application of physical design control techniques to the 'first cut' design, to refine it so that the designer can be sure it will meet the necessary performance criteria.
3. Creation of detailed file and program specifications for use in the programming phase.
4. Specification of the operating procedures associated with the operation of the system.
5. Creation of detailed plans for the subsequent development phases of the project.

7.1.3 Mapping Version 3 and Winway SSAD

There is a good correlation between V3 and the generic Winway model:

- Winway problem definition corresponds to V3 Stage 1.
- Winway requirements specification is covered by V3 Stage 1, and steps 200–210 of V3 Stage 2.

- Winway requirements definition is covered as follows:
  - business options by Step 220 in V3 Stage 2.
  - Technical options by V3 Stage 3, Steps 310 and 320.
  - Requirement consolidation by V3 Stage 2 Steps 230–260 and Steps 330 and 340 of V3 Stage 3.
- Winway logical data design, logical process design and physical design all map neatly on to V3 Stages 4, 5 and 6.

Using V3 within the Winway method is therefore not a problem. There is some difference in the order of completion of later analysis work, but this can be handled without difficulty.

7.1.4 Mapping Version 3 and Winway information systems planning

V3 was defined before the need for a comprehensive strategic plan for the organization and IT had been properly understood. This meant that, prior to V3, projects were started in something of a vacuum until Stages 01 and 02 were introduced to provide a basic business justification for the project.

Stages 01 Problem definition and 02 Project identification, should not really be needed if a strategy study has been completed.

Stage 1 Analysis of system operations and current problems, would use the information systems portfolio results as the basis for starting work, but could be extended to encompass a simple reconsideration of the problems and benefits defined earlier.

Stage 2, Specification of requirements, would be largely unchanged except that Step 240 would need to be completed in the context of the ISP data model. It is also possible that some options in Step 220: Identify and select from business options, would have already been considered.

Stage 3, Selection of technical options, could also be greatly simplified as the ISP should contain a technical plan identifying the hardware and software platforms to be used for different systems.

Logical design, in Stages 4 and 5, would refer less to the ISP and more to the other systems in operation or under development. This is particularly important for data design.

Stage 6 would also need to refer back to the ISP, particularly for Step 630 regarding performance and Step 680 for implementation planning.

7.1.5 Techniques

The major techniques used in SSADM are:

- LDS: logical data structure, a method for deriving entity/data models. This is also known as entity relationship analysis.
- DFDs: data flow diagrams, a method of representing flows of information through a system and between the system and the outside world.

- ELHs: entity life histories, a technique for developing a model of how the system cycles operate, and how events must be handled by the system.
- Process outlines: a method of converting ELHs into definitions describing how transactions must be processed by the system.
- TNF: third normal form data analysis, a technique for defining data and creating unambiguous logical data sets. Also called relational data analysis (RDA).
- First-cut data design: rules for converting logical data models into physical files/databases.
- First-cut programs: rules for converting logical processes into transactions and program run flows.
- Physical design control (PDC): a process for tuning designs to meet acceptable performance criteria.

The key techniques are LDS, DFD, ELH and RDA, and they are described in Chapter 10.

7.1.6 Documentation

Every organization is likely to have its own view of how computer systems development fits into its structure and operations. V3, as a generally applicable development method, is intended to cope with widely differing project circumstances.

While V3 provides copies of all the forms needed to support individual techniques, it does not include very much guidance about the contents of the various reports which should be produced as the project progresses. There is, for example, no detailed specification for the 'Statement of requirement', which is the input to SSADM. It can be as simple (and as vague) as a few lines broadly outlining the area for investigation, or as detailed as a preliminary study which may have involved some man-years of effort to produce. Obviously the more detailed the statement of requirement, the less effort is required in the analysis phase. Winway provides a precise documentation framework and contents for this and all reports in Chapter 12. The following map Winway reports on to V3 reports:

- Winway ISP/feasibility study (if completed) corresponds to the Version 3 feasibility study
- Winway draft system requirements specification has no real equivalent in Version 3, but it is the document which should be produced at the end of Stage 1: analysis of system operations and current problems.
- Winway system requirements specification equates to the required system specification produced at the end of Stage 3: selection of technical options, which incorporates the work of Stage 2: specification of requirements.
- Winway system design specification incorporates the Stage 5: logical system design and the documents from Stage 6, Steps 610–660 and 670, which are part of what is loosely defined as the system specification.
- Winway system implementation specification includes the various user documents created during Stage 6, Steps 660 and 690.

7.2 WINWAY AND SSADM (VERSION 4)

7.2.1 Background

The origins of SSADM were covered in Sec. 7.1.1. It had long been realized that there were many shortcomings with earlier versions of SSADM: indeed a number of problems had been embodied into the first release of the method against the advice of the authors in 1983.

Version 4 (V4) was intended to resolve as many of these problems as possible, but it suffered from a long gestation period and was not published until July 1990. The authors had already successfully predicted all the important changes in their SSADM (Version 3) Interface Guide for the Unify Corporation's Accell/SQL 4GL, and Unify 2000 RDB published in 1989.

V4 has addressed most of the major issues and will undoubtedly replace V3 over the next few years. Most importantly, V4 is now promoted as an open method, so that users can select those parts of the method they wish to use and integrate them with other methods and techniques, so long as the integrity (inputs, activities and outputs) of the selected parts is maintained. For more information consult the SSADM V4 Reference Manual[13]. One of the most significant changes is in the new versions structure.

7.2.2 Structure

SSADM V4 consists of five modules. Each module consists of a number of stages, and each stage is broken down into a number of steps. This is shown diagrammatically in Fig. 7.2. The steps are further expanded into tasks. A revised notation is used for presenting the block diagrams for V4, so that, at each level, activities can be seen as 'black boxes' performing a discrete, self-contained task. This is derived from the SADT notation described in Chapter 10. The modules are grouped under three headings as follows:

Feasibility study A short assessment of the proposed system, to confirm that the business requirements could be implemented in a cost-effective way. It consists of one module with one stage:

- Module 1: Feasibility, also called FS.

Full study This is the heart of the method, where the complete specification of the requirement is produced. It contains three modules and their component stages:

- Module 2: Requirements analysis, or RA
- Module 3: Requirement specification, or RS
- Module 4: Logical system specification, or LSS

Physical design The final part of V4 is identified as being part of development work. It consists of one module:

- Module 5: Physical design, or PD

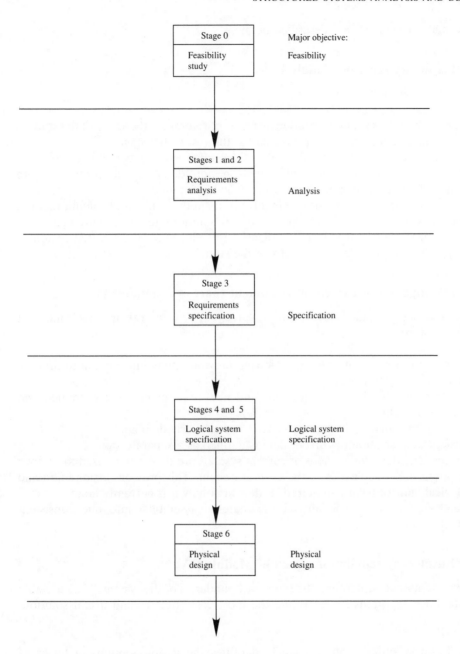

Figure 7.2 SSADM Version 4 © Crown Copyright.

The individual stages of V4 are described below.

Stage 0: Feasibility (part of Module FS)

There are four steps in this stage:

1. The *feasibility study* is set up by producing terms of reference, the scope of the study is reviewed and detailed plans are produced for the rest of the stage.
2. *Problem definition* adds a level of detail to the outline issues covered by the scoping document. It identifies the data requirements in more detail, defines problems more precisely and identifies new facilities which may be required.
3. *Select feasibility option* is intended to involve users in the study, and commit them to subsequent work by identifying various logical solutions to the requirements and helping them to choose one. Detailed plans are produced for the selected option.
4. *Report production* publishes the results of the study.

Stage 1: Investigation of current environment (part of Module RA)

This stage provides a detailed description of current systems and their environment. It consists of six steps:

1. The first step is a preparatory one, reviewing previous study information to prepare for the detailed analysis work.
2. Next the previously identified problems and new requirements are examined and documented in detail.
3. The flows of information in current systems are similarly defined.
4. The structure description of current data is defined as a separate step.
5. The process and data descriptions of current systems are then rationalized to remove all the physical characteristics of the current system. This provides a simplified and more logical view of what is required, rather than how it is currently done.
6. The final step is to consolidate all the material assembled into one consistent statement of requirements.

Stage 2: Business system options (part of Module RA)

This allows end users to determine the scope or boundaries of the system. They are able to evaluate various options to determine the most cost-effective and useful solution. There are two steps:

1. Refine business system options, which identifies the various options in terms of functionalists, inputs, outputs, data, interfaces, costs, benefits, timescales, etc.
2. Select business system options, where the most appropriate option is selected.

Stage 3: Definition of requirements (part of Module RS)

This takes the chosen business system option and expands it to provide a detailed specification for the proposed solution.

- Both data and processing requirements are reexpressed to provide a more precise statement of the processing flows and data structure required to implement the chosen option.
- The processing is then translated into specific outline functions and enquiries with associated inputs and ouputs.
- Relational data analysis is conducted to further refine the data model.
- Prototypes of selected processes are prepared and agreed with users.
- The update procedures are reexamined and documented in greater detail.
- The objectives of the system are reviewed, and revised or confirmed as appropriate.
- Finally, a specification document is assembled to complete the stage.

Stage 4: Technical system options (part of Module LS)

This is intended to review the various technical ways in which the system could be implemented:

- Options are defined in terms of hardware, software, networking, capacity and service levels.
- One option is selected, although typically it will be revised to include desirable features of other options.

Stage 5: Logical design (part of Module LS)

This is intended to produce a detailed specification of the requirements which can be implemented on a range of technical environments, and which maximizes the opportunities to reuse elements even if the technical environment were to change. In particular:

- User dialogues and menu structures are defined.
- Update processes are produced for each event, to identify the precise database amendments to be made.
- Enquiry processes are described.

Finally, all the processing requirements are reviewed to ensure they integrate to provide a full and workable solution to the requirements.

Stage 6: Physical design (part of Module PD)

This translates the logical data structure and various process descriptions on to the chosen technical environment. After preliminary preparation and planning work to better understand the technical environment:

1. The logical data model is translated into a physical database, using the storage and indexing options of the chosen database management system. This is subsequently optimized for performance and space utilization, and then reviewed to ensure that all requirements have been sensibly provided.

2. Each function in the system has its physical input/output layouts defined, error routines documented, etc. Additional processing logic is produced so that there is sufficient information for the programmers to code the function.

Finally, all the components of the physical design are assembled to ensure that they are consistent.

7.2.3 Mapping Version 4 and Winway SSAD

V4 maps on to the generic Winway SSAD model as follows:

- Winway problem definition corresponds broadly with Stage 0: Feasibility, which includes a specific step for problem definition.
- Winway requirements specification is covered by Stage 1: Investigation of current environment, with a high-level description using Stage 3: Definition of requirements.
- Winway system definition is covered as follows:
  - User options by Stage 2: Business systems options.
  - Technical options by Stage 4: Technical systems options.
  - Requirements consolidation by Stage 3: Definition of requirements.
- Winway logical data design is already covered in Stage 3, Steps 320 and 340.
- Winway logical process design is reflected in Stage 5: Logical design.
- Winway physical design matches Stage 6: Physical design.

As with version 3 there is a high correspondence between the two, and so V4 can be used within the Winway framework. The only areas of difference are that the Winway requirements specification would cover somewhat more ground than V4's requirements analysis, and that in V4, the logical data design will have been completed earlier than anticipated in Winway.

7.2.4 Mapping Version 4 and Winway information system planning

V4 acknowledges that an information system planning (ISP) activity may well have preceded any use of V4 for a single project. It therefore includes a number of references back to ISP source/controlling information.

Stage 0: Feasibility would generally not be needed where an ISP exists, unless the ISP was nearing the end of its life. If this stage is conducted then considerable reference back to the ISP will be appropriate, to identify objectives, plans, goals, scope, etc.

Stage 1: Investigation of current environment would obtain source information regarding business plans and objectives, data descriptions and business plans, and basic processing data from the ISP, and validate its results against ISP models.

Stage 2: Business systems options would be unchanged.

Stage 3: Requirements analysis would be unchanged but would validate its data and process models against those in the ISP.

Stage 4: Technical system options should be greatly simplified, as the ISP should contain a technical architecture setting out the basic implementation and operation environments.

Stage 5: Logical (process) design would be unchanged.

Stage 6: Physical design would also be largely unchanged.

7.2.5 Techniques

V4 utilizes 13 different techniques to support each Module of work. The most widely used are:

- Data flow diagram (DFD) as described for Version 3.
- Dialogue design. These use Jackson-style notation, similar in construction to ELHs.
- Logical data modelling (LDS) as described for Version 3.
- Relational data analysis (RDA), also described in Version 3.
- Entity life histories (ELH), also described in Version 3.
- Requirements definition is intended to provide a more effective means of identifying, quantifying and recording users' requirements using the requirements catalogue. It is therefore more a list of issues for consideration and less a formal procedure. The DFD, LDS, ELH and RDA techniques are described in Chapter 10.

7.2.6 Documentation

V4 has also addressed the documentation shortcomings of Version 3 and gives much greater priority to the production of formal reports, or Products as they are called. They are defined as Management, Technical or Quality products. The technical products include a subcategory of application products, and it is these which are mapped against the Winway reports shown in Fig. 1.5.

- Winway ISP feasibility study matches the V4 feasibility report produced from Stage 0.
- Winway draft system requirements specification equates to the V4 analysis of requirements report produced from Module 2: Requirements analysis.
- Winway system requirements specification maps on to the V4 requirements specification from Module 3: Requirements specification.
- Winway system design specification incorporates the logical system specification from Module 4: Logical design, and the physical system specification from Module 5: Physical design. V4 includes the required system logical data model in the preceding requirements specification.

7.3 WINWAY AND LSDM

7.3.1 Background

The Learmonth and Burchett structured development method (LSDM) is based on their early method for database design called LDBD. LSDM was developed in parallel with

SSADM by Learmonth and Burchett Management Systems plc, who were responsible for both products in the eighties. There were therefore many similarities between the two during the early years. The current version of LSDM looks very different to SSADM Version 4, but still has many underlying similarities.

LSDM is probably more widely established in the private sector than SSADM and has therefore evolved at a somewhat faster pace. LSDM:

- Is data-driven and not function-driven.
- Separates logical and physical views of requirements.
- Encourages accurate 'logical' definitions of systems data and processing.
- Enables systems logic to be identified and checked before programming.
- Supports the parallel development of three separate system views, data flows, data structures and time cycles.
- Includes a series of prescriptive rules, checklists and guidelines.
- Covers physical design, including definitions of files or databases, programs and runflows, and resource usage estimation and optimization.

7.3.2 Structure

The method consists of three basic stages (see Fig. 7.3), each broken down into a number of steps. Each step uses specific techniques and produces defined outputs. Detailed guidelines ensure that no ambiguity exists on what is required or on how it should be achieved.

Stage A: Analysis

This has two parts. The first is optional and is used only where an existing system needs to be considered. The second focuses on defining the required system in detail.

Step A1: Initiate project This is the start-up activity to begin the stage and to establish the basic framework for the system.

Step A2: Investigate generic data structure Provides a definition of the data in the existing system.

Step A3: Investigate current system processes Provides a definition of the current functions.

Step A4: Identify current system problems This documents all the problems and shortcomings of the existing system.

Step A5: User review of current system This is a management review of the preceding steps, to ensure that the current system has been completely and correctly documented.

Step A6: Identify user requirements This is the first mandatory step in Part 2 of Stage A. It ensures that users' requirements for the new system (as opposed to those of any current system(s)) are properly recorded.

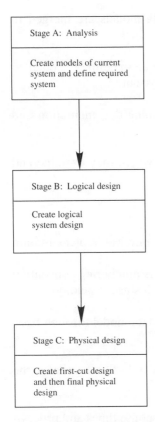

Figure 7.3 LSDM © LBMS plc.

Step A7: Identify business system options and select optimum The list of problems and requirements is analysed to produce a number of options for the scope and operation of the proposed system. The user and IT community evaluate these together to choose the most appropriate solution.

Step A8: Further define the chosen option This produces an outline specification for the chosen option.

Step A9: User review of required system The outline specification is reviewed with users and signed off.

Stage B: Logical design

This converts the above requirements into a hardware- and software-independent design, covering both data and processes.

Step B1: Relational data analysis Third normal forms (TNF) are produced to provide a simple and unambiguous statement of data structures required in the new system.

Step B2: Create final logical data design The RDA and data models are merged to produce the consolidated logical data design.

Step B3: Define system logic Uses the entity life history technique to define the detailed procedural logic associated with every event in the required system.

Step B4: Finalize logical design This completes all the remaining documentation and detail needed for input to the physical design stage.

Step B5: User review Similar to previous user reviews this is where they examine and approve the logical design.

Stage C: Physical design

The final stage translates the logical designs into an optimized physical implementation on the chosen hardware and software environment.

The individual steps in these stages are described below. The numbering convention for steps uses the parent stage letter, so that it is clear to which stage it belongs.

Step C1: 'First-cut' physical data design Processes the logical data model through basic transition rules to create an initial database design.

Step C2: Create process outlines for major transactions Like C1, this translates the logical process model into physical transactions.

Step C3: Create performance predictions This identifies the response times and processing loads, and tunes the data and process models to achieve acceptable levels of performance.

Step C4: Create file/database definitions This is a self-explanatory task.

Step C5: Create program specifications Provides the final level of processing documentation needed for the programmer to begin work.

Steps C6–C9: Complete physical design tasks This includes a number of tasks which form the baseline for subsequent development work, including the creation of:

- A system test plan
- An operating schedule
- A development plan
- A user manual

7.3.3 Mapping LSDM and Winway SSAD

As with the previous methods, there is little problem in mapping LSDM on to the generic SSAD model.

- Winway problem definition broadly equates to Part 1 (Analysis of current system) of Stage A and the early part of Step A6: Identify user requirements.
- Winway requirements specification broadly equates to Step A6.
- Winway system definition is covered as follows:
  - User options by Step A7: Identify business system options and select optimum.
  - Technical options are not really addressed by LSDM.
  - Requirements consolidation by Step A8: Further define chosen option, and A9: User review.
- Winway logical data design maps on to Stage B, Steps B1: Relational data analysis, and B2: Create final logical data design.
- Winway logical process design equates to Step B3: Define system logic. This, and the preceding data design, are finally brought together in B4: Finalize logical design.
- Winway physical design is the same as Stage C and its nine component steps.

7.3.4 Mapping LSDM and Winway information system planning

LSDM acknowledges the possible existence of an information system strategy. There will be control feedback to the ISP as follows:

Step A1: Initiate the project must be done within the framework of the ISP.

Steps A2 to A5 review any existing systems and will be largely unchanged. However, the problems and requirements list in Step A4 should be compared to that in the ISP.

Step A6 to identify user requirements should be largely unchanged, although the emerging data and process documentation should be reviewed carefully against those in the ISP.

Steps A7–A9 should also be largely unchanged, except for the need to review any options addressed in the ISP.

Steps B1–B5 should be little affected by the ISP, except for the need to rationalize the emerging data structure (B1 and B2) with that in the ISP.

Steps C1 and C2 will be constrained to the technical environment specified in the ISP's technical architecture.

Step C3 must reflect any service levels, performance measures, etc., defined in the ISP.

Steps C4–C9 should be unaffected.

7.3.5 Techniques

LSDM utilizes 10 different techniques, the major ones of which are:

- Data flow diagrams (DFDs)
- Entity relationship analysis (ERA)
- Entity life histories (ELH) and process outlines
- Third normal form (TNF) or relational data analysis (RDA)

These are described in Chapter 10.

Each technique is fully supported by formal documentation, and has a set of rules allowing a precise approach to be taken towards its use. LSDM focuses on the analysis of the systems data at the business level, as this provides a stable foundation upon which the information system can be constructed. The necessary bias towards the flexibility of a data-driven approach is, however, tempered by a recognized need to reflect and meet current processing requirements — thus balancing the method between flexibility (data) and functionality (process).

LSDM, like SSADM, places considerable emphasis on using different techniques in parallel, so that results can be verified from more than one source. Users are involved to a large extent, so misunderstandings and errors can be minimized.

7.3.6 Documentation

LSDM does not specify end-of-stage documentation report contents, so LSDM users would need to refer to the Winway documentation recommended in Chapter 12.

- Winway ISP feasibility study has no real equivalent in LSDM, but would not be needed anyway where an ISP exists.
- Winway draft system requirement specification would be produced after Step A6.
- Winway system requirement specification would be produced after Step A9 once a business option had been chosen and fully defined.
- Winway system design specification would be produced at the end of Stage C, Step C8: Create development plans. A draft version, reflecting only the logical design, could be produced after Step B4, the final logical design.
- Winway system implementation specification would derive some of its material from Step C9: Finalize user procedures (the user manual and manual procedure) and C7: Operating schedule.

7.4 WINWAY AND PRISM

7.4.1 Background

LSDM is also used as the method for structured analysis and design in the PRISM methodology marketed by Hoskyns. This encapsulates LSDM into a wider management and control framework, with a clearer definition of reports and documentation to be produced. While LSDM has evolved in later releases with the new structure defined in this Section, PRISM's core structure has remained largely unchanged and is therefore closely related to early versions of SSADM.

7.4.2 Structure

PRISM identifies two phases of SSAD:

1. Definition phase, covering problem analysis and definition. It has three tasks: problem definition, feasibility study and requirements definition.
2. Design phase, which focuses more on developing solutions to the above problems. It has two tasks: functional system design and computer system design.

These phases are subdivided into tasks, and tasks into activities. Activities are manageable blocks of work controlled by guidelines and procedures. A diagrammatic representation of the SSAD elements of PRISM is seen in Fig. 7.4.

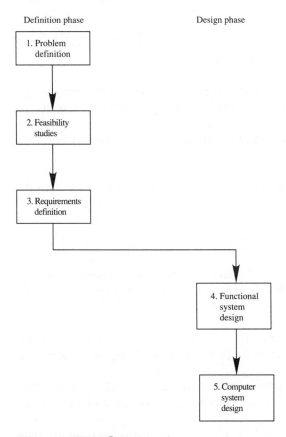

Figure 7.4 PRISM © Hoskyns plc.

Phase 1: Problem definition

This is designed to identify, quantify and document the problems and/or opportunities which exist in the user area. It has four tasks:

1. Initiate the phase concerned with establishing the scope, duration and resources of the study.
2. Study problem background, which identifies current procedures and organization, identifies opportunities for improvement and produces a proposed scope, objectives and constraints list for the project.
3. Describe present situation, which produces a detailed statement about existing systems.
4. Analyse current costs — this is self-explanatory

The final tasks are concerned with planning subsequent stages of the project and producing a formal report.

Phase 2: Feasibility study

This is intended to identify various ways for meeting the requirements and to select the most appropriate for further study. It has five tasks:

1. The phase is initiated by revising plans produced in the problem definition report.
2. A number of different alternative solutions are then defined in some detail, including the scope of the option, proposed functionality, data and interfaces.
3. These options are then evaluated in terms of the costs, benefits, feasibility and risks associated with their implementation.
4. One option is selected.
5. A plan for the next phase is prepared and issued as a formal report along with the option and selection information.

Phase 3: Requirement definition

The requirement definition phase produces a detailed statement of requirements for the new system. The phase is initiated in the same way as all the other phases, and the following tasks are performed:

- The current system is described in full in terms of existing processes and data, interfaces, control and security features and operating costs. A logical view is then constructed of the requirements.
- The user requirements for the new system are then defined. This includes identifying the scope of functionality and data, and the detailed processes and data to be provided.
- A number of business options are defined for the selection of the most appropriate one.

As with the other phases, the final tasks are concerned with planning the next phase and producing a formal report.

Phase 4: Functional system design

This phase translates the requirements into an initial design via the intermediary activities of logical design. The following tasks are included:

- A logical data model is produced.
- A logical process design is prepared to cover all processing requirements.
- An initial technical design is formulated to identify which processes will be automated, and their priorities.

Phase 5: Computer system design phases

This creates the full technical design for the system from the outline design produced above.

7.4.3 Mapping PRISM and Winway SSAD

PRISM maps on to the generic SSAD as follows:

- Winway problem definition broadly equates to PRISM Phase 1: Problem definition.
- Winway requirements specification is broadly equivalent to the PRISM feasibility study (Phase 2).
- Winway system definition is covered as follows:
  - User options by PRISM Task 3.3
  - Technical options by PRISM Tasks 2, 3 and 4.
  - Requirements consolidation by PRISM Phase 3.
- Winway logical data design maps on to Phase 4: Functional systems design, Task 4.2: Specify logical data model.
- Winway logical process design is the same as Task 4.3: Specify logical process design.
- Winway physical design covers Task 4.4: Review physical solution options and Phase 5: Computer system design.

7.4.4 Mapping PRISM and Winway information systems planning

PRISM does not assume that a strategic study has been completed. There will be control feedback into the ISP as follows:

Phase 1: Problem definition must be planned and conducted within the boundaries and constraints set by the ISP for the project. In particular, the initiation work and the problem definition phase should refer carefully to ISP material.

Phase 2 will continue with only limited reference to the ISP for:
  - Any alternatives that may already have been considered.
  - The potential costs, benefits and risks already identified.

Phase 3 should proceed unchanged, although as data and process models evolve, these should be validated against ISP models.

Phase 4 will also refer heavily to ISP models. The review of physical design options should be somewhat simplified by adherence to ISP technical standards.

Phase 5 should also draw heavily on the technical architecture specified in the ISP.

7.4.5 Techniques

PRISM uses the following techniques, the major ones of which are described in Chapter 10:

- Data flow diagrams (DFD)
- Logical data structure (LDS)

- Entity life histories (ELH)
- First-cut program design
- First-cut data design
- Physical design control
- Dialogue design

7.4.6 Documentation

PRISM contains far greater detail on project reports and deliverables. These map on to Winway documentation as follows:

- Winway ISP feasibility study corresponds with the PRISM problem definition report.
- Winway draft system requirement specification does not map easily on to a PRISM report. However, the PRISM feasibility report would cover this ground.
- Winway systems requirement specification is equivalent to the PRISM requirements definition report.
- Winway systems design specification would be produced at the end of the functional system design and computer system phases.

7.5 WINWAY AND INFORMATION ENGINEERING

7.5.1 Background

The Information Engineering Methodology (IE) is a James Martin Associates product. The principles of IE are that it is:

- Understandable to the business user due to the use of clear, simple diagramming techniques.
- Relevant to the business and its needs since it stresses the need to relate projects back to corporate goals.
- Based on a set of compatible and consistent techniques.
- Able to speed up the development life cycle.
- Conducive to scoping projects that are manageable through a well defined and structured set of stages and tasks.

While IE has much in common with the SSADM/LSDM family of methods, it has many novel features and uses a number of different techniques. A simple diagram of the IE approach is seen in Fig. 7.5.

2.5.2 Structure

There are three parts of IE which relate to that part of the life cycle covered by SSAD — business area analysis, business system design and technical design.

Business area analysis (BAA) The objectives of this stage are to develop a full understanding of the business area, to define specific data needs and priorities, to collect

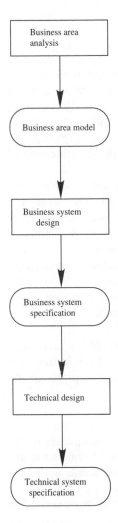

Figure 7.5 Extract of Information Engineering © JMA.

quantitative information (volumes, frequencies, etc.) for use in design, and to prioritize individual systems within the area. BAA includes the following tasks:

- Plan the project, in which a discrete business area is selected for further analysis. The scope and terms of reference for the project are defined.
- Gather information. This involves the individuals who perform or manage the work. It identifies business activities, information needs and priorities. It also obtains supporting details. It is split into two parts — obtaining an initial understanding of the business area and then gathering the detailed information from users.
- Produce a detailed business area model — concerned with three things: producing a detailed entity relationship diagram, producing detailed process models and reviewing these two models for consistency and completeness.

- Analyse interaction. This is broken into two activities:
  - Entity-type life-cycle analysis.
  - Process logic modelling.

  These show how processes use data and vice versa, identify the usage of attributes and the connection/disconnection of relationships. Finally the two models are reviewed to see if either needs to be enhanced.
- Analysis of current systems. This is in three parts: analysis of current system procedures; analysis of current systems data to understand the scope, strengths and weaknesses of these arrangements; problem definition, including the identification of potential solutions.
- Confirm business area model. This consist of five tasks, designed to ensure the stability, completeness, correctness and consistency of the model. The three 'C's involve comparing the various documents produced so far, and using a variety of checklists to identify shortcomings. Stability is gauged by assessing the possibility of the business changing, and assessing the impact of potential changes.
- Planning for business area design is the final task. It is concerned with prioritizing business processes and data and selecting groupings for implementation. From these activities a design plan is produced. A BAA might identify a number of design areas, each of which becomes the subject of a separate system design strategy.

Business system design (BSD) BSD focuses on those aspects of design which affect users. Its objective is to design the business system to implement the selected BAA processes and data. This design is completed at a logical level, so that it does not prejudge the technical platform to be used to implement it.

BSD consists of a number of discrete tasks:

- Plan BSD project — this inherits planning details from the BAA and updates them.
- Data structure design — translates the entity model into an initial data structure diagram which can then be extended as missing entry points and access paths are identified.
- System structure design. This identifies the basic procedures and data flows needed to support them, and the required control procedures.
- Transition design — specifies any special concession routines, how the new system will be introduced, and training needs.
- Define interactions — produces a matrix to show all the accessing of data by process. It also produces individual access diagrams to show the order in which data is retrieved.
- Design procedures. This is in three interacting parts: constructing individual dialogue flows, design of screen layouts, and the completion of detailed action diagrams.
- Confirm design reviews the whole with users, to ensure that it is complete and correct, and that it appears to provide a usable system.
- Plan for technical design, which involves a further management review and the production of an implementation plan.

Technical design (TD) This translates the logical design understood by users into a technical implementation for the chosen hardware and software environment. It includes a number of tasks:

- Define technical context, which sets out the technical environment to be used, standards, etc.
- Design data structure and storage — applies the storage and indexing features of the chosen database management system to the logical data design. The design is optimized for storage considerations.
- Transition plans produced during BSD are revised to show precisely how data will be moved from existing sources to the new database.
- Operating procedures are defined to cover issues such as security and recovery.
- Software design identifies the programs to be developed and their testing plans.
- Technical design verification ensures that the desired performance levels can be achieved and that identified business problems have been resolved.
- System test definition produces the IT department's system test and user's acceptance test procedures.

7.5.3 Mapping IE and Winway SSAD

IE is somewhat different from the SSADM – LSDM family of methods, so it is slightly more difficult to map on to the generic model.

- Winway problem definition would have no parallel in IE because IE assumes that an ISP has been completed, and therefore it is superfluous.
- Winway requirements specification broadly equates to BAA activities up to and including confirming the business area model.
- Winway systems definition is covered by the BAA Task: Plan the design, but would also involve somewhat more emphasis on documenting the scope of the selected processes and data.
- Winway logical data and logical process design are covered by the business systems design stage.
- Winway physical design is covered by the technical design stage of IE.

7.5.4 Mapping IE and Winway information systems planning

IE assumes that ISP has been completed, and therefore integrates well with ISP.

Business area analysis tasks will all make considerable reference to ISP source material. The scope of the project will have been defined by ISP and information and process models will also originate from it. Throughout the rest of the BAA, evolving work will need to be integrated with corporate-level ISP models. The last task, Planning for business system design, needs to be carefully related to ISP priorities and objectives for cost–benefit analysis work.

Business system design should have relatively little feedback to ISP documentation. Transition design may need to refer to any outline proposals in the ISP. The final task plan for technical design will involve comparing the revised benefits and timescales, etc., with those in the ISP.

Technical design will have some interaction with ISP. The first task, that of defining the technical context, should be undertaken within the parameters defined in the ISP

7.5.5 Techniques

IE uses a number of techniques which are different from other methods. These include functional decomposition — a variation of SADT for function analysis — dependency diagrams (at both function and process level), action diagrams, dialogue flow diagrams and data flow diagrams. It also uses entity relationship modelling for data, and entity life cycle modelling, which is a variation of the ELH technique. The main techniques are described in Chapter 10.

7.5.6 Documentation

IE produces a BAA and a BSD report, which relate to Winway documentation as follows:

- Winway ISP feasibility study. As IE only operates within the context of an ISP this report is not required.
- Winway draft system requirement specification would be a draft of the BAA report produced at the end of the Confirm the Business Area Model Task.
- Winway system requirement specifications equates to the final BAA report.
- Winway system design specification is covered by:
  - The BSD report for logical design work.
  - The technical design report for physical design.

The contents of these reports are not clearly defined in IE. Winway suggested contents are in Chapter 12.

7.6 WINWAY AND OTHER METHODS

There are numerous other structured system analysis and design methods, although none with the level of market penetration achieved by those described above. Users of these methods should readily be able to judge how their method integrates with Winway by following the comparison method used in each of Secs 7.1–7.5.

8

CONSTRUCTION TO PRODUCTION

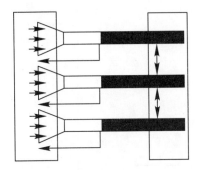

This chapter contains the detailed breakdown of the extended Life Cycle Stages (β and 7–12). The diagrammatic representation and mechanics used for this are consistent with those adopted for SSADM Version 3 documentation. Each stage diagram identifies all the steps involved in that stage, and subsequently identifies each task in each step. The stage level contains a narrative overview of each step and the inputs and outputs produced by the stage. The step level contains a detailed narrative of every task contained in the step.

8.1 STAGE β: ACQUISITION, SUPPORT AND CONTROL OF THE ENVIRONMENT (Fig. 8.1)

8.1.1 Objectives

The objectives of Stage β are to provide the total man and machine environment, and the supporting procedures to enable system development and implementation to proceed in an orderly and controlled manner, leading to continuous system operation.

8.1.2 Description

This stage runs in parallel with the applications software development life cycle activities, starting with Stage 1. This includes things such as the presence of an existing computer installation and the use of prototyping techniques, both of which would dictate the

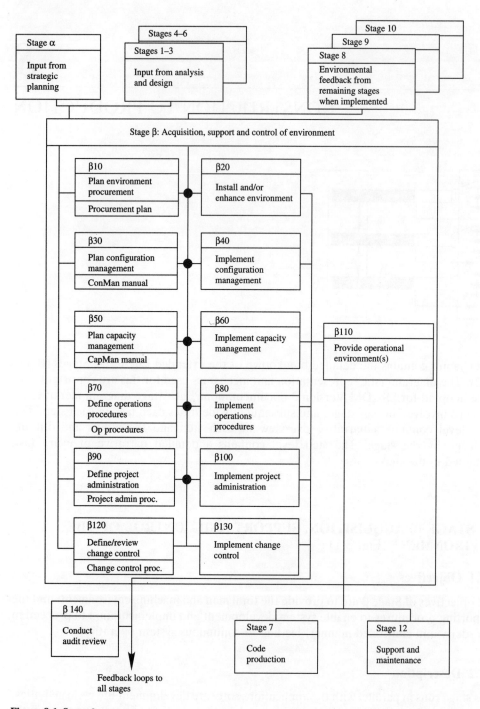

Figure 8.1 Stage β.

establishment of clearly defined support procedures. It supports and controls the activities which enable system development and delivery to proceed in a timely and effective manner.

The following documentation contains a comprehensive list of activities and procedures that should be considered in all projects. Inevitably, the precise subset of tasks within steps applicable to a specific project will be determined by a number of considerations:

- Previous projects
- Site procedures and constraints
- Corporate objectives and controls
- Existing hardware, software and communications networks

STEPS

β10 Plan environment procurement

.10 Review selected technical option
.20 Specify hardware requirements
.30 Specify software requirements
.40 Specify communications requirements
.50 Confirm performance/sizing requirements
.60 Review and refine accommodation requirements
.70 Review and refine environmental requirements
.80 Produce final accommodation/environment procurement plans
.90 Review procurement/enhancement plans with project board

β20 Install and/or enhance environment

.10 Procure and commission accommodation
.20 Procure and commission environment
.30 Procure and install hardware
.40 Procure and install software
.50 Procure and install communications
.60 Undertake trials
.70 Commission installation

β30 Plan configuration management

.10 Identify components to be subject to configuration management (ConMan)
.20 Establish hardware base configuration
.30 Establish software base configuration
.40 Establish network base configuration
.50 Establish component relationships
.60 Define ConMan procedures

.70 Define organizational structure for ConMan
.80 Subject to approval and change control

β40 Implement/enhance configuration management

.10 Create organization for ConMan
.20 Implement ConMan procedures

β50 Plan capacity management

.10 Identify components to be subject to capacity management (CapMan)
.20 Identify hardware components to be monitored
.30 Identify software components to be monitored
.40 Identify communications components to be monitored
.50 Establish component relationships
.60 Identify CapMan tools required and plan their procurement
.70 Define CapMan procedures
.80 Define organizational structure for CapMan
.90 Subject to approval and change control

β60 Implement capacity management

.10 Create/enhance organization for CapMan
.20 Procure and install CapMan tools
.30 Implement CapMan procedures
.40 Review and refine performance and sizing parameters
.50 Tune components
.60 Subject to approval and change control

β70 Define operational procedures

.10 Define operations group organization and staffing requirements
.20 Define/refine operations procedures and manual(s)
.30 Define application database dumping and transaction logging requirements
.40 Define application automatic data and transaction recovery requirements
.50 Define application manual data and transaction recovery requirements
.60 Define standby/alternative-site procedures
.70 Define application reversion-to-manual system procedures
.80 Define access control mechanisms to data and/or processes within applications
.90 Define access control mechanisms to application(s) within system
.100 Define access control mechanisms to application(s) within site/installation
.110 Subject to approval and change control

β80 Implement operational procedures

.10 Create/enhance operations group
.20 Implement operational procedures

β90 Define data administration

The functions and activities of the 'data administrator' within projects are fairly well understood. The following tasks include more documentation, filing and clerical administration control and management than is usually the case, and as such the role becomes more that of a 'project administrator' rather than that of a data administrator.

.10 Produce project quality plan
.20 Define data definition control procedures
.30 Define data dictionary system(s) control procedures
.40 Define project quality control practices and procedures
.50 Define project documentation control procedures
.60 Define project standards
.70 Define project quality and document continuum
.80 Define project librarianship organization requirements
.90 Subject to approval and change control

β100 Implement data administration

.10 Create project administration organization
.20 Implement project administration

β110 Provide operational environments

.10 Integrate results of Steps β20, β40, β60, β80 and β100
.20 Determine application development requirements
.30 Define development environment(s)
.40 Build development environment(s)
.50 Document development environment(s)
.60 Determine application live-running requirements
.70 Define live-running environment(s)
.80 Build live environment(s)
.90 Document live environment(s)
.100 Subject to approval and change control

β120 Define/review change control

.10 Define change control procedures
.20 Design change control proforma
.30 Identify change controller duties
.40 Specify change control board (CCB) terms of reference
.50 Identify CCB

β130 Implement change control

.10 Conduct impact analysis
.20 Produce cost/benefit analysis

.30 Refer to project board at corporate level to assess impact with or relationship to any other development
.40 Produce enhancement plan
.50 Assign resources
.60 Implement and test enhancement
.70 Submit to delivery process

β140 Conduct internal audit

Many of the activities listed for these periodic 'independent' reviews overlap with those that will be considered by the management board reviews specified in Step 1140. It will be for each particular project to determine the precise delineation of responsibilities and the relationship between these steps, in that some projects may not maintain a full management board capability once a project is live, and even if they do, it may be felt that periodic independent reviews, for example by internal audit, might be beneficial, indeed may be mandatory in some organizations.

.10 Review conformance to SLA
.20 Review conformance to SMA
.30 Review changes applied to the system since the last review
.40 Review current hardware, software and network configuration
.50 Review project cost/benefit returns
.60 Make recommendations for operational running and proposed enhancements of the system
.70 Produce audit report

Stage β Inputs

Stage β inputs are any corporate and project standards/documentation that exists for capacity and configuration management, data administration, change control or any other support or environment management and control documentation.

Stage β Outputs

- Contingency document (to Stage 9)
- Test environment details (to Stages 7–9)
- Live environment details (to Stage 11)
- Configuration planning and management documents (to Stages 7–11)
- Capacity planning and management documents (to Stages 7–11)
- Change control (all stages)
- Project administration procedures (all stages)
- Feedback on any of the above to corporate standards and strategies, i.e. Stage α as appropriate.

Step β10: PLAN ENVIRONMENT PROCUREMENT (Fig. 8.2)

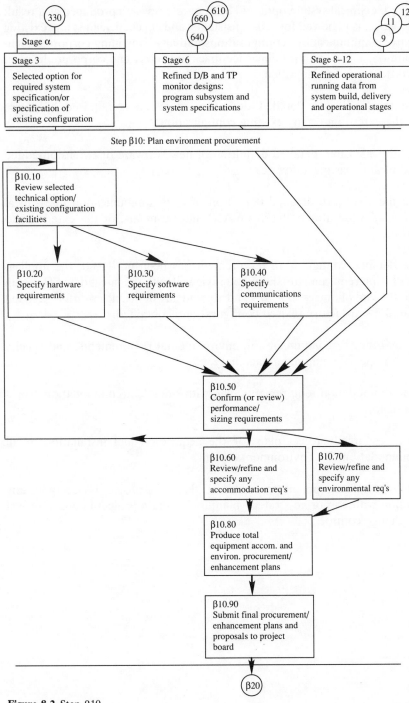

Figure 8.2 Step β10.

Tasks

β**10.10** The selected technical system option (TSO), or any revision produced as a result of subsequent activities, is reviewed for self-consistency and checked against any existing hardware, software, communications configurations and any overriding corporate technical strategies and objectives, and produces feedback at project and corporate levels if any deficiencies/differences are identified.

β**10.20** Translate the TSO into detailed definition of the new required hardware configuration or the extension of any existing configurations.

β**10.30** Translate the TSO into detailed definition of new software or extension-added facilities required of any existing software.

β**10.40** Translate the TSO into detailed definition of new communication lines, local area networks (LAN), wide area network (WAN) and terminals, or the extension to existing network(s).

β**10.50** Once the detailed configuration requirement has been produced, the applications performance/sizing requirements should be reviewed with the latest data. This step should be done at the end of Stages 6, 7, 8, 9 and 10, and any deficiencies/differences fed back to β10.10 until a satisfactory revised configuration is obtained.

β**10.60** Review any office or computer-room environmental requirements, and specify procurement for any special equipment/machinery.

β**10.70** Review accommodation requirements plan with suitable accommodation representation in attendance.

β**10.80** Produce a resourced project plan for the acquisition and installation of all equipment, accommodation and environmental plant.

β**10.90** Final review of all equipment procurement plan with project board (with any necessary interaction with corporate strategy planning), obtain project board approval and place under change control.

STEP β20: INSTALL AND COMMISSION NEW AND/OR ENHANCED ENVIRONMENT (Fig. 8.3)

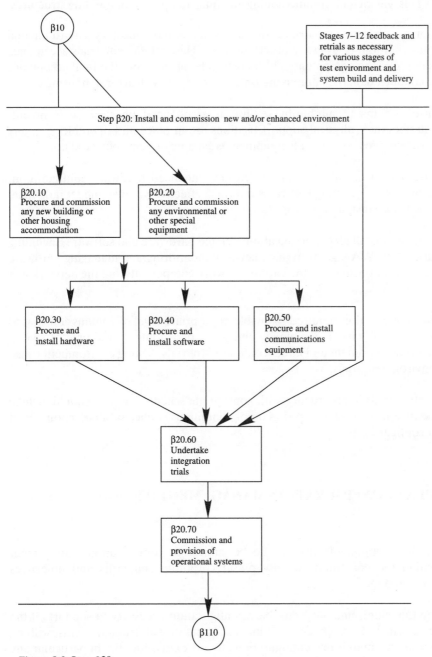

Figure 8.3 Step β20.

Tasks

β20.10 Authorize and implement any building programmes required (false floors and ceilings, etc.) This will include commissioning and final acceptance of building structures.

β20.20 Authorize, procure and install any necessary and/or ancillary environmental equipment, air-conditioning, standby generators, etc. This includes site trials acceptance and commissioning of the equipment. This may well be phased, but the final acceptance trials must be conducted on the equipment 'on site', in any new structural 'housing'.

β20.30 Procure and install all hardware into new/enhanced physical environment. Ensure that all necessary physical support facilities are in place and operable, e.g. any ducting of power supplies, and that all equipment is capable of being powered up.

β20.40 Procure and install all software on to new/enhanced hardware configuration. Ensure that any new and existing softwares interface effectively, and conduct individual and collective software installation tests.

β20.50 Procure and install all communications-related hardware and software, including terminals, tails, LAN, WAN gateways and network monitoring and managing hardware and software. Trial connectivity of the various network components and the network as a whole.

β20.60 Create configuration required to enable appropriate level of commission trial to be conducted. This will vary in complexity and scale, depending on the type of trial in respect of project development and initial configuration trials, testing environment trials, operational environment trials.

β20.70 Run actual trials in accordance with appropriate schedule, but all should include sufficient repetitive tests to ensure provision of continuous service of all components of the particular configuration.

STEP β30: PLAN CONFIGURATION MANAGEMENT (Fig. 8.4)

Tasks

β30.10 Determine components that are to be subject to configuration management (ConMan) within the constraints of any preset corporate standards and objectives established for ConMan.

β30.20 Define the mainframe hardware base configuration necessary to support all the project environments: development, testing and operational running. This will be necessary even when a mainframe configuration already exists. Identify in particular any switching and fallback provision, and criteria for their invocation.

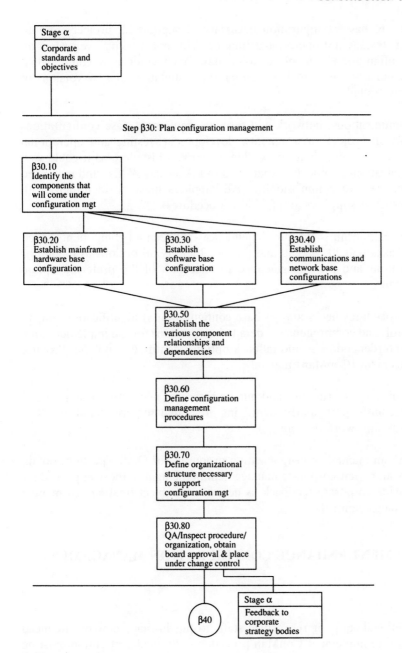

Figure 8.4 Step β30.

β30.30 Define software base configuration necessary to support all project environments: development, testing and operational running. This is necessary even when an existing software configuration is in place, as it may well include new components. Particular attention must be given to how testing and installation of new versions of software are to be controlled.

β30.40 Define communications, network and terminal equipment base configurations necessary to support all project environments: development, testing and operational running. This is necessary even when an existing network is installed, as it could well involve new communications protocols, expansions to LANs and WANs and may need extensive simulation prior to commissioning. All suppliers must be identified, with contingency for alternative suppliers and fallback procedures.

β30.50 Identify the relationships and interdependences between all components specified as a result of Tasks β30.20, β30.30 and β30.40. Identify all options available for major fallback situations and provide guidance for selection of the preferred option under what circumstances.

β30.60 Define all procedures necessary for base configuration(s) identification, implementation and control, and comprehensive, detailed instructions for the implementation and control of the interdependences and fallback options identified in β30.50. Produce configuration management (ConMan) manual.

β30.70 Define organizational structures and human resources necessary to support and effect ConMan procedures, particularly identifying areas that require round-the-clock attention and perhaps shift work on rotas.

β30.80 Submit ConMan manual and organization proposals for QA/Inspection; obtain project board approval; review corporate management in the light of those approved for the project and provide corporate feedback as necessary. Subject final agreed manual and procedures to change control.

STEP β40: IMPLEMENT/ENHANCE CONFIGURATION MANAGEMENT
(Fig. 8.5)

Tasks

β40.10 Recruit additional staff, or reorganize staff, to put in place new or enhanced organization structure to implement ConMan procedures. Particular attention must be given to terms and conditions necessary to support 'out-of-normal-hours' working.

β40.20 Implement ConMan procedures themselves. Again, particular attention must be given to any differences of procedures and organizational support for different phases of the project, viz. development, testing and operational running, and how a smooth transition from each phase is put in to effect.

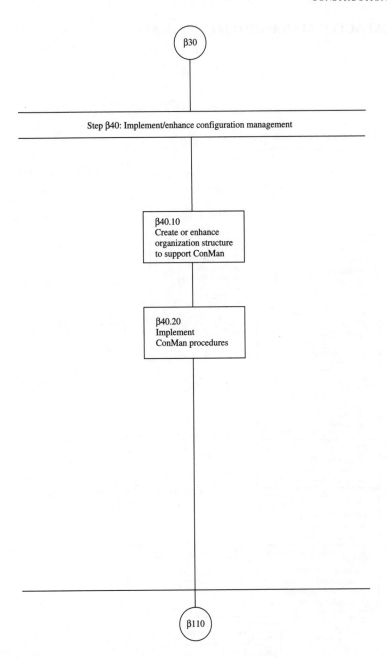

Figure 8.5 Step β40.

STEP β50: PLAN CAPACITY MANAGEMENT (Fig. 8.6)

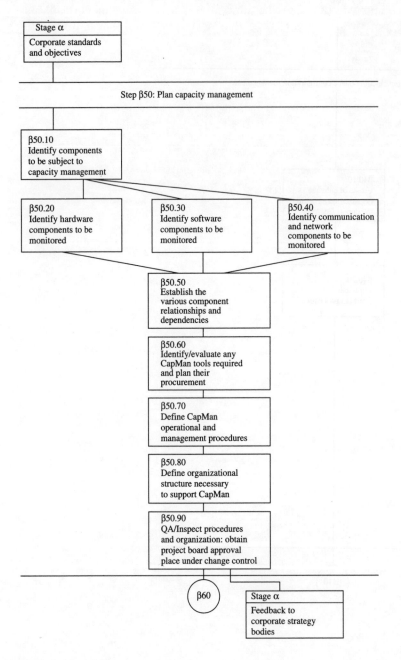

Figure 8.6 Step β50.

Tasks

β50.10 Determine components that are to be subject to capacity management (CapMan) within the constraints of any preset corporate standards and objectives established for CapMan.

β50.20 Identify any hardware component that should be subject to capacity management. The criteria used in the selection should be: any component that has particularly high throughput, that cannot be duplexed or otherwise provided with alternatives to maintain processing, and is known or suspected to be less reliable than other components that interface or relate to it.

β50.30 Identify any software component that should be subject to capacity management. These are likely to be superstructure products or elements of the operations system that are capable of being tuned, e.g. transaction processing (TP) monitors, number of streams per virtual machine profiles, database design, system access etc. These are most likely to require online statistics/volumes collection, which may or may not be inherent in the software component.

β50.40 Identify any communications equipment and network component that should be subject to CapMan. This would involve looking at both hardware (H/W) and software (S/W) components as described in Steps β50.20 and β50.30, respectively. There will, however, be unique requirements relating to network management and control and line (network) monitoring.

β50.50 Identify and define the relationship and any interdependences of the components identified by Tasks β50.20, β50.30 and β50.40. Examine any possibilities of combining the management of any individual or groups of components.

β50.60 Identify any tools available for monitoring any component(s), both as an inherent part of a manufacturer's facility (H/W or S/W) and any OEM tool produced for a specific function or component. Evaluate the various tools, and combination of tools options, and make recommendations for preferred selections.

β50.70 Define the procedures necessary to optimize effective return from the recommended tools, and the actions to be put in train as a result of the monitoring. This would include both operational procedures for immediate action and managerial procedures for longer term and strategic evaluation, including possible feedback loops to corporate strategy planning bodies. Produce CapMan manual.

β50.80 Define the organizational structures and human resources necessary to introduce and support CapMan, particularly identifying any areas/procedures that require out-of-normal-hours support, shift working, rotas, etc. and any special conditions, human and machine, that need apply. This would include staff remuneration, etc.

β50.90 Submit CapMan manual and organizational proposals for QA/Inspection and obtain project board approval. Review corporate standards and strategy for capacity management in the light of those approved for the project, and provide corporate feedback as necessary. Place final agreed CapMan manual and procedures under change control.

STEP β60: IMPLEMENT CAPACITY MANAGEMENT (Fig. 8.7)

Tasks

β60.10 Create organizational structure to support capacity management. This should be recognized as part of, and integrated with, existing operations/system support groups. In most cases, the activities required will be conducted for normal 'prime' shifts and reports compiled for operations control management. Work outside prime shifts should rarely, if ever, be required to support this activity, as it is non-operational. If the site has existing capacity management capabilities these must be reviewed in the light of any additional requirements.

β60.20 Procure and install any new tools to monitor hardware, software and network components, that have been identified as being necessary. Where CapMan tools already exist, review their use and capability for supporting increased workloads/throughput.

β60.30 Implement CapMan procedures, conduct acceptance tests and trials of any new H/W, S/W and N/W tools and extended use of existing tools, and procedures. Review results and, on meeting acceptance criteria, make operational.

β60.40 Having captured initial operational data, review total configuration sizing and performance, particularly response times and network traffic. Identify any new or potential bottlenecks for particular devices, operating system and super-structure products.

β60.50 Tune/retune all configuration components, possibly including the CapMan tools themselves, reset levels and reiterate capacity management cycle until optimum configuration for new workload is established.

β60.60 Submit all CapMan procedures and documentation for QA/Inspection and obtain project board approval. Review any previous corporate standards for CapMan procedures, and update feedback in the light of those currently being approved. Place finally agreed procedures under change control.

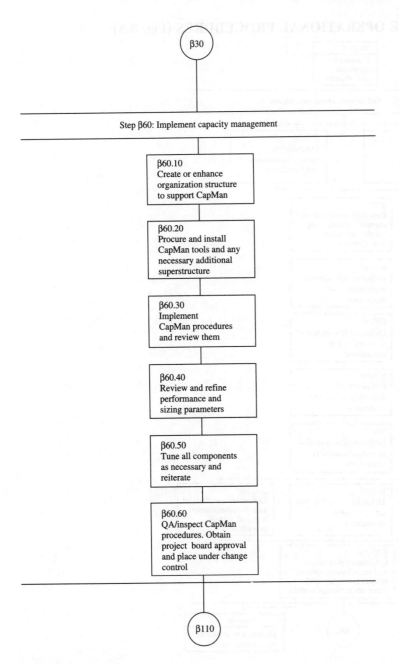

Figure 8.7 Step β60.

STEP β70: DEFINE OPERATIONAL PROCEDURES (Fig. 8.8)

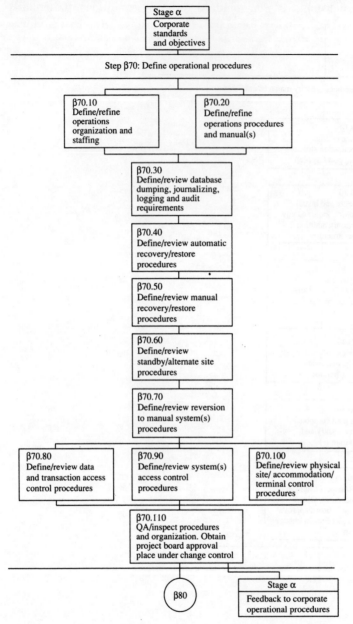

Figure 8.8 Step β70.

Tasks

β70.10 Create or review operations group organization and staffing. The group to be considered not only involves the (obvious) operations staff, but also software support, technical services, development services support (as opposed to the actual operational applications) and applications acceptance/delivery services. Particular attention must be given to the need for out-of-hours, i.e. non-standard, working conditions, particularly shift work. Just to provide online services to support 'prime' shift working will require operations support to set up and shut down services, to take dumps, journals, etc., involving potentially substantial resources at the start and close of each session. However, the use of unattended operation, for example overnight batch processing, could reduce the requirement for on-site operations staff.

β70.20 Define/review all supporting documentation and procedures for operational and development services. Quite apart from the specific manuals outlined in the succeeding tasks, there must also be comprehensive operating instructions (this could also affect or be affected by the whole training process); 'bug' reporting and fixing procedures; and systems delivery procedures (again this could affect/be affected by testing and trials procedures).

β70.30 Define/review all data consistency/security procedures. This would cover all aspects of system recovery strategy, including frequency, timing and the number of generations retained of database/file dumps; processing journals; audit logs; inputs (batch and online); and magnetic media, microfiche, etc., and copies of selected outputs. Data integrity procedures, file and database restructuring and reorganization must also be considered.

β70.40 Define/review automatic recovery and restore procedures, including roll-forward and roll-back on process failures. Particular attention should be given to what, if any, automatic recovery facilities should be provided for online transactions.

β70.50 Define/review manual recovery/restore procedures. These will include different recovery procedures to be invoked for various types of system failure, from identification of journals, logs, audit trail 'tapes' to be applied, to more fundamental restoration from previous dumps, system files or database.

β70.60 Define/review computer standby/alternative-site procedures. In circumstances where critical time periods would elapse before any automatic and/or manual recovery procedures could be put into effect, some consideration must be given to computer standby and alternative site arrangements. Provision can be made by ensuring duplication of given H/W S/W configurations, and retention of spare capacity on them. This would provide configuration standby within a single site; if a whole site were to be rendered out of commission, then similar provision should be sought at alternative sites. This would clearly be more easily achieved if it were included as part of a corporate plan, but where corporate resources would not permit such an arrangement, then similar facilities should be sought with other companies offering mutual standby capabilities. Where the site is a node of a telecommunications network, then gateways from the alternative configurations must be provided, preferably via the prime-site network control centre, or directly into the network if this is feasible. Where the alternative site has no networking capability then the reversion-to-manual procedures must address this. All recovery/restore/fallback procedures should be considered for inclusion as part of the infrastructure testing and trials processes.

β**70.70** Define/review reversion-to-manual system procedures. These are an adjunct to reversion to alternative-site/standby procedures, and will only be applied, if at all, in catastrophic circumstances. It may not be possible to revert to manual procedures in many circumstances, and certainly will not be unless proper planning is put in train. Critical processes, e.g. financial invoice generation, bill and receipts payments, and corporate core business such as production control processes, goods issued and received, must all be examined for provision of emergency manual standby capability, in case of lengthy deprivation of computer support.

β**70.80** Define and/or review data and transaction control procedures. This involves defining or reviewing procedures for specifying data privacy or security markings; determining user rights of access to data (read/write; etc.), and procedures for implementing them; determining what users have what use of what transaction facilities, and procedures for implementing them.

β**70.90** Determine what user has what rights of access/use to what system and subsystem facilities, and review user authentication, passwording and any other software system access control mechanism.

β**70.100** Define and/or review physical access control procedures. This will include control of access to the site and specific locations within it by pass, badge or any other mechanisms; control of access to terminals and any electronic radiation protection required (e.g. TEMPEST), and the need for any specific network protection, encryption or other devices.

β**70.110** Submit all operational procedures, organization and staffing proposals for QA/Inspection and obtain project board approval. Review corporate standards and strategy for all operational procedures in the light of those approved for the project, and provide any corporate feedback as necessary. Place the finally agreed operational procedures for the project under change control.

STEP β80: IMPLEMENT OPERATIONS PROCEDURES (Fig. 8.9)

Tasks

β**80.10** Staff need to be recruited and put in place to reflect the newly created or enhanced operations organization. Appropriate experience in the chosen hardware, software (and N/W) configuration is clearly essential, and this will have been ensured by the recruitment policy or specific training, in most cases a combination of both. In any event, site-specific training will be essential for the procedures to be adopted to support the site systems if they exist already, the new applications development environment(s), and the new applications operational environment(s).

β**80.20** Detailed implementation of operations procedures must of necessity reflect the particular stage of the development being supported, and this is reflected in Step β110. However, basic (manufacturers') environment setup procedures can be practised and any other work practices trialled and implemented.

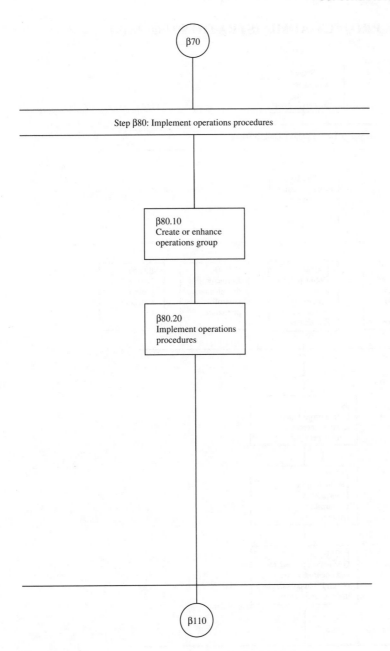

Figure 8.9 Step β80.

STEP β90: DEFINE PROJECT ADMINISTRATION (Fig. 8.10)

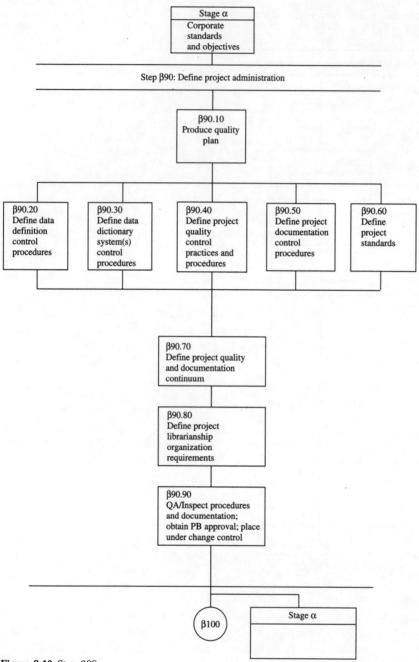

Figure 8.10 Step β90.

Tasks

β**90.10** Produce quality plan. This will indicate for the particular project what quality functions will be applied at what times within the project life cycle; what documentation will be produced when; and what standards, practices and procedures will be applied for the various activities and phases of the project. This includes production of the quality gate diagrams described in Sec. 9.

β**90.20** The data definition control procedures will encompass all those functions commonly called data administration, and control the definition, naming and formatting of every element of data in the system. They will ensure that the definitions will conform to, and be consistent with, the corporate model (or virtual DB) and the company naming standards where they exist. Where these do not, they will be created to cover the scope of the project.

β**90.30** Procedures will be created (or reviewed if they exist) for the use of a project dictionary, which may be an automated tool or a series of tools. Where project information is held on more than one repository, then the procedures should define the authoritative source for all project information and the interfaces and controls to be applied across repository boundaries. Although there can be only one authoritative source for any particular item of information, various subsets of this information could well reside across several tools/workbenches/dictionaries, etc.

β**90.40** All the various quality control and assurance practices to be used in the project, and where and when used, must be defined, and be consistent with corporate practice where they exist. In particular, stage, document, and facility reviews must be clearly defined. Facility reviews will take place at major points where various options may be available to the users/project owners, for example, business and technical options, design, and implementation options, etc. The use of independent, i.e. non-project, development staff should be clearly specified, and procedures defined in terms of project objectives, notification and scheduling. If, for instance, Fagan techniques are used, the appointment of a suitable moderator from a corporate quality management section pool, and the use of users, technical support staff and others for specific inspection roles.

β**90.50** This will include the reviewing of all committed corporate deliverables, where they exist, or the definition of project deliverables where they do not. In particular it will define the content and format of the FRS, SRS, SDS and SIS. It will also define how the components are to be produced, delivered, signed off and base lined. All these responsibilities will be part of the project librarian function.

β**90.60** This will embrace the review (or generation) of standards to be applied for particular aspects/phases of the project, such as program specification production, programming standards, etc. It will also define standards to be used for any particular tool or support workbench, e.g. data dictionary systems or analyst workbenches. It will also cover the use of any proprietary DBMS, TP monitor or program languages (4GLs or AGs).

β**90.70** When the quality and documentation procedures have been defined, they will be reviewed to determine their interrelationships, with particular regard to the establishment of audit trails and the ability to trace back to the source of an error at whatever stage of the project the error is detected. The combination of all these considerations will result in the definition and production of the quality and documentation continuum.

β**90.80** The establishment of all the necessary control procedures, documentation registry, assembly and distribution, and their maintenance throughout the life cycle will demand an appropriately defined and staffed project organization.

β**90.90** All the project administrative procedures, quality control, standard(s) proposals and the necessary organizational structures will themselves be subject to QA/Inspection and submitted for project board approval. It may be necessary for the QA/project board approval to be invoked at various points of the project — for example when standards have been developed for a novel procedure or tool, or both. This should be clearly identified at the first submission and any subsequent QAs can usually be subsumed into other 'standard' project QA points.

STEP β100: IMPLEMENT PROJECT ADMINISTRATION (Fig. 8.11)

Tasks

β**100.10** Staff need to be recruited and placed in post. The recruitment process (or specialist training) should ensure that the staff have the appropriate quality ethos and documentation experience. There will however be a need for site-specific training, to introduce staff to control and QMS practices and procedures, and to familiarize them with any existing standards.

β**100.20** The initial administrative procedures, as approved, should then be implemented. It must be recognized that it is inevitable that project administration will be involved in the revision, and perhaps creation, of practices and standards throughout the project life cycle.

STEP β110: PROVIDE OPERATIONAL ENVIRONMENTS (Fig. 8.12)

Tasks

β**110.10** The output from all appropriate preceding steps needs to be reviewed and integrated. Clearly the procurement installation (β20) must have taken place; however, all other procedures ConMan (β40), CapMan (β60), operations procedures (β80) and data administration procedures (β100) must be rationalized .and coordinated. The rationalization will need to reflect the differing needs and requirements of the H/W, S/W and N/W configurations to support the different stages of the project development and live running. There will be additional problems in determining these requirements if the development is to take place on an existing configuration already supporting other

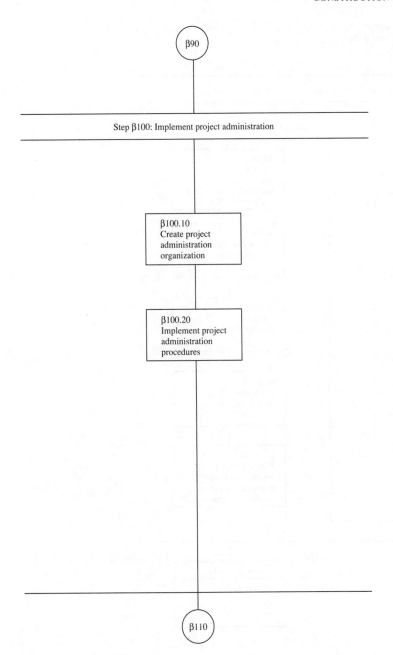

Figure 8.11 Step β100.

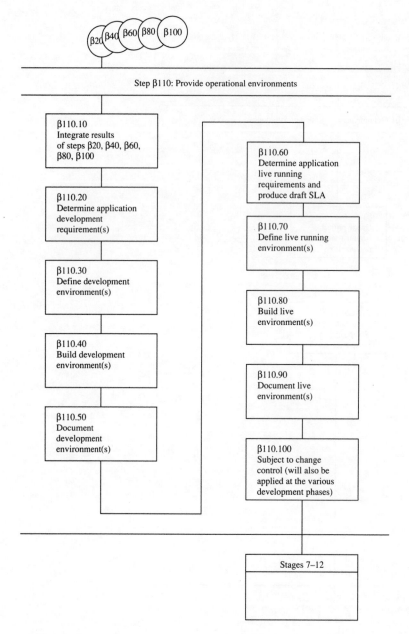

Figure 8.12 Step β110.

development and operational systems. In these circumstances, total site and system scheduling will need to be reviewed and reappraised.

β110.20 To determine the application development environment, the following need to have been determined already:

- Language to be used 4GL or 3GL?
- Implementation data structures; conventional files; codasyl or relational database; or an integral element of the 4GL package selected?
- Batch environments?
- Online management system package to be utilized. As for file/DBMS section above, the relative merits of any manufacturer's product and those available in the open marketplace, including those that play an integral part of any 4GL package, must be considered.
- Select any programmer and/or analyst workbenches to be used at the various stages of the project life cycle.
- Consider use of any test-data generators and/or test harness.
- Determine what, if any, automated dictionary will be used as the prime (central) respository for all project data. Define interfaces and control procedures for ensuring consistency of data with other tools holding project data.
- Consider use of any appropriate CASE product that may subsume some of the above but require an effective and efficient interface to be established with the remainder.

β**110.30** Having determined the required development environment, identify all specific software packages required, including relevant versions, and review configuration management procedures to ensure that they are adequate and compatible for the development environment.

β**110.40** Procure all development software, install, test and integrate where necessary, to build total development environment.

β**110.50** Document details of all the components of the delivered development environment, and subject to change control.

β**110.60** Determine the application live environment requirements. These will be derived from those components specified in β110.20, obviously excluding those that are specifically required to support the development but adding those which will be necessary for live running, e.g. online runtime statistics, performance and line monitors, etc. By this stage the contents of the first-draft service-level agreement (SLA) which represents the 'contract' between the service suppliers (usually operations) and the project owner must have been drawn up.

β**110.70** Define precisely those elements of base, superstructure and ancillary software required for the live-running environment.

β**110.80** Procure, trial and accept the total live environment; build and deliver.

β**110.90** After accepting live environment, document precisely each component selected, including relevant version number and define interfaces and relationship between the various components.

β**110.100** Submit documentation of development and live environments for QA/Inspection and obtain project board approval. Review corporate standards and strategy for the use of development tools and operational environments, including review of attendant related documentation such as ConMan and CapMan. All documentation approved by project board will then be put under change control.

STEP β120: DEFINE/REVIEW CHANGE CONTROL (Fig. 8.13)

Tasks

β120.10 Define, or review if they already exist, the change control procedures to be applied to the project. This must be conducted at a very early stage of the project, as, dependent on project circumstances, change control may be applied from as early as the end of Stage 3, when the SRS is produced. The procedures must address the 'levels' of approval necessary, the criteria for determining the appropriate level of approval, impact analysis and the agencies for that analysis, and the role any automated package, particularly the project dictionary, has in it.

β120.20 Determine/review all the proformae required to support the change control procedures.

β120.30 Identify the change controller duties to be applied within the project, with specific reference to registry, distribution, control and receipt of all change control requests and proposals.

β120.40 Specify the project change control board's (CCB) terms of reference, with particular regard to any delegated responsibilities for change control approval and the criteria to be applied.

β120.50 Identify and assign project staff to the project change control board. This identification should relate to specific project posts and duties, *not* to individuals.

STEP β130: IMPLEMENT CHANGE CONTROL (Fig. 8.14)

Tasks

β130.10 There will be changes that may require major enhancements to the current system. These could be identified by predetermined parameters such as size of change, operational implications, strategic changes of direction. There will also be changes submitted for defect correction that in the event require more time/resources than are within the remit of the maintenance team. In these cases a more rigorous review process will be necessary.

β130.20 The standard impact analysis process will be conducted. However, this is likely to be extended to the formal corporate analysis skills group for a more detailed preliminary evaluation.

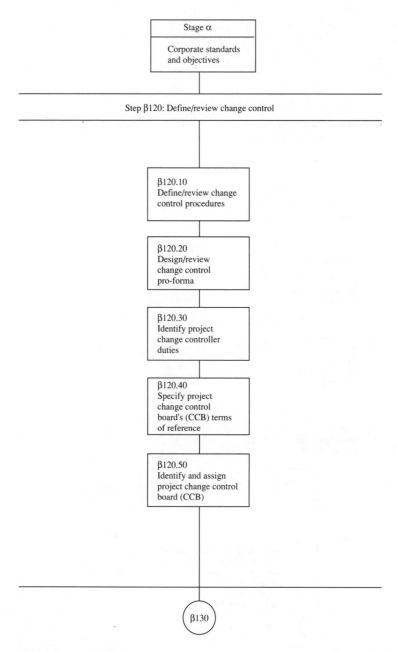

Figure 8.13 Step β120.

β130.30 As an adjunct to the impact analysis, a formal cost/benefit analysis of meeting the requirement will be conducted. Indeed this will very often be a determining parameter for identifying changes meriting enhancement status in the first instance.

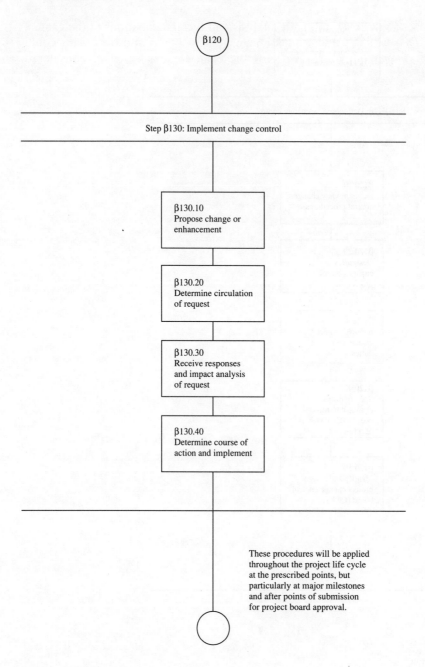

Figure 8.14 Step β130.

β**130.40** The impact analysis, cost/benefit analysis and recommendations of the change control board (CCB) will be submitted for management board approval. This could generate the full project initiation process if the change/enhancement is considered significant enough.

β**130.50** Full detailed production plans will be drawn up for those enhancements approved for discharge within existing project resources or granted the resources required.

β**130.60** Resources will then be allocated in accordance with the project plan, and production initiated.

β**130.70** The production and testing will again follow the philosophies and procedures adopted for direct correction, but may be a little more extensive and intensive, as determined by the management board.

β**130.80** On completion to the team leader's satisfaction for fitness for purpose and quality, the enhancement will be submitted for the delivery process.

STEP β140: CONDUCT AUDIT REVIEW (Fig. 8.15)

Tasks

β**140.10** The audit will examine all facets of the service-level agreement, to ensure conformance and to report any deviation from it.

β**140.20** A similar review of the system maintenance agreement will be conducted.

β**140.30** All changes applied to the system since the last review will be analysed, trends identified and a report on implications for the future direction of the system produced.

β**140.40** The current H/W, S/W and N/W configurations will be reviewed for their adequacy for the current and continued support and running of the system at the prescribed performance levels, and any recommendations for enhancements produced.

β**140.50** The actual cost benefits achieved since the last review will be produced and incorporated into a report on the overall cost benefit of the system to date.

β**140.60** The audit will make overall recommendations for improved operational running, updating of management procedures, and any configuration enhancements necessary.

β**140.70** The whole will then be assembled into the required audit report (suggested contents appear in Chapter 12) and submitted to the project management board.

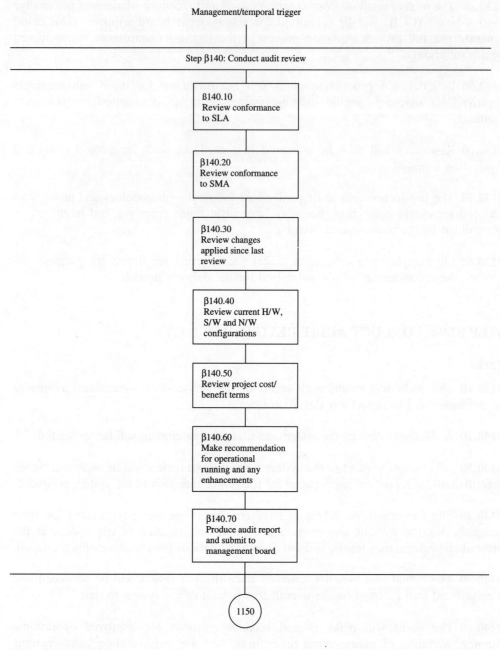

Management/temporal trigger

Step β140: Conduct audit review

β140.10
Review conformance
to SLA

β140.20
Review conformance
to SMA

β140.30
Review changes
applied since last
review

β140.40
Review current H/W,
S/W and N/W
configurations

β140.50
Review project cost/
benefit terms

β140.60
Make recommendation
for operational
running and any
enhancements

β140.70
Produce audit report
and submit to
management board

1150

Figure 8.15 Step β140.

8.2 STAGE 7: CODE PRODUCTION (Fig. 8.16)

8.2.1 Objective

To generate individual modules of code, based on agreed specifications and physical design criteria.

8.2.2 Description

This stage involves the production of clean, unit-tested modules to specification for input to link testing and system building. Existing documentation is revised to reflect the current position. A random sample (say up to 10 percent) of unit code is selected for inspection. This outlines the activities that can be completed in this stage. It does not specify any particular techniques, although structured programming techniques such as Jackson or the structured design method (SDM) could be mapped on to these procedures.

If prototyping (see Chapter 11), and 4GLs or AGs have been or are being used, this will mainly affect Stages 4, 5 and 6. However, just as the use of these tools in no way obviates the need for a thorough analysis of the requirement, so also is the need for thorough testing at all levels as identified in stages, 8, 9, 10 and 11, in no way obviated. What may well change are Steps 720 and 730. These will reflect that which is necessary to create the particular tools environment. In Step 740 the code may well be generated automatically or semi-automatically, by use of specific 4GL/AG. However generated, the object code should then be subjected to exactly the same processes identified in Step 760 onwards.

This, and subsequent stages employ the principles encapsulated in the quality and documentation continuum, specifically the quality gate and inspection procedures detailed in Chapter 10.

STEPS

710 Review code production process

  .10 Review and refine code production plans
  .20 Review programming team organization and responsibilities
  .30 Determine parameters for code inspections
  .40 Plan and schedule code inspections
  .50 Identify any production environment features affecting code production
  .60 Identify units of code for external tests
  .70 Determine parameters for external tests
  .80 Plan and schedule external test inspections
  .90 Review/produce test environment standards
.100 Review use of data dictionary systems (DDS)
.110 Review use of test harness, test data generators and any appropriate CASE tools
.120 Implement testing environment
.130 Conduct stage review and produce any feedback loops

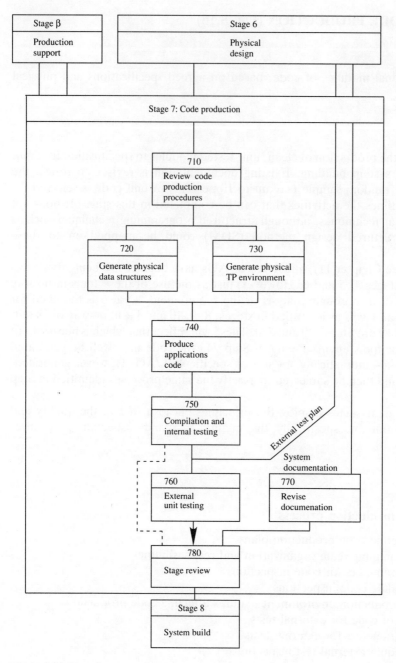

Figure 8.16 Stage 7.

720 Generate physical data structures

.10 Check existence of physical data structure specifications
.20 Map on to chosen DBMS
.30 Generate required physical data structures
.40 Copy any predefined test data into the database
.50 Generate physical test harness environment

730 Generate physical TP environment

.10 Specify actual or simulated development TP environment
.20 Generate required TP, and/or simulation environment

740 Generate applications code

.10 Code module
.20 Generate and load any additional test data
.30 Update module specification with value-added implementation features

750 Compilation and internal testing

.10 Submit code for compilation
.20 Check for errors and rework where necessary
.30 Submit to required number of levels of programming line management and rework where necessary
.40 Declare suitable for formal inspection
.50 Declare available for external testing

760 External unit testing

.10 Review/refine external test schedule
.20 Document expected test results
.30 Conduct test and document
.40 Compare actual results with expected results
.50 Update module/unit history
.60 Rework where necessary
.70 Inspect code of selected unit(s)
.80 Make available for system testing

770 Revise documentation

.10 Produce/revise user guides/manuals
.20 Produce/review operation guides/manuals
.30 Produce/revise fallback/recovery procedures
.40 Produce/review manual procedures and interfaces

780 Stage review

.10 Review inspection results; if sample reflects acceptable error rates, sign off specifications else conduct further selection and repeat Step 760.
.20 Authorize feedback to inspection/productivity information database.
.30 Report on adequacy of program specification contents and format and project standards for code production and control.
.40 Produce report for feedback to corporate steering committee on experiences and recommendations on technical options and tool(s) usage.
.50 Review link/integration plans
.60 Sign off stage and authorize proceeding to Stage 8.

Stage 7 inputs

- Operational and test environment specifications (ex Stage β)
- Configuration management manual (ex Stage β)
- Capacity management manual (ex Stage β)
- Data administration manual (ex Stage β)
- Operations procedures manual (ex Stage β)
- Module specifications (ex Stage 6)
- File/database definitions (ex Stage 6)
- Internal program test plan (ex Stage 6)
- External program test plan (ex Stage 6)
- System documentation (ex Stage 6)

Stage 7 outputs

- Tested clean modules
- Revised program specifications
- Code inspection reports
- Test system/results inspection reports
- Review of code production standards and procedures
- Report to corporate body on technical options and tool usage
- Revised Stage 8 plans.

STEP 710: REVIEW CODE PRODUCTION PROCESS (Fig. 8.17)

Tasks

710.10 High-level plans for the code production process as published in the SRS are revised and refined. These will provide detailed schedules for unit production, to be allocated to individual programmers or programming teams depending on the project size. At least three months' detailed schedules should be produced; again, the total elapsed time for this phase of activity will depend on the project size. For larger projects this process will be repeated at periodic intervals to produce progressively detailed schedules for manageable amounts of work, i.e. approximately three months' work, and

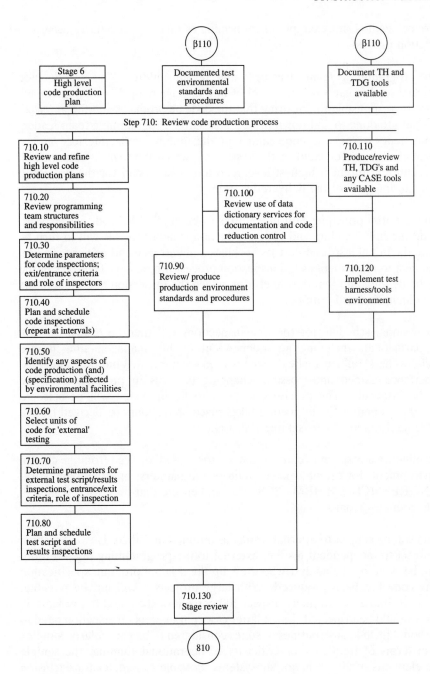

Figure 8.17 Step 710.

to inject experience gained, for example in confirming estimation procedures accuracy, into the production process.

710.20 Review programming team structures and responsibilities. This will include building-in internal quality gates at each level of line management. For example, each programmer will be responsible for ensuring that the code he produces and the 'internal' tests he carries out are done to laid-down project standards. Programming team leaders will ensure consistency across the code, and that the units of code interface and/or integrate to produce the sub-element of the system for which the team is responsible. This will be repeated at the next highest level as often as necessary for the project to ensure the ultimate integrity of the delivered system.

710.30 Determine initial principles and procedures to be applied for code inspections. This will include the initial coding and code production standards. This will in turn be used to generate the initial inspection error checklists and entrance and exit criteria. All these will be subject to refinement as the inspection process progresses. The roles of the inspectors will be defined and the personnel from which the inspection and moderators are to be drawn identified and notified.

710.40 The provisional schedule for the first inspections will then be drawn up with management, participants including an independent quality management/assurance group if this exists. This should again be drawn up at no greater than 3-monthly intervals, to reflect experience gained and possible changing patterns in production of the documents to be inspected. The precise document to be inspected will be selected approximately 10 days before the inspection takes place, and should be derived from a statistically generated random cross-sample (hit list).

710.50 Finally, identify any specific features that are to be used, derived from the chosen production environment, for example screen editors and painters, programming work-benches, for INGRES, ICL AM, IBM CICS, etc., and ensure that they are reflected in the appropriate coding standards.

710.60 All code will be subject to internal testing as outlined in 710.20. However, some code will be subject to independent testing, external to the programming organization. Ideally this will be done by the analyst who drew up the original program specification from which the code has been produced. With large projects it will not be possible, practical or even desirable to externally inspect 100 percent of the code, but at least 50 per cent or more should be inspected. In the latter case, parameters for selection need to be made, and should include any routines or suites considered to be particularly complex or important in terms of frequency or criticality of operational running; the sample should include elements of all the major subsystems. Possible candidates for exclusion are units that would otherwise be tested extensively as part of systems testing, such as access control mechanisms, major batch processes, housekeeping routines and common routines that are called or used by many subsystems.

710.70 Principles and procedures need to be drawn up for test script and test results inspections. In practice it is usually more effective to combine both the script and the results into one inspection. Again, script and result standards will have been drawn up, together with error checklists and entrance and exit criteria, which will be subject to review as a result of the initial inspections.

710.80 A test script/result schedule will be drawn up identifying and notifying suitable candidates to fulfil the various roles of inspectors and the moderator. Again, the specific document to be inspected will be distributed some 10 days prior to the inspection, against another, perhaps different, hit list. If inspections are scheduled to take place weekly, for example, the periodic drawing up of the inspection schedule will probably reflect the changing emphasis on different documents being inspected as the project progresses through the different phases of production.

710.90 The various individual standards may well have been reviewed as part of the inspection procedures, but the totality of all standards to be applied during the code production cycle needs to be reviewed. This may include standards for documents not explicitly being inspected, for example, environment-generated structure charts, run charts, etc., and the various control mechanisms that might be applied in addition to the quality gates — program library(s) control, code assembly, compilation and running, report/listing control and distribution.

710.100 The control of all project-produced documentation needs to be examined as part of the role of the project librarian. This would include the maintenance of the central documentation repository, dictionary, naming standards and version control(s) of the various elements. Increasingly the central repository will in itself be automated, by perhaps more than one tool or DDS. The relationship of all automatic and/or manual dictionary components needs to be defined, and the use of any proactive facility such as automatic data definition of code elements reflected in the appropriate code-production standards.

710.110 Similar reviews need to be conducted on any test harness, test data generators or CASE tools recommended or mandatory for the project or organization. The test environment to be utilized during code production must then be specified.

710.120 Instructions must be issued to ensure that all the H/W and S/W and environments specified are in place at the commencement of code production.

710.130 Submit all revised standards, procedures and plans for inspection and/or approval by the project manager (or project board as appropriate), and provide for explicit feedback loops for experience gained on proposed changes in standards, procedures, practices, etc.

STEP 720: GENERATE PHYSICAL DATA STRUCTURES (Fig. 8.18)

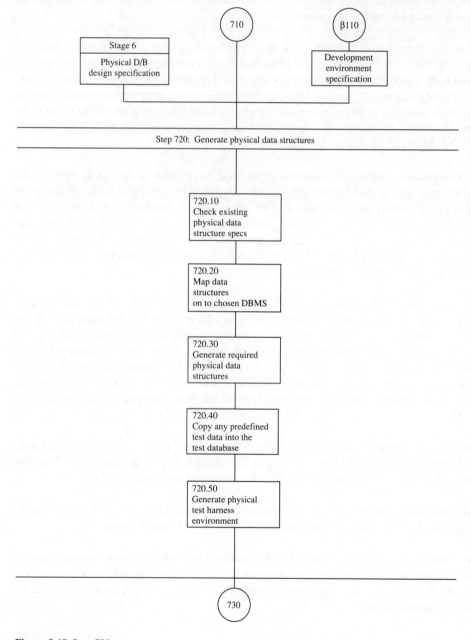

Figure 8.18 Step 720.

Tasks

720.10 Review existing physical data structure specifications, produced during Stage 6.

720.20 Create actual physical data structures specification for the chosen database management system.

720.30 Generate actual physical data structures of chosen DBMS on chosen hardware.

720.40 Copy any predefined test data into the test database, and/or initialize test database.

720.50 Generate test harness and any ancillary environmental facilities. This will include setting up test libraries control and code delivery procedures. Ideally the test harness should include facilities for generating test data, comparing actual with anticipated results, generating reports on any discrepancies and reinitializing the database.

STEP 730: GENERATE PHYSICAL TP ENVIRONMENT (Fig. 8.19)

Tasks

730.10 Review/specify the online environment within which the application will be developed, if applicable. This will often involve two distinct environments, viz. a pseudo online environment for program development, and the genuine online transaction processing environment for later stages of system testing.

730.20 Generate online simulation/development environments and actual transaction processing environments when required.

STEP 740: PRODUCE APPLICATIONS CODE (Fig. 8.20)

Tasks

740.10 Receive program specification allocated by detailed production plan (via programming team leader or whatever level of programming team organization is deemed necessary for the project).

740.20 Generate any specific 'internal' test data that the programmer deems necessary. This should be done entirely independently of any formal external test scripts being devised by the specification author/analyst. Nevertheless, they should be documented to a reasonable standard, together with any appropriate code listing outputs and an initial documentation 'docket'.

740.30 Discussions with programming management, analysts involved and coding itself will almost inevitably generate some minor changes/expansions to program specification. This will particularly be the case in certain 4GL and AG environments, reflecting the use of any facilities these environments afford, such as screen editors, painters, etc.

740.40 Code is produced as prescribed by the development environment.

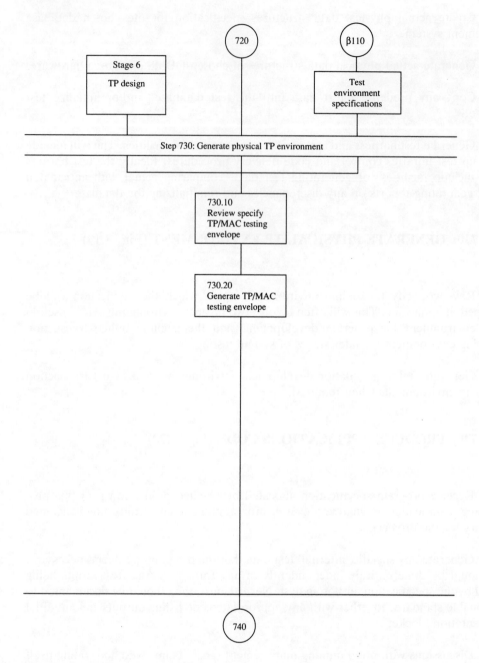

Figure 8.19 Step 730.

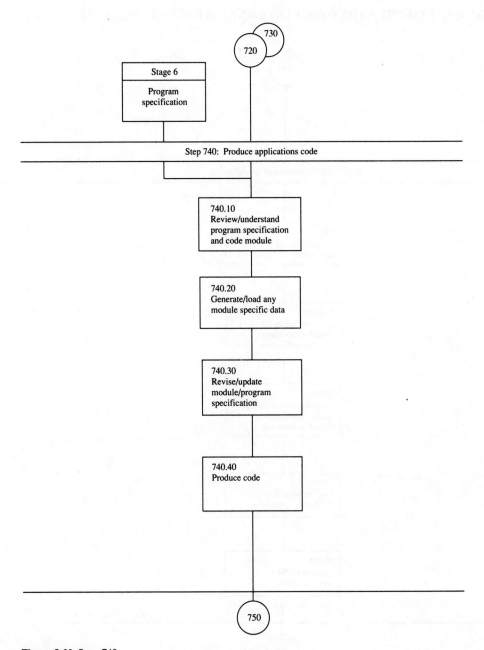

Figure 8.20 Step 740.

STEP 750: COMPILATION AND INTERNAL TESTING (Fig. 8.21)

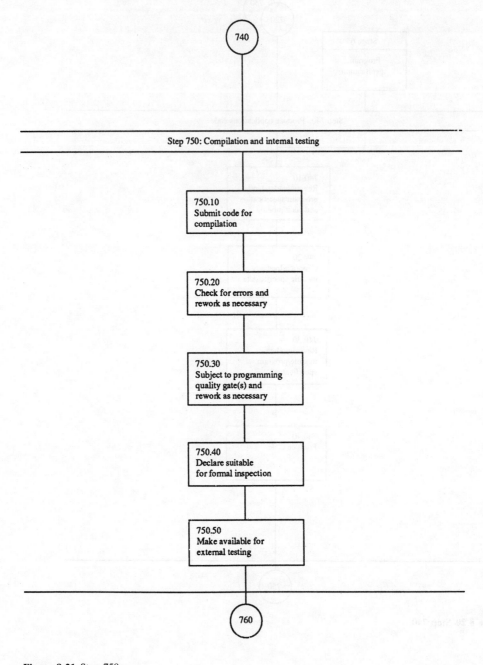

Figure 8.21 Step 750.

Tasks

750.10 Submit code for conversion into machine instructions, and test run. The conversion process was variously known as 'assembly', 'interpretation' or 'compilation'. With current 4GLs, AGs and more sophisticated database/TP environments, this can be a multiphase process. Specific management control mechanisms may be required when this process is conducted online, to obtain optimum return from both human and machine resources. The latter can be achieved by scheduling, etc., the former may require explicitly defined desktop checking procedures, for example, to ensure that code and any subsequent errors are adequately checked prior to submission to the 'code conversion/compilation' process.

750.20 Programmers will check output from each run against their anticipated results. This again will be documented to the level demanded by the programmers' line manager for his understanding, and may form part of the delivered documentation.

750.30 When the programmer is satisfied that the code produced matches the requirements defined by the specification, he will then formally deliver the code, any specifications amendments and the internal test history to the required project standards. This will then go through various programming quality gates, the number of which will usually be determined by the programming team structures. Each line manager will check the documentation for consistency and adherence to standards at the appropriate unit, subsystem and system levels. Other quality gates might exist either in their own right or absorbed by the appropriate quality gate, to ensure adherence to certain technical aspects such as efficiency of use of DBMS structures, database navigation, use of TP facilities, etc.

750.40 When the documentation has been subjected to all internal quality gates and assurance determined by the overall program team manager, it will be declared suitable for consideration for formal Winway inspection, as described in Chapter 11. It will not be usual for all code documentation to be inspected, but it is all equally likely to be chosen for inspection, to ensure that all is produced to a consistently high quality.

750.50 At this stage, all those programs that have been identified as being subject to external testing (710.80) will be made available to the independent external testing team, who should be derived from the analysts who produced the original specifications.

STEP 760: EXTERNAL UNIT TESTING (Fig. 8.22)

Tasks

760.10 Review and refine the original external test schedule. This can be fairly dynamic during code production, in that it may be necessary to reassess the schedule in the light of the degrees of complexity within function areas, and whole function areas relative to each other. This could cause a change of emphasis in which areas should be tested when the initial results of the external tests become available. This assumes of course that less

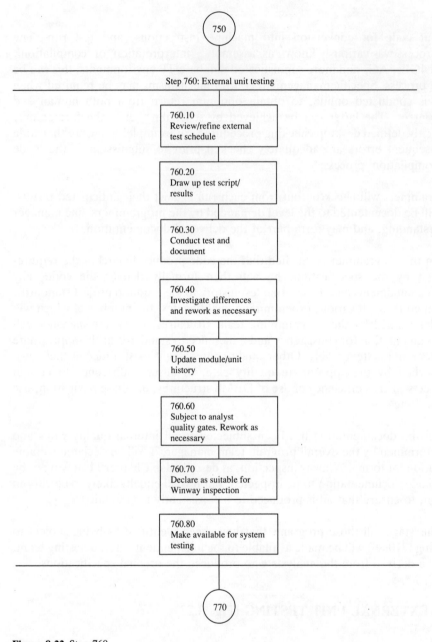

Figure 8.22 Step 760.

than 100 percent of units are subject to external testing. The proportion chosen for external testing could again change, depending on the results of the process itself. The allocation of work to the testing teams will obviously need to reflect the dynamic nature of the situation, and will usually not be more than two or three weeks ahead of the release of the program/module code. The external test team members should be drawn from staff who are completely independent of the code to be tested. Ideally they will be from the analyst team that produced the original specifications, but they could be experienced programmers who worked on different areas of the system.

760.20 Individual analysts will draw up and document detailed test scripts in accordance with the standards appropriate to the development environment. These will always include definitions of test data to be used, and expected test results.

760.30 The test itself will then be scheduled and run, and the results documented. This may consist of outputs produced by the testing environment, but the actual data results obtained from the test must be recorded.

760.40 Any differences between anticipated and actual results must be investigated, any necessary rework conducted and the whole process documented.

760.50 When external tests have been completed to the analysts' satisfaction, the results should be formally lodged with the program documentation. This will usually be a simple 'tidying up' of the documentation produced during the process itself.

760.60 The documentation will then be subject to a series of 'quality gate' assessments depending on the size and structure of the external test team organization. This assessment will in fact be critical scrutiny of the work against project standards, by the management team leaders and overall team manager. This could include examination of any specific technical aspects of interest in the particular environment (the process in fact mirrors the programming team quality gates outlined in 750.30). Any rework deemed necessary will be discharged and documented. At this point, some internal change control procedures should be put in place. In larger projects these may have already been introduced during code production. They are now, however, essential to control rework that may have been identified during external testing, to establish the control of differing versions of programme code, and the release of updated software to this 'official' systems testing environment.

760.70 On completion of the whole process, the test team manager will 'sign off' the external test as being suitable for Winway inspection procedures.

760.80 This of course also implies that the code is now available for the next phase of systems testing. The test team manager will maintain a list of all such code, including code that will not be subject to external tests but which has been 'signed off' as acceptable by the programming team manager.

STEP 770: PRODUCE/REVISE DOCUMENTATION (Fig. 8.23)

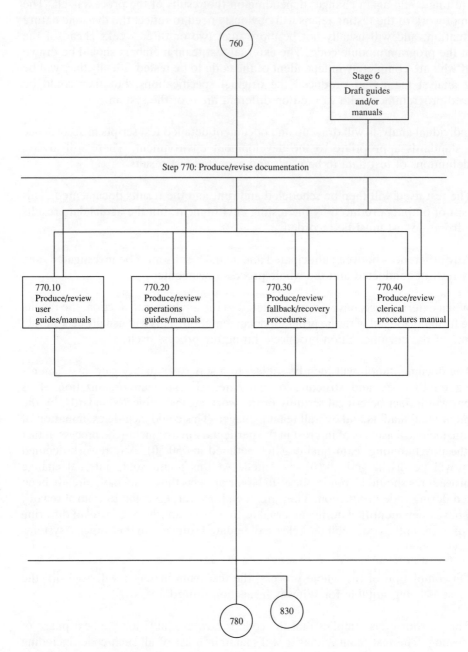

Figure 8.23 Step 770.

Tasks

All the elements of documentation referred to in this step may, to a greater or lesser extent, have been drafted during Stage 6. Depending on the document itself, the draft may consist merely of a corporate standards contents list. It may also contain some elements that have been derived from the analysis and design stages. In all cases, further input for later consolidation and rationalization should emerge from the code production and testing stage.

770.10 Produce and/or review user guides and manuals. There should now be sufficient material to produce an outline of the system and its major components in lay terms. Full details of complete batch runs will probably become available during system trials. Sufficient information on individual online transactions should be available to produce the first draft of the detailed manuals immediately after the external test, when all the details are current in the analysts' thoughts. Error messages should be consolidated and rationalized. Details of data-field definitions and validations applied at that level should be available to translate into lay terms. The glossary of terms should be revised to include any that have emerged during testing that will be relevant to the end user.

770.20 Produce and/or review operations guides/manuals. This includes all operation instructions, system maintenance guides, network commissioning, management and control, bug reporting and release procedures, and HelpDesk facilities. Some lower level operational instruction details will begin to emerge at the testing of units of code. Most of the detail for the rest of the documentation will arise from system testing, but fuller appreciation of the context required should be gained during unit testing. Bug reporting and release procedures should be reviewed, as in some cases simplified versions can be used to good effect during user acceptance testing (UAT).

770.30 Produce and/or review recovery and fallback procedures. Although it is unlikely that sufficient detail will be available on the procedures themselves, there should be sufficient information in Job Run/Systems Structure charts to produce a strategy for considering which recovery mechanisms should be placed at which points, the number of generations of key files that should be kept, and the number of copies of report files to be held, depending on the frequency of production, etc. This should also include any dumping, journalizing and before and after look strategies to be employed. These may well be part of established corporate procedures on a mature site.

770.40 Produce and/or review clerical and manual procedures. Detailed clerical and desktop procedures should be produced by the users as part of their input to the UAT. However, some clearer view should emerge as to what, if anything, can be done in terms of reverting to manual procedures in circumstances of partial or total loss of the computer system.

STEP 780: STAGE REVIEW (Fig. 8.24)

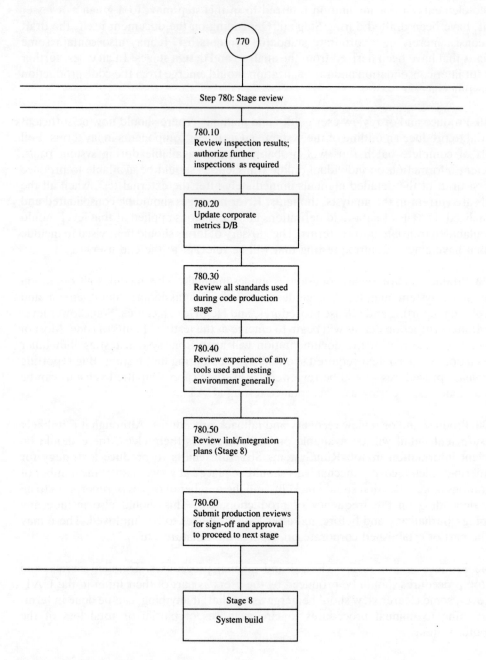

Figure 8.24 Step 780.

Tasks

780.10 Review inspection results and procedures. Documents that will have been candidates for inspection during this stage would include program code, test scripts and results, and some draft user manuals. The inspection process may be extended depending on the particular project and its precise development philosophy. The procedures of the Winway inspections will be reviewed, to identify changes and/or enhancements that may be considered necessary as a result of experience gained in their use during development. The actual results will be analysed, to ensure that all document inspections have achieved the level of error detection necessary to ensure that quality has been achieved. Any that have not will be subject to continued review (Stage 760) until such time as they have. This need not inhibit continuation into Stage 8, but Stage 8 plans will have to be revised as a result.

780.20 The acceptability of the inspections having been established, the statistics of the error patterns (usually expressed in terms of the number of errors per page of the document inspected) are fed into the corporate metrics database. The errors detected at the various stages of code testing, both internal and external, together with the identification of the source of the error, will also be recorded and fed into the corporate metrics D/B.

780.30 Review all standards that have been applied throughout the code production process. It is almost inevitable that some 'adjustments' will have been made during the early stages of the Winway inspection process. These need to be documented and analysed to assess if there is a need to change corporate standards, and a report must be produced.

780.40 A review must be conducted of any tools used, test harnesses produced and any test data generator used, and the total test environment. This will be compared with the appropriate element of the technical options and a report produced, which again will be assessed in terms of any implications for corporate strategy.

780.50 The plans for link/integration testing will now be reviewed in the light of all the above. Special regard should be given to the units subjected to external testing, to ensure that attention is given to any areas identified as being particularly complex or otherwise significant and to ensure that all subsystems are adequately tested and user training considered prior to release to UAT.

780.60 All reviews, reports and revised plans will be submitted to senior project management for sign-off and authorization to proceed to Stage 8.

8.3 STAGE 8: SYSTEM BUILD (Fig. 8.25)

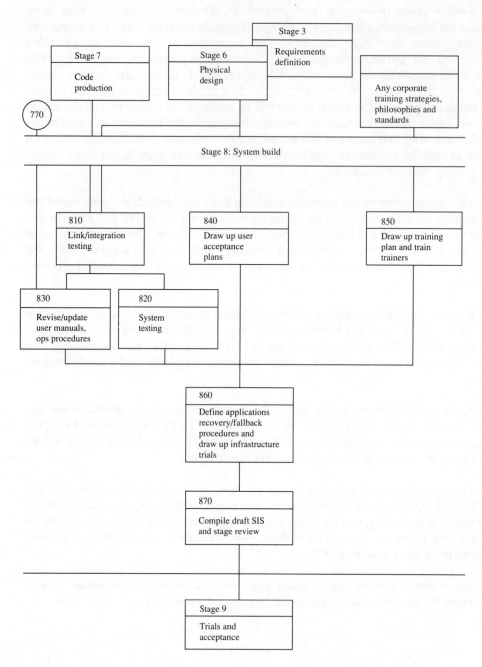

Figure 8.25 Stage 8.

8.3.1 Objective

The aim of this stage is to build the delivered code into an integrated system, to prove the suitability and accuracy of supporting documentation, and to draw up a user training programme.

8.3.2 Description

This stage takes units of code 'inside-tested' by the code producer and 'outside' tested by analysts, and progressively assembles them into function, subsystem and system components by link, integration and system testing (outside testing) in accordance with predetermined plans produced by the analyst/designers of the system and carried out by them.

   All relevant system manuals and procedures will be reviewed in the light of this process (including, where relevant, the infrastructure support documentation). Comprehensive user training programme(s) and documentation will be drawn up and applied to the level necessary for acceptance trials.

STEPS

810 Link and integration testing

.10 Allocate link tests to teams
.20 Review test script standards and begin test script production
.30 Identify any job control procedures required and design code and test
.40 Conduct tests and document
.50 Compare actual with anticipated results and rework as necessary
.60 Subject test results to quality gates
.70 Declare suitable for Winway inspection process
.80 Make available for system testing

820 System testing

.10 Refine/review system testing plans
.20 Identify and allocate system test components
.30 Conduct test runs
.40 Review tests and rework as necessary
.50 Update system performance metrics DB
.60 Produce report and conduct stage review

830 Review/revise manuals and guides

.10 Produce initial/revised draft of the user guide/manuals
.20 Produce initial/revised draft of operations guides/manuals
.30 Produce initial/revised draft of fallback and/or recovery procedure
.40 Produce initial/revised draft of clerical production manual

840 Draw up user acceptance plans

.10 Review any existing plans and/or procedures
.20 Define user roles and draw up job descriptions
.30 Draw up organization charts for staff required for user acceptance trials (UAT)
.40 Define hardware and communications environment(s) required for UAT
.50 Produce any documentation and procedural standards required to support UAT
.60 Determine what QA/QC and sign-off procedures might be required and applied
.70 Draw up the detailed user acceptance trial plans
.80 Allocate resources to the user acceptance teams and install any necessary equipment

850 Produce training plans and train users

.10 Review any existing training plans and policies
.20 Train the trainers, and expose to systems applications and documentation
.30 Involve trainers in batch input and transaction testing
.40 Prepare course materials and training manuals
.50 Draw up training schedules
.60 Coordinate and rationalize user manuals and desktop/clerical procedures
.70 Prepare/review bug reporting/HelpDesk facilities
.80 Commence user training

860 Define recovery/fallback and draw up infrastructure trials

.10 Identify application recovery requirements
.20 Identify mainframe resilience and H/W redundancy requirements
.30 Identify communication and N/W resilience requirements
.40 Determine volumetric trials requirements
.50 Review standby/fallback requirements
.60 Draw up infrastructure operational trials (IOT) plan
.70 Allocate resources and identify logistic requirements

870 Compile draft SRS and conduct stage review

.10 Review link and system testing
.20 Review user acceptance test (UAT) plans
.30 Review all training plans and materials
.40 Review all infrastructure operational trial (IOT) plans
.50 Compile draft SIS
.60 Stage review and resource allocation

Stage 8 inputs

- Test environment (ex Stage β)
- Configuration management manual (ex Stage β)
- Capacity management manual (ex Stage β)

- Project administration manual (ex Stage β)
- Operations procedure manual (ex Stage β)
- Draft user manuals (ex Stage β)
- Tested modules (ex Stage 7)
- Integration test plan (ex Stage 6)
- System build plan (ex Stage 6)
- System test plan (ex Stage 6)
- System manual(s) (ex Stage β).

Stage 8 outputs

- Tested clean program/system (to Stage 9)
- Draft system implementation specification (SIS)
- User documentation
- Trained users
- Stage review documentation for project board submission
- Report to corporate strategy body on any relevant feedback

STEP 810: LINK/INTEGRATION TESTING (Fig. 8.26)

Tasks

The objective of link and integration testing is to ensure that all the individual units of code are assembled and tested, cohesively and progressively, through the logical grouping of processing (subsystems) to a point where the total system can be assembled and made available for testing (Step 820). Where the system includes elements of online and real-time processing, account should be taken of the fact that the development environment is often different from the operational environment and special trials may need to be run to confirm coordination and rationalization of the components in the operational environment. These may not be finally proved and accepted until systems testing has been completed.

810.10 Allocate individual link/integration tasks, as defined by the revised stage plan, to the test teams. They will usually be the logical extension to the external testing of unit code. As such the testing team(s) should be derived from analysts — ideally those involved with the original requirements definition. This provides the necessary independence from the code producers, yet maintains the necessary continuity of production.

810.20 Test script standards and procedures established for external testing should be reviewed in the light of their suitability for link/integration testing. Changes, if any, should be minor. Individual analysts will produce test scripts, test data and results in accordance with the revised standards.

810.30 In many projects, the development and operational environment will require the production of 'job control' programs (commonly referred to as JCL or SCL or similar,

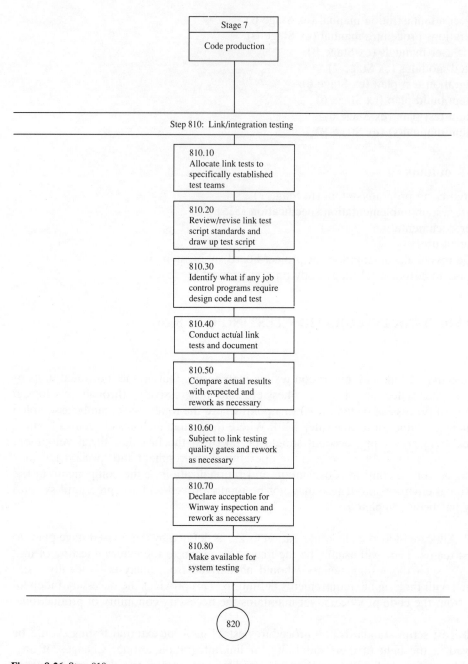

Figure 8.26 Step 810.

depending on the particular manufacturer). These will provide the automatic linking of the various units of code components, control of magnetic media and hardware peripherals, and communication with operating staff. This will require specifying, coding and testing according to the general principles established for normal code production in Stage 7. The detail required, and the precise timing for its production, will be very much dependent on the specific development environment; however, in most cases final refinements will not take place until just prior to operational running, as final details of the sizes, job timings and recovery mechanisms become available.

810.40 Tests will be scheduled and run, and the results documented. As the tests will now potentially involve many individual units of code, the link-testing documentation will exist as an independent series of documents, but some cross-referencing must be made in the individual units' documentation.

810.50 Any discrepancies between the anticipated and the actual results must be investigated, documented and any necessary rework conducted. This must in turn be fully documented.

810.60 When the link/integration tests have been completed successfully to the analyst's satisfaction, the full documentation will be presented to the analyst's next/immediate manager and subjected to the usual quality gate inspections as determined by the test team organization. At each level, the leader/manager will confirm general conformance to standards and quality, and progressive coordination and integration in the more generally accepted sense of the word. These quality gates may include conformance to any specialist facilities/techniques demanded by the specific development environment.

810.70 When all quality gates have been successfully passed, the senior test team manager will sign off the test and declare it suitable for the Winway inspection procedures. Where applicable, the necessary JCL code will have been subjected to the same processes, usually as an adjunct and/or by-product of the individual link/integration tests. Any rework generated by the inspection process will be conducted as necessary.

810.80 All documentation of link/integration testing will be assembled, coordinated and made available for full system testing. However, project management must be reassured that the formal Winway inspections have achieved the 'ambient' level of error detection necessary to confirm that the requisite level of quality has been achieved.

STEP 820: SYSTEM TESTING (Fig. 8.27)

Tasks

The prime objective of system testing is to simulate actual operating conditions in terms of the functionality of the system. In addition to replicating operational functionality, the normal anticipated usage of the system by the various elements of the user population should be simulated. This is particularly the case for online systems where online input, correction and amendment transactions are available.

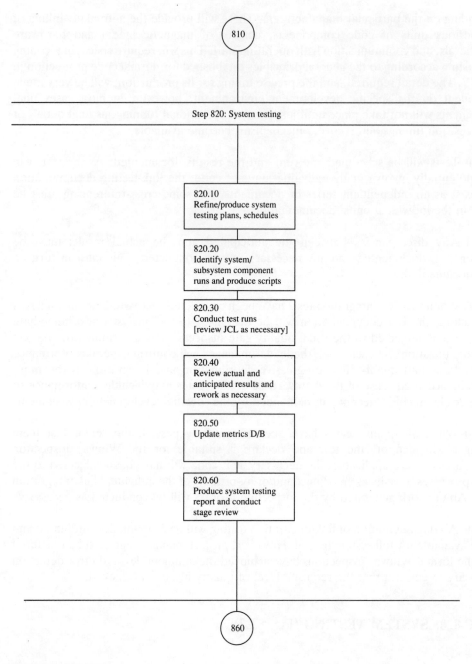

Figure 8.27 Step 820.

820.10 Review and revise system testing plans and schedules in the light of information and experience gained during link/integration testing. Allocate tests to the system testing team(s), who will be derived from the teams established for link/integration testing: they may need some minor reorganization to reflect the support/expertise required to run the larger subsystem components.

820.20 Review the appropriateness of link test script standards; expand/amend as necessary and produce the necessary system test scripts.

820.30 Run actual system tests. This could involve amendment/expansion of any job control procedures, reflecting larger job runs, more information available, viz. file sizes, job run timings, etc. It should be noted that because of the dynamic nature of the use of job control procedures, a more flexible approach to their testing and documentation is required than that for unit, link/integration and system testing.

820.40 Any differences and/or discrepancies between the anticipated and the actual results must be investigated and documented. Any rework deemed necessary must be conducted and documented.

820.50 All performance and quality metrics must be fed into the project and corporate metrics databases. These will predominantly be bugs identified in the system code and errors in the system procedures. The testing itself should be subject to quality assurance processes, which could involve inspections of individual test runs, but it is more usual to have a formal review of the whole process as documented in the systems testing report.

820.60 Produce system testing report, which will consist of an explanation of the philosophy applied, identification of all test runs conducted and results obtained, and an analysis of full metrics obtained throughout the testing. This is a necessary precursor to ensuring that the system is considered sufficiently stable to embark on UAT.

STEP 830: REVIEW/REVISE MANUALS (Fig. 8.28)

Tasks

830.10 The first complete draft set of user guides/manuals should be drawn up and integrated into a full working set, in preparation for UAT. In many cases the online transactions components of the manuals will have been produced during link/integration and systems testing, and should have been subjected to the usual quality gates scrutiny and Winway inspection processes, in which case they merely have to be coordinated, rationalized and assembled. Some components of the user manual may not, however, be able to be produced until the final stages of system testing. These will include the overall statement of the system and its various subsystems and how they relate and interface, final rationalized error lists, and a glossary of terms. Any user-relevant technical details of the particular equipment being used, particularly terminals and keyboard layouts, should also be integrated here. The whole assembly should then be subjected to a preliminary QA/product review prior to release for UAT.

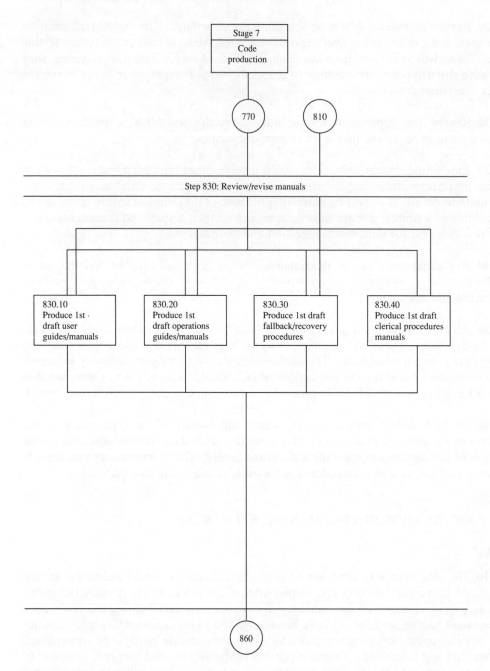

Figure 8.28 Step 830.

830.20 Many details of the operational procedures will also have become available during systems testing, and they too will need to be coordinated, rationalized and assembled for the first complete working draft. There will also be a need to produce overall system and subsystem integration information, system run charts, etc. The obvious difference is that the recipients of the information will be operations staff, as opposed to end users. In terms of the quality assurance processes to be applied, it is probably more appropriate to work directly with representatives of operations as the procedures develop, reflecting the more dynamic nature of their production rather than the more formal Winway inspections that inevitably involve some element of time lag. Even if operations cannot be directly involved, they should be exposed to the draft instructions as they are produced. The whole assembled operation instructions/manuals should be subjected to a high level QA/review prior to IOT. These should take place in a parallel timeframe with UAT, but their very nature will demand separate scheduling. Full details of UAT and IOT are contained in Stage 9. However, the essential difference is that the UAT will prove the applications code and the IOT will prove the environment(s) within which the code runs.

830.30 The strategy for recovery and fallback should have begun to be shaped during system testing, and indeed some of the considerations may well have influenced the production of any job control procedures and programs. However what will need refinement is:

- What recovery mechanism needs to be put where
- What files/journals need to be preserved
- The number of generations required
- How many generations of the database need to be taken, and at what frequency
- What recovery options are available for different system failures vis à vis restoration by journals/restore mechanisms, by reprocessing, or by a combination of the two.

Some strategic decisions such as the use of duplex databases and before and after look journals, will have been taken at a much earlier stage (Stage 6, or even technical options stage) or may be predetermined by corporate strategy. However the proving of these should be reflected in the IOT, and use of the facilities should be in the recovery/fallback manuals/guides. The manuals/guides should also address the problem of priority in processing in circumstances of reduced mainframe components and/or hardware failure, so that 'graceful degradation' of services can be achieved. Again, fallback strategy in terms of reverting to a separate configuration or even disparate geographical sites, or mutual standby facilities with other divisions or companies using similar hardware configurations, will usually have been decided at a corporate level. None the less, these should be trialled in the IOT and details of procedure be reflected in the fallback manuals/guides.

830.40 The need for any clerical procedures or desktop instructions and HelpDesk procedures to augment or complement the existing draft user manuals should be determined. At this stage, little more can be determined than what needs to be produced, and an outline of the production schedule. The proving of the detailed content of their final production will almost inevitably have to await the UAT itself.

STEP 840: DRAW UP USER ACCEPTANCE PLANS (Fig. 8.29)

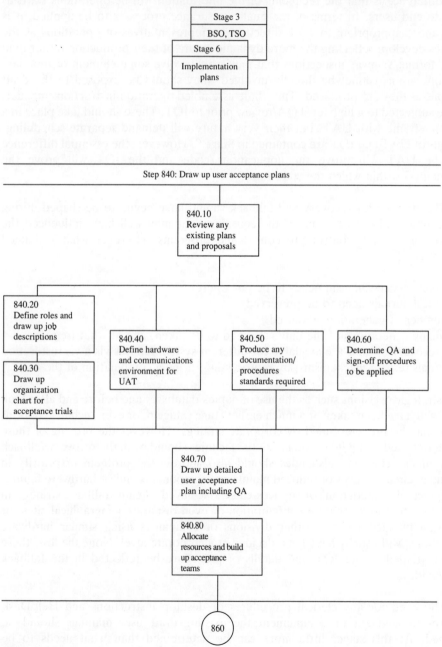

Figure 8.29 Step 840.

Tasks

840.10 Review any user acceptance plans that may have been drawn up as part of the implementation plans, or objectives that may have been specified as part of the business or technical options. Any corporate strategies required for acceptance testing should also be reviewed. The overall review process should establish the objectives to be applied to the user acceptance process: these must include proving of all functionality defined in the SRS, and ensuring that all issues identified in the PRL have been properly addressed.

840.20 Define the roles required to discharge agreed acceptance objectives and draw up terms of reference/job descriptions for main areas of user responsibility. Although the main tasks will be determined by the objectives of the acceptance trials, detailed tasks will vary depending on the needs of each specific project and the user areas within them.

840.30 Organization charts detailing the teams required to support the tasks for each user area should be drawn up, resources required for them quantified, and provision made for any necessary training as determined in Step 780.

840.40 The environment necessary to conduct user acceptance trials should be defined. Whereas the mainframe hardware requirements should be similar to, if not the same as, those needed for systems testing, specific filestore, data, database and TP services may well be required. In addition, any communications network(s) and protocols will need to be put in place, together with terminals and LANs in the user locations, as appropriate and necessary for projects involving online communications facilities.

840.50 Standards need to be reviewed/produced for any documentation that will be required to record the acceptance trials themselves. This will include test scripts, results expected, and definition of the data required to support them. Formats produced during systems testing may provide a basis, but these will need to be expanded to reflect specific user requirements. In addition, separate tests will need to be drawn up for any supporting administrative and clerical procedures. Trials will also need to be defined, as to how the user community will ensure that the functionality and requirements, as defined in the SRS, are met, particularly those contained in the PRL. All these issues will be encapsulated in the user acceptance trials completion report, and will determine its content and format.

840.60 The quality assurance procedures to be put in place during user acceptance need to be determined. These will include Winway inspections of appropriate documentation, defined in 840.50, and a formal review and sign-off of the UAT completion report.

840.70 A detailed user acceptance plan should be drawn up, reflecting all the requirements that emerge from the preceding tasks of this step, including clearly scheduled quality assurance processes.

840.80 User resources required to discharge the detailed UAT plan should be approved and committed, and provision made for any necessary training in the equipment to be used, the applications to be trialled, and the clerical and system administration support procedures needed.

STEP 850: PRODUCE TRAINING PLANS AND TRAIN TRAINERS
(Fig. 8.30)

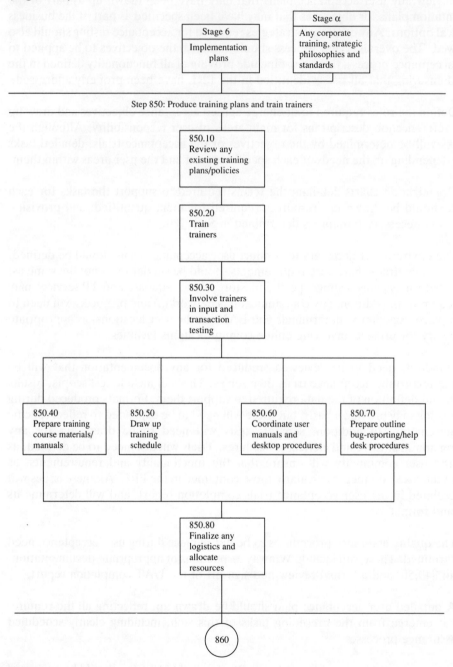

Figure 8.30 Step 850.

Tasks

850.10 Review/produce strategy to be adopted for initial training required for UAT and for the long-term ongoing training of new users introduced to the system. The latter will need to take into account any strategic plans for general staff induction, IT training generally and any existing applications/systems either being replaced by, or interfacing with, the current project. Training needs must be determined by reviewing roles and responsibilities in the new system and assessing the levels of current skills. The most appropriate media — courses, computer-based training — should be selected.

850.20 A training schedule for the trainers of the new system should be drawn up in the light of the revised strategy. If there are personnel dedicated to the training function, they themselves should be directly involved in drawing up this program. If no dedicated trainers exist, then the most appropriate experienced users in the applications areas should be released and used to draw up the initial longer term training plans. This is done in conjunction with senior analysts and management personnel, including the project manager, if appropriate.

850.30 An essential part of drawing up the training plans is the early involvement of users with the emerging systems applications. In this regard, some consideration should be given either to the direct involvement of 'trainers' in the final stages of link/integration (Step 810), system testing (Step 820) and user manual reviews (Step 830.10), or the release of the various components, 'without prejudice' as soon as the development team have completed the relevant tests. This qualification acknowledges that some deficiencies may exist in the components because, in some instances, they will be released before system testing has been completed. If, however, both parties fully recognize and accept this, considerable advantage can accrue to them both.

850.40 Trainers with early exposure to the system and all the attendant documentation will begin to prepare the formal programme for long-term ongoing user training. The training must be determined by reviewing the roles and responsibilities in the new system, and assessing the level of current skills, and the appropriate media selected.

850.50 Training schedules should be drawn up, indicating what training of what parts of the system are required by what users. Also an initial programme for the training of those staff who will be responsible for the acceptance, delivery and live running of the system must be developed.

850.60 There will be a requirement, particularly for online systems, to draw up procedures for how the existing manual, and perhaps other computer, systems will interface with the new system. It is unlikely that all these aspects will be covered by the user manuals since these are produced by the development team analysts and will tend to concentrate on the facilities inherent in the new system. Trainers will be required to produce documentation — clerical procedures or desktop instructions — to make good any deficiencies in these areas.

850.70 The procedures for reporting any perceived deficiency, errors or any other observations, need to be defined in advance of UAT. Bug-reporting procedures may already exist at a corporate level, or 'internal' procedures may have been produced by the development team during system testing. Any existing procedures must be reviewed to determine their adequacy for the new system and users, and new procedures produced as necessary. These procedures may include or be augmented by HelpDesk facilities, which will provide a point of first contact for users during 'office hours' for operational running. The HelpDesk will also act as a focal point for the dissemination of information, broadcasting messages, initial networking contact point, etc. Again these facilities may exist at a corporate level or within other systems, but they will need to be reviewed or new facilities provided.

850.80 When all the preceding tasks have been completed their results need to be coordinated and rationalized, training facilities and logistics, for example any specific accommodation, provided, courses scheduled and promulgated, and trainers and students allocated.

STEP 860: DEFINE RECOVERY/RESILIENCE/FALLBACK PLANNING AND INFRASTRUCTURE TRIALS (Fig. 8.31)

Tasks

860.10 Finalize recovery mechanisms to be built into the application to provide the necessary system resilience. The systems flow chart should be re-examined to determine:

- The number of generations of backup files to be preserved for input and output files
- The master files and/or a number of databased dumps to be held
- The frequency of the dumping process
- The number and type of any journal files to be used
- What checkpoint/restart points are to be built into the system
- Any recovery of data extracts required for input to other processes/systems

860.20 Identify or review any mainframe hardware resilience and/or redundancy requirements. This may already be an inherent aspect of the configuration design if an existing development is being used. However the new system may demand additional resilience requirements, additional switching capability of various hardware components, duplexing of files/databases, etc. The new system may also necessitate changes in work practices that may affect hardware and software recovery procedures. For example, moving from one-shift to two-shift working, or even 24-hour working may require a radical review of dumping procedures.

860.30 Identify or review any network and communications resilience/redundancy requirements. Again this may already be inherent in the network design if one already exists, but even so, the traffic on the network will inevitably be increased. This will require any existing line utilization to be reviewed, including tails to local area networks

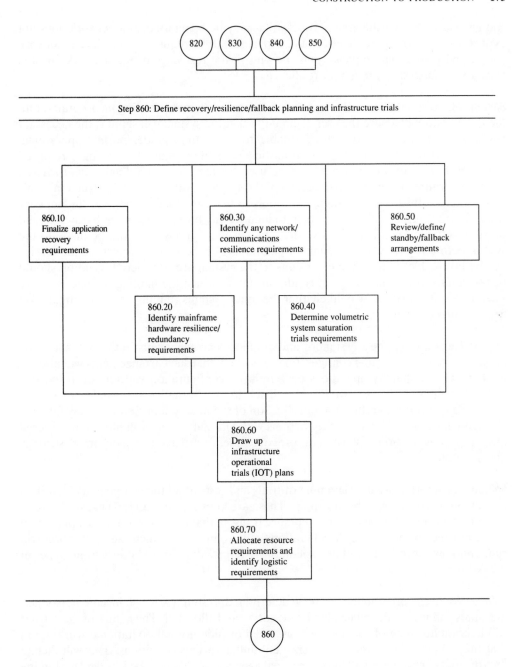

Figure 8.31 Step 860.

and gateways to any wide area networks that may be being used. If a network does not exist, then very considerable effort and expertise will be required to produce a network design and substantial emphasis must be put on the resilience of the network and the trials to be applied to prove that resilience.

860.40 There should be an element of rudimentary volumetric testing incorporated into the UAT. This will assure the user community that the system will support the necessary levels of concurrent access with acceptable response times under normal operational conditions. However, a much more sophisticated level of volumetric testing is required to establish the working parameters to be used for the service level agreement (SLA), and to determine the limiting parameters of the system by driving it to 'destruction'. This may require software and/or simulation tools to drive the mainframe, and the network where it exists. The trials will also help to identify any bottlenecks in the hardware (and possibly software) configurations so that any necessary adjustment can be made to the system before it goes live. The limiting parameters of the various aspects of the service will be invaluable if and when extensions to the system are considered. Caution should be used, however, in defining the conditions under which the limiting parameters were established; it is extremely unlikely that the other systems running on the configuration will remain constant.

860.50 Review or define any standby and/or fallback arrangements. If the system is to be implemented on an existing configuration, it is likely that such arrangements will already exist; however, standby operations on a reduced configuration will require respective system priorities to be reviewed, and fallback to an alternative site would need to be rehearsed and rerun to reflect the introduction of the new system. If no standby/fallback arrangement exists, then some negotiations with alternative sites will have to be entered into at a much earlier stage and the outcome(s) reflected in corporate strategy documentation.

860.60 A comprehensive programme of trials and tests of all the components identified in previous tasks needs to be drawn up. These are known as the IOT. These trials are as important as the system and user acceptance trials, in that the latter prove the application itself, but the former prove the operational environment in which the application will run, and how the systems will be expeditiously returned to service after various types of breakdown.

860.70 When the programme has been determined, resources, which include personnel, machines and material, will need to be identified and allocated. The nature of these trials will necessitate some of them being conducted outside normal operational working, in that they require the system to be 'crashed' under various conditions. This will dictate 'out-of-hours' working. In addition, external agencies are likely to be involved in standby and fallback trials and network/communications trials. Close cooperation with maintenance and facility management teams will also be necessary.

STEP 870: PRODUCE DRAFT SIS AND STAGE REVIEW (Fig. 8.32)

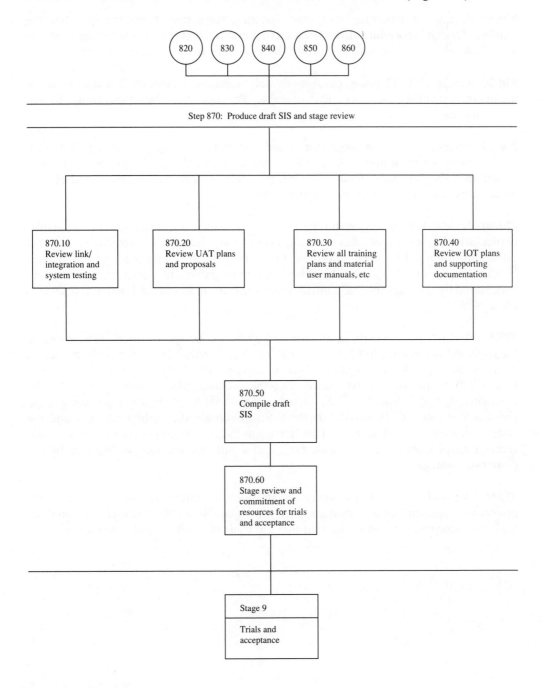

Figure 8.32 Step 870.

Tasks

870.10 Review all link/integration and system testing results and ensure that the requisite QA/QC procedures have been carried out. Subject the system testing report to a full QA review and sign off to declare the system fit to be released for UAT.

870.20 Review all UAT plans, ensuring that all necessary documentation and standards are in place, that the objectives and deliverables are understood by all involved, and that necessary resources are available.

870.30 Review all training programmes and material, ensuring particularly that sufficient training has been undertaken or allocated to enable the UAT to commence. Also ensure that the necessary documentation, particularly draft user manuals and clerical procedures/desktop instructions, are available.

870.40 Review IOT plans, ensuring that all necessary documentation is available, particularly operation procedures, network control and HelpDesk instructions, and that sufficient training has been allocated to ensure all these aspects can be trialled effectively. Ensure that the objectives and deliverables for each component are understood by the relevant staff and all necessary man, machine, and material resources are available.

870.50 Produce the necessary draft system implementation specification (SIS) to enable the trials and acceptance to be undertaken. The SIS is a draft in the conventional sense, in that some of the elements will be subject to expansion and review, but also in the sense that it will be incomplete compared with the ultimate SIS. It will be compiled by reviewing and updating the SDS, including relevant documentation emerging from previous tasks in 870. In particular, the SIS will contain the embryonic SLA and the system security policy statement. This latter will include all aspects of system security, access control violation procedures, etc., and a full risk analysis as required by the corporate strategy.

870.60 The draft SIS, and any other relevant documentation, will be presented to the project management for approval and sign-off, to enable all the resources required for trials and acceptance to be committed and the trials themselves embarked upon.

8.4 STAGE 9: TRIALS AND ACCEPTANCE (Fig. 8.33)

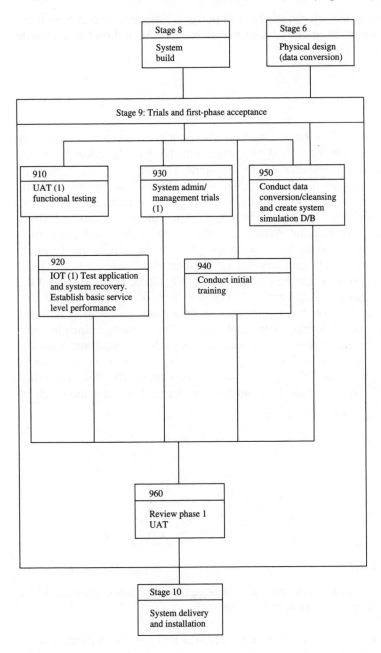

Figure 8.33 Stage 9.

8.4.1 Objectives

These stage trials prove that the offered system will perform as specified, that both users and management are adequately prepared for its implementation, and that an adequate continuity of service can be provided.

8.4.2 Description

The delivery phase of the project hinges on how the final user acceptance trials are conducted. This will consist of two essential components: proving the functionality of the system, and proving the operational aspects of the system. The latter is more often done by what is commonly known as parallel running, where the existing system and the replacement system are run side by side, and all aspects of the systems are compared. This will include administration and the proving of the interfaces with all other complementary or supporting systems. Where a current system does not exist, or it diverges so much as to render meaningful comparisons with the replacement system impossible, then alternative system simulation trials must be run.

Quite often the distinction between the two types of UAT will be blurred; indeed the two may be elected to be run as a single entity. This will have a corresponding impact on the proving of the other aspects of the system, such as operations procedures, network management, infrastructure trials and data conversion. The guiding principle must always be that as much testing as possible is conducted as early as conditions allow.

Stages 9 and 10, as detailed here, reflect the situation where a clear delineation can be drawn between the two phases, and this is the recommended approach. However, when this is not possible all the tasks detailed should be completed, but some may well be merged.

STEPS

910 Conduct Phase 1 UAT

.10 Review function test plans and resource allocation (ex 840.80) and commence UAT
.20 Draw up UAT test scripts and anticipated results
.30 Conduct Phase 1 UAT tests
.40 Submit test documentation to quality gate procedures and rework as necessary
.50 Declare test documentation acceptable and make available for Winway inspections
.60 Note any proposed changes to user manuals, desktop instructions and any other relevant existing documentation
.70 Produce Phase 1 UAT report and review

920 Conduct Phase 1 IOT

.10 Review IOT plans and resource allocation (ex 860.70) and commence IOT
.20 Draw up specific test programmes and schedule them
.30 Conduct IOT recovery and hardware degradation plans, and schedule any necessary returns
.40 Draw up basic volumetric trials for mainframe application, and schedule trials
.50 Conduct volumetric trials and schedule any necessary reruns
.60 Note any proposed changes to operational manuals and any other relevant existing operations documentation
.70 Produce Phase 1 IOT report and review

930 Conduct system administration/management trials

.10 Review/produce any specific system administration and/or management trials plans
.20 Conduct system administration trials and schedule any necessary reruns
.30 Conduct management trials of non-IT and/or clerical and other support facilities, and schedule any rework as necessary
.40 Note any proposed changes to any existing administrative support documentation
.50 Review activities and determine any requirement for Phase 2 UAT, and produce report

These activities can be integrated with Step 910 in smaller systems.

940 Conduct initial training

.10 Review training programs and resource allocation (ex 850.80) and commence user training
.20 Conduct training of all initial user areas
.30 Review course and material, and revise as necessary
.40 Complete user training of sufficient users to conduct full parallel running/system simulation
.50 Finalize ongoing training programmes for all future users of the new system, and provide feedback to corporate training strategy planning

950 Conduct data cleansing/conversion

.10 Produce/review data conversion/cleansing plans
.20 Schedule and run initial data conversion/cleansing
.30 Review results of initial run and schedule any reruns as necessary
.40 Schedule parallel run/system simulation database conversion/creation runs
.50 Run system simulation database creation and review
.60 Produce plans for data conversion/load of operational database

960 Review Phase 1 trials

.10 Collate all Phase 1 trials documentation/metrics
.20 Aggregate all proposed amendments to user, operations and systems manuals
.30 Produce Phase 1 trials report
.40 Produce plans for Phase 2 trials and system delivery
.50 Submit report for review and acceptance, and seek authority to commence simulation/parallel running and system delivery

Stage 9 inputs

- Test environment (ex Stage β)
- Configuration management (ex Stage β)
- Capacity management manual (ex Stage β)
- Project administration manual (ex Stage β)
- Operations procedure manual (ex Stage β)
- Tested, clean programs/system (ex Stage 8)
- Fallback/standby plan (ex Stage β)
- Volume test plan (ex Stage 6)
- Acceptance plans
- Management readiness plans
- Prepared users (ex Stage 8)
- User manuals (ex Stage 8)
- System manual(s) (ex Stage 8)

Stage 9 outputs

- Fully operational programs/system to operations and maintenance groups (to Stage 10)
- User documentation (to Stage 10)
- Prepared users (to Stage 10)
- Parallel running plans where appropriate
- Stage review and detailed plans for Stage 10 for project board submission
- Report to corporate strategy body on any relevant feedback.

STEP 910: CONDUCT FIRST PHASE OF UAT (Fig. 8.34)

Tasks

910.10 Review/confirm user acceptance test plans and resource allocations drawn up by Task 840.80. Establish team(s) as defined and allocate tasks and responsibilities to them; commence Phase 1 UAT.

910.20 Collate test scripts and anticipated results in accordance with project standards. This task can and should commence as early after Stage 6 as possible. The documents produced should be subjected to informal quality gate production procedures. Some

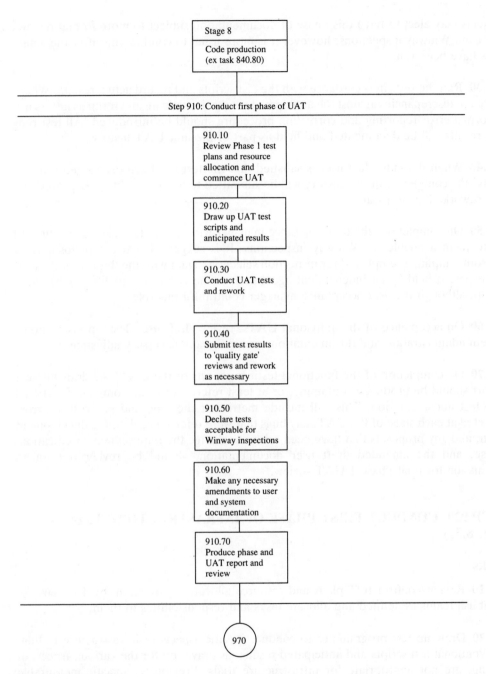

Figure 8.34 Step 910.

projects may elect to have this phase of documentation subject to more formal reviews and even Winway inspections; however it is more usual to conduct this after the actual tests have been run.

910.30 Run the tests in accordance with the test scripts and record actual results. Where there are discrepancies against the anticipated results, investigate and rerun as necessary. A formal error-reporting and correction procedure should be introduced. All test runs and results will be documented and held as part of the unit UAT history.

910.40 When the individual user is satisfied that the test has been discharged satisfactorily, the complete unit test history will be submitted to formal quality gate procedures and reworked as necessary.

910.50 On completion, the user assurance manager will declare the tests successful and make them available for Winway inspections. It is suggested that the philosophy of random sampling is employed for inspection selection, again with the 'hit list' of those to be inspected held by an independent agent such as the corporate quality management group, although the user acceptance manager could fulfil this role.

910.60 On acceptance of the individual UATs, review draft user desktop instructions, system administration and documentation, and make any necessary adjustments.

910.70 On completion of the functional testings aspects of the UAT, the draft Phase 1 report should be produced containing, or at least referring to, the complete functional unit test documentation. This will include metrics of the type and severity of errors detected at each stage of the UAT, any bugs that were referred back to the development team, and any proposals that have been raised to change the requirement specification. These, and the amended draft user documentation, should be reviewed prior to submission for final Phase 1 UAT review.

STEP 920: CONDUCT FIRST PHASE OF INFRASTRUCTURE TRIALS
(Fig. 8.35)

Tasks

920.10 Review/confirm IOT plans and resource allocations drawn up by Task 860.70. Establish teams as defined and allocate tasks and responsibilities to them.

920.20 Draw up test programmes to conduct specific aspects of infrastructure testing. Conventional test scripts and anticipated results, as drawn up for the various aspects of testing, are not appropriate for infrastructure trials. Previously, specific measurable outcomes, usually data results, could be predicted and actual outcome measured against them. However, these trials will be geared to testing certain events happening, or being generated for specific circumstances, and then remedial events or programmes of work being put in train to enable a situation to be contained and resolved. None the less it is

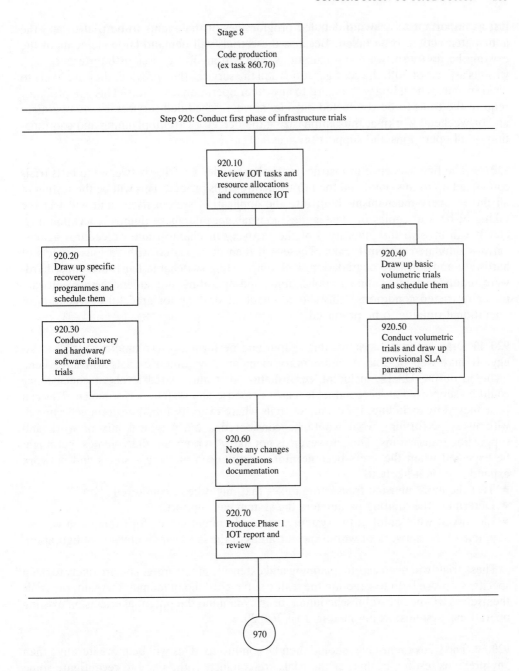

Figure 8.35 Step 920.

just as important to draw up detailed programmes of the events to be trialled and the anticipated action to be taken. Because these trials will demand large elements of the existing hardware/software configurations, and will involve conscious interference with various aspects of both the configurations and the services they provide, they are likely to need specific scheduling with regard to any other operational services. This will probably require the trials to be conducted outside 'normal' scheduled services — say overnight and/or weekend working, thus emphasizing the need for careful planning and coordination of all operations and support services.

920.30 The first aspect of infrastructure trials provides a bridge between the tests/trials conducted up to this point and the infrastructure trials proper. This will be the testing of all the recovery mechanisms built into the application system itself, and will test the taking of backup copies of master files, journalizing, database dumps, checkpointing, etc. It will involve the invocation of the recovery mechanism and procedures against various simulated system breaks. These will then be repeated with various aspects of hardware and software degradation, including testing switchable hardware units, hardware redundancy and running applications, and operating and superstructure software under restricted conditions. This should enable a strategy for graceful degradation of operational running to be produced.

920.40 Draw up initial systems throughput and performance (volumetrics) trials strategy. It may well be that a rudimentary element of volumetric trials will have been included during UATs, including confirmation that anticipated levels of concurrency could be supported at 'acceptable' levels of response and system performance. This can be achieved by including, for example, trials where every terminal position is occupied, with users performing what would be considered a fairly typical mix of work and supporting transactions. This, however, is not likely to replicate the volumes that might be expected when the users become more experienced and the systems and network expand. Nor is it likely to:

- Test the more unusual transaction mixes that might be encountered
- Determine the limiting parameters the system can support
- Identify at what point in the system bottlenecks might occur, for example in various points of the network or within specific areas of the hardware/software configuration.

These trials will need careful planning and extensive monitoring, and are likely to need specific software both to generate the traffic and record the outcome(s). Again, the trials themselves will need careful scheduling, bearing in mind the potential effects on existing operational systems, as outlined in Task 920.20.

920.50 The trials themselves should then be conducted. This will be more iterative than any previous testing, in that, as the trials are conducted, the need to reconfigure some elements of the network may arise. At the end of the trials, sufficient information should be available to draw up meaningful and realistic initial performance metrics, such as throughput or response times for various working conditions, for input to the first draft of the SLA.

920.60 On completion of the recovery and volumetric aspects of the infrastructure trials, which may be conducted in parallel, all operational instructions and documentation should be reviewed. The original operations instructions will be revised as required.

920.70 A report of the findings of the first phase of the infrastructure trials should be produced, consisting of:

- The various test/trial programmes and their results
- Volumetric summaries and metrics
- Notes on any amendment changes
- New operational input to SLA documentation

These need to be assembled for review and input to determine the strategy for the second phase of the trials.

STEP 930: CONDUCT SYSTEM ADMINISTRATION/MANAGEMENT TRIALS (Fig. 8.36)

Tasks

It may well be that various aspects of the tasks outlined in this step are integrated into the other tests and trials, notably the UAT, and possibly the IOT. This will be the case particularly for a smaller or less technically sophisticated project. However, they are addressed separately here because they require consideration in their own right, even if they are integrated into other tests/trials.

930.10 Review/define the system administration and management trials. Some of the issues to be considered may have been addressed during design (Stage 6), evolved during code production (Stage 8), or may not yet have been addressed, but they should cover such things as controlling:

- Who has what use, rights of, and access to, the system.
- What actions need to be taken if any violations, attempted violations or the illegal access to the system take place.
- How and by whom any system tables, code lists, etc., are controlled and maintained.
- How any ancillary, non-IT support services are to be managed and controlled.

Plans for the trials of the management and administration of the system need to be reviewed/drawn up, assigned and scheduled.

930.20 Conduct all application system administration trials. These will not usually need to be carried out outside normal working, indeed aspects of it may demand that they are run in parallel with, or even part of UATs. In batch-oriented systems, this will include administrative checks on all inputs to, and outputs from the system, including registration

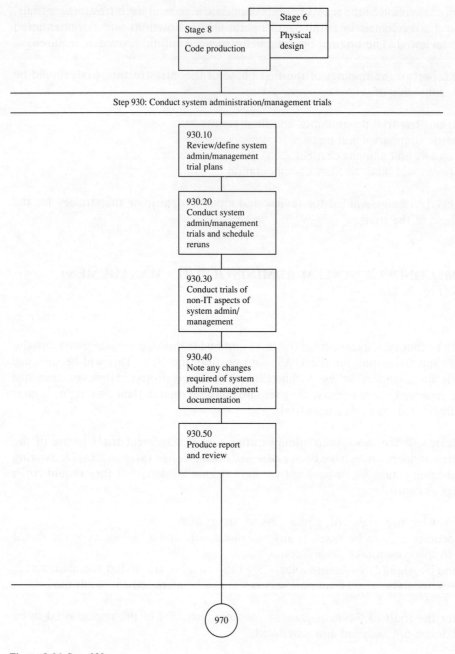

Figure 8.36 Step 930.

and control of restricted inputs and outputs. For online system transactions controlling the introduction of new users to the system, the allocation of passwords and privileges, and restricted transactions will have to be tested. In both cases, procedures to be invoked when administration and management controls/facilities are violated will need to be trialled. It may be that the procedures themselves may need to be refined in the light of the trials, and amended procedures rerun.

930.30 Trials of non-IT aspects of the system will also need to be conducted. Earlier trials should have proved that the IT system and infrastructure function correctly: the non-IT trials should prove that the user's organization and manual procedures are appropriate to make effective use of the IT system. They will ensure that IT systems, and manual systems, are effectively and efficiently interfaced. These will also include support and distribution services for inputs, tapes, PCKS and outputs, prints, magnetic media, fiches, etc. Distribution may require trialling of public services such as post, parcel and vehicular, and the equivalent in-house facilities. It should also address the control of physical access to buildings, parts of buildings and particular facilities.

930.40 The trials should confirm, consolidate, refine and/or expand any system administration and management control documentation. These could form a discrete element in any user manuals or desktop instructions.

930.50 A report should be produced that covers all the documentation of the various trials and their outcomes, together with any proposals for procedure changes or documentation that require higher level project consideration. All this will be reviewed before the second and final phase(s) of acceptance testing are determined.

STEP 940: CONDUCT INITIAL TRAINING (Fig. 8.37)

Tasks

Precisely how much training is given to whom and at what time will depend on particular project circumstances. What is encapsulated here represents more ideal circumstances than will normally exist. Training, in various guises and intensity, may well fluctuate across Stages 8, 9 and 10, and in some instances initial users may be being trained on 'go live' date and beyond. The philosophy to be aimed at is that trainers are exposed to the system and draw up initial training plans during the later phases of Stage 8 (Step 850). These people are involved in:

- Initial UAT function testing.
- The progressive training of staff to provide the necessary numbers to fulfil the various stages of UAT.
- Providing a definitive programme for ongoing user training.

940.10 Review training programme and resource allocation determined in Step 950. There should be sufficient trainers and 'trained' staff both to allow functional testing of

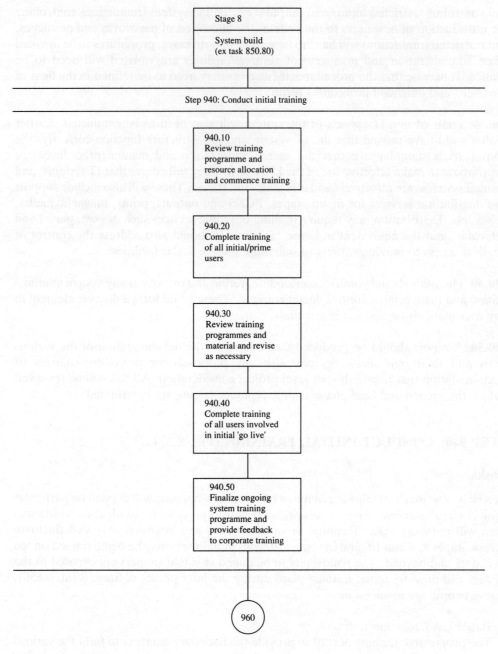

Figure 8.37 Step 940.

the system to begin and to provide for the far more detailed training that will be necessary to conduct parallel running and/or system simulation. Having confirmed this, the first training is commenced.

940.20 The recipients of initial training should be representatives of users in the major areas affected by the system. They should be experienced in their areas but as yet will have no formal exposure to the new system. The frequency of training will, of course, be entirely dependent on the size of the new system and the user population.

940.30 After the initial training, the programme and material will be revised both by trainers and students to produce a programme for ongoing training. The initial students will form the kernel of the staff involved in the detailed parallel running and/or system simulation trials.

940.40 Complete the training of all users who will be involved in using the system from day one. This programme, while beginning during Stage 9, will almost inevitably continue during Stage 10 and probably up to 'go live' date itself.

940.50 As the full training programme progresses, it should be further reviewed to finalize the ongoing programme. Feedback to corporate training should be provided, both in terms of:

1. Any novel aspects of the new system that require wider exposure, such as the use of new training techniques, or exposure to the use of windows/mice in the human–computer interface.
2. How training for this particular system is to be integrated into the overall corporate training programmes.

STEP 950: CONDUCT DATA CLEANSING/CONVERSION (Fig. 8.38)

Tasks

Data creation, cleansing and/or conversion is another activity that will vary enormously from project to project, but will in any event include some iteration that is likely to cross Stage 9 and 10 boundaries. It will be affected by the source of the data from the existing system, e.g. paper-based, magnetic media-based or transfer from an existing computer system. Again, the underlying philosophy is that whatever route is taken, all concerned must be convinced of the successful migration of the data from the old system to the new. The 'conversion' process must take into account the need to provide sufficient data for parallel running and/or system simulation. The conversion process itself must be fully trialled prior to the creation of the live database.

950.10 Produce/review data conversion plans. Some outline plans/strategies for data conversion may have been proposed during design (Stage 6) or may have emerged during system testing (Stage 8). In any event, a review needs to take place on how to capture

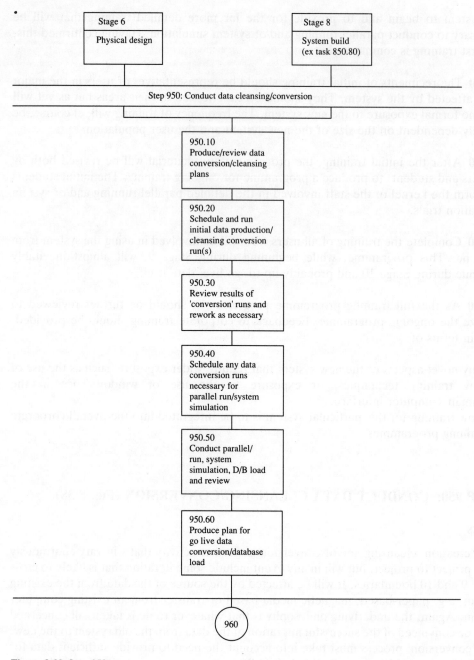

Figure 8.38 Step 950.

data from existing system(s) and the strategy necessary to migrate existing data. The data-capture process must recognize the need to convert the existing data into a form acceptable to the new system. Input to the system may utilize routines that will be an integral part of the new system, but in some cases 'special' conversion routines may have to be written and separately trialled: these need to be clearly identified. Irrespective of the source, it is usual for any new system to subject data to more stringent validation rules than the system it replaces. This will inevitably identify deficiencies, inconsistencies, errors and corruptions. It may also require considerable user resources to cleanse this data.

950.20 Schedule and run initial data capture/conversion processes. This may require the equivalent of fairly extensive unit, link and integration testing as outlined in Stages 7 and 8; if this is the case it should have been recognized in Stage 6 and integrated into Stages 7 and 8 as part of overall systems testing. These may have to be scheduled outside normal working because of the nature of the source data and its capture.

950.30 When the process itself has been satisfactorily proved, actual conversion runs are completed, critically examining the output and the source data. It is often difficult to plan precisely how to check this data, other than in specific areas where peculiarities are known. In these circumstances sufficient comparisons of random samples should be conducted for the user to be confident about the migration of the whole. Inevitably discrepancies will be found that will need amendment to the source data, the conversion process or both. Reruns will have to be scheduled after the necessary amendments have been applied, until there is sufficient confidence in the conversion process.

950.40 A specific run should be scheduled, to provide as realistic data as possible for parallel running and/or system simulation. In some circumstances, the initial live database load will in fact be a combination of various data conversion runs and initial data capture. It is advisable to conduct at least one full rehearsal of the whole process: this could be combined with the trials, to provide the data for parallel running/system simulation.

950.50 Run the final data conversion/database creation process for parallel run/system simulation trials. The outcome of these runs plus the creation of any specific data, such as code lists or systems tables, must be reviewed and accepted by users as being fit for purpose to embark on parallel running/system simulation.

950.60 Data capture, conversion and cleansing exercise(s), the creation of the system simulation database, and any other initialization runs must be reviewed. This determines any data-conversion or operation load rehearsal(s) requirements, and the strategy for the loading of the operational database.

STEP 960: REVIEW PHASE 1 UAT (Fig. 8.39)

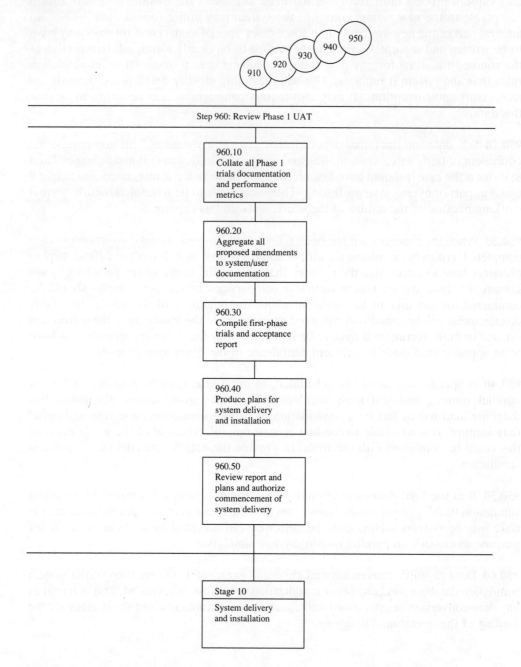

Figure 8.39 Step 960.

Tasks

960.10 Collate all documentation and system performance metrics produced during the various Phase 1 UAT activities, coordinate and rationalize the results.

960.20 Examine all proposed amendments and enhancements to the system and user documentation, and incorporate them into the relevant draft manuals in preparation for full parallel run/system simulation trials.

960.30 Compile first-phase user acceptance trials report. The formality of the report production and the detail of its content will depend on the size of the project and the requirements of management. It may be verbal, but must include any salient conclusions and recommendations necessary for the review at Task 960.50.

960.40 Plans for the conduct of Phase 2 of the acceptance trials and system delivery and installation must be drawn up in the light of the experience gained during Phase 1.

960.50 The Phase 1 report and Phase 2/system delivery plans must be submitted to project management. Approval must be sought to commence Stage 10. This will not normally require submission to the project board for formal sign-off: the project manager should have sufficient authority to determine whether or not to proceed.

8.5 STAGE 10: SYSTEM DELIVERY (Fig. 8.40)

8.5.1 Objectives

The objectives of this stage are to conduct a period of full parallel running or system simulations where appropriate, to install a fully operational system and to obtain full acceptance by the appointed commissioning authority.

8.5.2 Description

This stage identifies and schedules all resources necessary for data conversion, parallel running and actual implementation of the project, as defined by the initial user requirement. It will also produce and deliver the system implementation specification (SIS) as the final act of acceptance and commissioning.

STEPS

1010 Parallel running/simulation (UAT2)

.10 Review/revise Phase 2 UAT plans
.20 Determine any QA mechanisms to be applied
.30 Run all necessary 'operational' schedules
.40 Review results of operational schedules

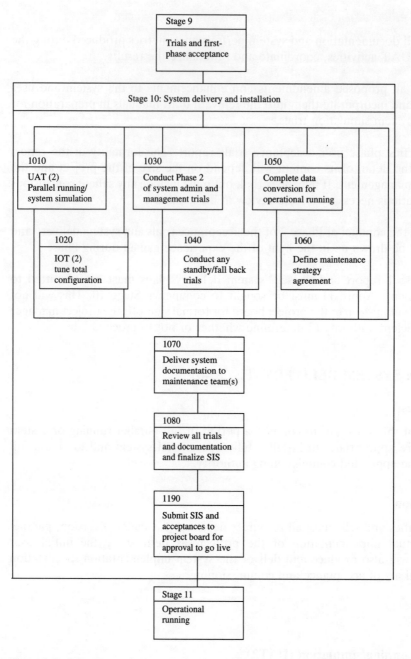

Figure 8.40 Stage 10.

.50 Record any proposed amendments to system and user documentation
.60 Produce Phase 2 report and consider final user acceptance report

1020 Tune total configuration (IOT2)

.10 Review/revise Phase 2 of IOT plans
.20 Conduct in-depth volumetric trials of all aspects affecting system performance and throughput
.30 Review results of volumetric trials
.40 Tune the operating system and all proprietary, network, communications, and applications software, and mainframe and communications hardware
.50 Obtain technical approval for operational configuration
.60 Record any proposed amendment to operations running documentation
.70 Produce Phase 2 report and consolidate final IOT trials report

1030 Conduct Phase 2 of system administration and management trials

.10 Review/define all system administration and management facets/facilities that need to be trialled for operational running
.20 Run trials of all system administration aspects, including user population control, system violation procedures, HelpDesk facilities, defect reporting, network management, etc., where appropriate
.30 Review results of various administration/management trials
.40 Record any proposed changes to administration/management procedures documentation
.50 Produce system administration and management trials report

1040 Conduct standby/fallback trials

.10 Determine scale and scope of standby/fallback trials and draw up schedule for their discharge
.20 Conduct standby/fallback trials
.30 Produce standby/fallback report
.40 Review report and prepare any corporate feedback

1050 Complete data conversion and operational database load

.10 Review live data conversion/database load plans
.20 Conduct any final data conversion runs
.30 Conduct database load exercise
.40 Review operational database and sign off

1060 Define maintenance strategy agreement

.10 Define/review operational HelpDesk facilities
.20 Define/review operational bug-reporting procedures

.30 Define/review change control procedures
.40 Define/review software restrictions and release procedures
.50 Define/review system delivery procedures
.60 Define maintenance strategy testing regime
.70 Identify all system/user documentation to be maintained
.80 Define procedures for maintenance of any test and training databases and documentation
.90 Prepare maintenance strategy agreement (MSA)
.100 Sign off MSA

1070 Deliver system maintenance documentation to maintenance teams

.10 Produce an inventory of all systems documentation and the media upon which it is held
.20 Agree programme for inspection/acceptance of all systems documentation
.30 Deliver all paper-based documentation
.40 Deliver all non-paper-based documentation
.50 Deliver operational version of application software
.60 Hand over and sign off delivery of system and documentation to the maintenance unit

1080 Review all trials, documentation and compile SIS

.10 Determine precise content and format of the system implementation specification (SIS)
.20 Draw up schedule for SIS production
.30 Collate all trial documentation and metrics
.40 Aggregate all changes to all system, operations and user documentation
.50 Publish SIS

1090 Seek approval to go live

.10 Submit SIS to project board
.20 Seek sign-off/acceptance of system for live operation
.30 GO LIVE!

Stage 10 inputs

- Manuals, procedures, users (ex Stage 9)
- Conversion plan (ex Stage 6)
- Implementation plan (ex Stage 6)

Stage 10 outputs

- Fully operational system (to Stage 11)
- System implementation specification (SIS)

STEP 1010: CONDUCT PHASE 2 OF UAT (Fig. 8.41)

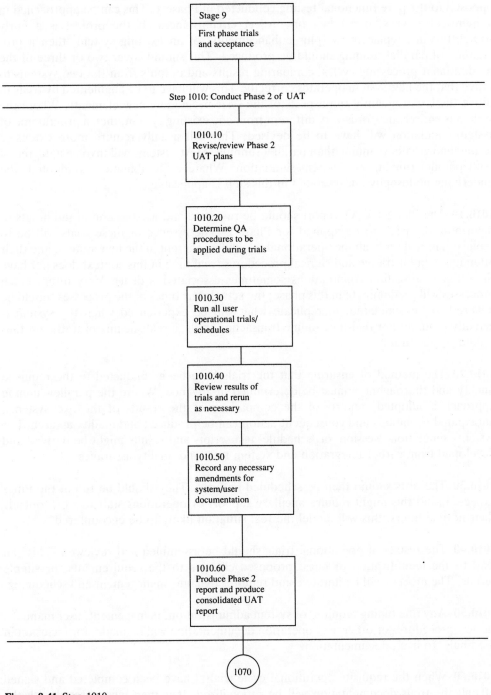

Stage 9

First phase trials
and acceptance

Step 1010: Conduct Phase 2 of UAT

1010.10
Revise/review Phase 2
UAT plans

1010.20
Determine QA
procedures to be
applied during trials

1010.30
Run all user
operational trials/
schedules

1010.40
Review results of
trials and rerun
as necessary

1010.50
Record any necessary
amendments for
system/user
documentation

1010.60
Produce Phase 2
report and produce
consolidated UAT
report

1070

Figure 8.41 Step 1010.

Tasks

Phase 2 of the UAT tests is to prove the full operational capability of the system, as opposed to the pure functional testing conducted in Phase 1. This can be approached in a number of ways, depending on project circumstances. If the project is a fairly straightforward replacement (plus enhancements) of an existing system, then a pro- gramme of parallel running should be produced. This should cover two or three of the predominant processing cycles, comparing results and outputs from the two systems to prove that the new system operates correctly. This will have to be augmented by trials to prove the less-frequently run aspects of the system, and any new elements. Where the system is entirely new or is very different from any existing system, then a programme of system simulation will have to be devised. This will usually require more extensive testing and greater planning than parallel running. Most systems will involve a degree of both parallel running and system simulation. Whatever combination is adopted, the underlying philosophy encapsulated in this step is applicable.

1010.10 The Phase 1 UAT report should be reviewed and used as one of the inputs to determine the trials to be applied for Phase 2. The essence of these trials will be to replicate, in real time, all the operational schedules inherent in the new system, and their attendant administrative and clerical procedures (real time in this context does not have the online transaction connotations sometimes associated with it). Very often, batch processes will predominate in this phase; the actual start times of the processes should be adhered to, or simulated, to replicate what will be experienced when the system is actually running. For real-time online transaction trials, a realistic mix of traffic profiles should be aimed for.

1010.20 The method of ensuring that the trials have been conducted to the requisite quality and thoroughness must be determined in advance. Where the parallel-running approach is adopted, reports of the comparison of the results of the two systems, anticipated deviations and consequent action can be produced and quality assured. For systems simulation, 'session' or 'schedule' test scripts and results might be derived and developed from earlier integration and system tests and quality assurance.

1010.30 The tests should then be scheduled and run. They should be run at the times expected, and this might require ancillary support or operations staff to work outside their normal hours: this will model the real situation likely to be encountered.

1010.40 The results of operational trials should be assembled and reviewed. This can lead to the identification of bugs, proposed changes to the requirements, or simple reruns. The process will be iterative and requires dynamic management and scheduling.

1010.50 Any fine tuning required of system administration, management, user manuals, clerical procedures or other user operation documentation will be made, for inclusion in the final, 'go live', documentation.

1010.60 When the requisite operational cycle trial(s) have been completed and signed off, all the trials documentation will be rationalized. It is then incorporated with the

Phase 1 documentation, and an overall signed-off UAT report is produced. The sign-off will be the user community's acceptance that the delivered system meets all functional and operational requirements. It may also contain caveats where this is not the case, and what course of action is to be taken in respect of them.

STEP 1020: CONDUCT PHASE 2 OF INFRASTRUCTURE OPERATIONAL TRIALS (Fig. 8.42)

Tasks

1020.10 Review the Phase 1 IOT report and any plans that may have been produced for consideration for Phase 2 trials. The delineation of what is conducted in Phase 1 and Phase 2 of the IOT is unique to every project, and dependent on its operational environment, particularly if communications networks are involved. All application and system recovery mechanisms built into the hardware, software and network configurations, and the basic volumetric trials, will have been trialled in Phase 1. The objective of Phase 2 is to drive the system to destruction:

1. To determine the limits of the various system components.
2. To establish the limiting operational parameters.
3. To allow for tuning the various components to give overall optimum performance of the system.

1020.20 To identify the limiting parameters of the system it is almost inevitable that some software tools or system generators will be required, for all but the simplest of batch systems. In this latter case, limiting conditions may be determined manually by increasing the number of transactions processed in particular runs, and conducting many 'streams' in parallel to achieve necessary limits. For online transactions generated over large telecommunications networks, the trials are likely to require two distinct phases, with specific tools/generators to support each. There are increasing numbers of network simulators and generators becoming available. Most will need some tailoring and in the worst cases software may need to be produced locally. Considerable effort will be required to generate the scripts or data required for the simulation exercise(s). They can consume considerable resources and demand extensive management planning and control. They will use the operational environment outside working hours and need to be scheduled with any existing systems. The two distinct phases of the testing will be:

1. To determine the capacity of the host, including any FEP to handle the IO traffic and to process the workload in acceptable times.
2. The capacity of the network to support the communications workload within the prescribed parameters.

The variations of network configurations and the relatively fewer proprietary tools available will mean that more demands are likely to be made on project communications staff, with all the usual attendant management control and scheduling problems. The objective should be to simulate actual traffic generation as far out into the network as

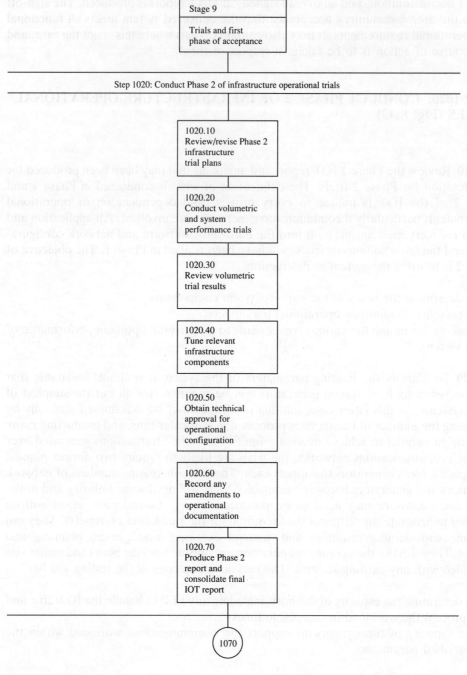

Stage 9

Trials and first
phase of acceptance

Step 1020: Conduct Phase 2 of infrastructure operational trials

1020.10
Review/revise Phase 2
infrastructure
trial plans

1020.20
Conduct volumetric
and system
performance trials

1020.30
Review volumetric
trial results

1020.40
Tune relevant
infrastructure
components

1020.50
Obtain technical
approval for
operational
configuration

1020.60
Record any
amendments to
operational
documentation

1020.70
Produce Phase 2
report and
consolidate final
IOT report

1070

Figure 8.42 Step 1020.

possible, ideally at individual terminal level. This will enable limiting factors to be determined for various terminal usage in LANs, across gateways into the WANs, and so on up to the FEP itself. It will also validate or test various aspects of communications protocols and polling strategy. This may be done:

- In isolation, i.e. on an 'empty' machine to establish pure online transaction limits.
- In parallel with a normal workload on the host and network, to establish the limits of the system under normal working conditions.

1020.30 The whole process(es) will be highly iterative and interactive, and it is unlikely that any such trials will ever be concluded, since they tend to be self-perpetuating. This must be strictly controlled by time and resource usage and by establishing a minimum subset of tests. The criteria for the tests are the levels of performance, throughput, and workloads defined in the SLA. The review of the trial results will also be iterative until at least the minimum subset of tests has been completed to continue all operational levels required by the SLA.

1020.40 The various components in the system will be subject to tuning, certain aspects of which will be conducted during the trials. The trials will cover various physical aspects of the hardware, such as the use of switches, placing filestore across physical media and tuning of software components. Consideration will be given to the network components, for example:

- What should be the capacity/utilization of the various gateways, communications ports and lines?
- What should be the relationships between the LANs and WANs, etc.?

Any communications software protocols may also need to be tuned.

1020.50 When the infrastructure trials are concluded, the final configurations and/or design of all the components subjected to refinement or tuning will need to be drawn up. These will represent the proposed overall operational configuration for the system, and should be offered for approval by the requisite operations and any other corporate bodies.

1020.60 Final amendments to operations and ancillary support documents should be reviewed and compiled. These represent the operational system documentation and will need to be approved by the relevant project (and corporate) agencies.

1020.70 Details of the trials conducted, their results, the operational configurations and documents need to be drawn together to compile a Phase 2 report, which will be integrated with the Phase 1 report to produce the final IOT and SLA. This will be included in the SIS.

STEP 1030: CONDUCT PHASE 2 SYSTEM ADMINISTRATION/ MANAGEMENT TRIALS (Fig. 8.43)

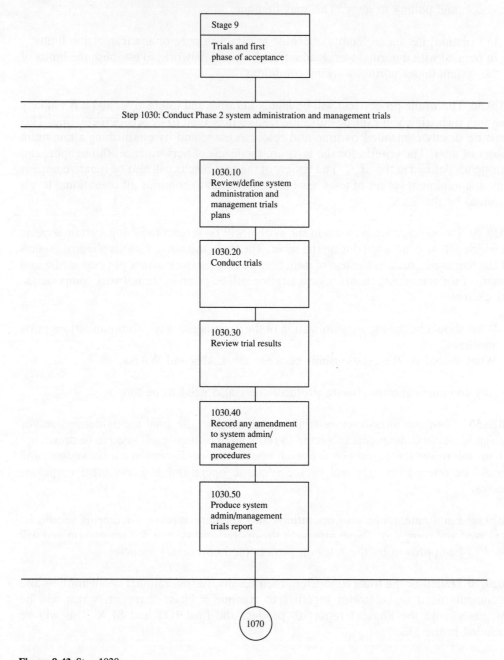

Figure 8.43 Step 1030.

Tasks

1030.10 Review the Phase 1 system administration report and management trials, and any outstanding issues to be resolved by Phase 2 trials. Produce a two-phase plan, which should include:

- User production 'control' numbers, names, access permission
- System violation procedures
- HelpDesk facilities
- System defect reporting
- Information dissemination, e.g. broadcasting
- N/W management and control

Most basic functions will have been trialled during Phase 1 and any outstanding tests will need to take into account the activities being conducted by Steps 1010, 1020 and 1040.

1030.20 Conduct Phase 2 trials. This can be a discrete activity or as part of the steps mentioned above. In the latter case, specific reports should be produced for integration into the systems administration report.

1030.30 Review all trial results; this cannot be completed until aspects being addressed by the other trials have been completed. When all tests have been completed they should be reviewed for coordination and consistency. If necessary, final rationalization should be carried out to achieve this.

1030.40 Any proposed amendments to documentation, procedures and system administration manuals, need to be identified and final operational documentation drawn up.

1030.50 The final system administration report is produced. This identifies all the trials, their results, and documentation changes required. It is rationalized and integrated with the Phase 1 report.

STEP 1040: CONDUCT STANDBY/FALLBACK TRIALS (Fig. 8.44)

Tasks

1040.10 Determine the scope and scale of any fallback/recovery plans as determined by the risk analysis and threat assessment study. An alternative site with compatible equipment and any necessary communications network connections should be provided if this is considered necessary. An alternative site may already exist as part of the corporate strategy, but this should be reviewed in a project context. Project plans for the trials of the import and export of proprietary and application software from the existing site to the alternative site must be scheduled.

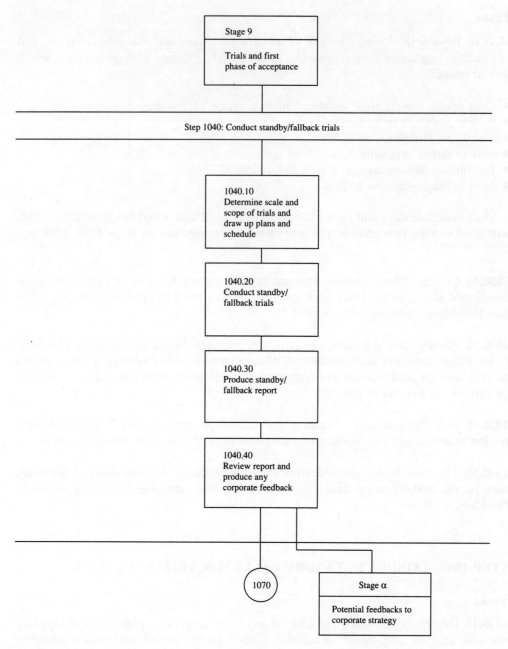

Figure 8.44 Step 1040.

1040.20 The export from the existing site and import to the alternative site must be rehearsed and the results fully recorded. It is likely that the exercise will need to be repeated several times before the process can be achieved with optimum effectiveness and efficiency. Reciprocal arrangements should also be trialled.

1040.30 A detailed report must be drawn up describing all the operational procedures to be carried out to achieve the optimal transfer. Provision must be made for periodic testing of the fallback procedure. Operational schedules should reflect the reduced capability available to local systems when reciprocal standby trials are held.

1040.40 The report must be reviewed for incorporation into the SIS and the potential requirement for feedback to corporate strategy.

STEP 1050: COMPLETE CONVERSION AND DATABASE LOAD
(Fig. 8.45)

Tasks

1050.10 The initial data conversion report produced as a result of the tasks in Step 950 must be reviewed to draw up the operational database load strategy.

1050.20 Loading the live database may be achieved, wholly or in part, by a data conversion run. In this case the pre-database load conversion suite must be scheduled and run.

1050.30 The live load should be completed in a number of phases. Initial systems data, codes, user details, network configuration details and so on, necessary to set up the operational system, are identified and loaded. This is followed by the loading of the operational data, and the exercise is completed by loading any specific operational or transaction tables as required.

1050.40 On completion of the database load, both the database design/structures and the initial contents must be signed off by the project owner. Any discrepancies between the data on the initial live system and the source from which it is derived must be identified. Proposals for remedying or accepting the situation should be drawn up, and the whole process documented and included in the SIS.

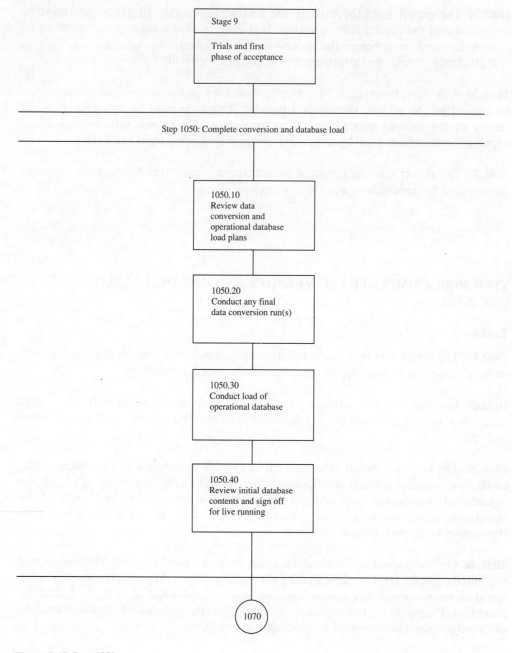

Figure 8.45 Step 1050.

STEP 1060: DEFINE MAINTENANCE STRATEGY AGREEMENT (MSA) (Fig. 8.46)

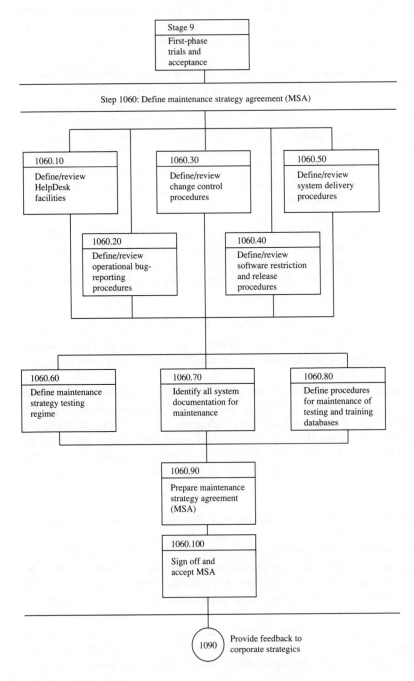

Figure 8.46 Step 1060.

Tasks

The first five tasks reflect procedures that will usually have been established at a corporate level. However, although there is considerable overlap among them, and the various elements may appear in different guises in different combinations, all the individual elements should be addressed in some way or other.

1060.10 Define/review HelpDesk facilities. A central focal point — the HelpDesk — should exist to act as the interface between the user community and the operations systems support teams. All queries, observations, requests for changes and enhancements will be dealt with by the HelpDesk in the first instance, by itself wherever possible, but otherwise giving some undertaking to the user of what will be done, and when. The query will then be directed to the relevant support agency. The HelpDesk will also disseminate information regarding the condition and status of the operational system, including the use of broadcasting facilities where these exist. The HelpDesk must be available during all periods of system usage.

1060.20 Define/review operational bug-reporting procedures. The HelpDesk will process all system defects, bugs and observations, augmented with any ancillary evidence or documentation. Procedures will allow for prioritization monitoring and control of all such defects. These could be derived from bug-identification procedures used during earlier testing.

1060.30 Define/review change control procedures. Even if these do not exist at a corporate level they should have been defined and specified in Stage β. They must be reviewed to ensure that they are appropriate to support the operational system.

1060.40 Define software restriction and release procedures. There may be defects which could inhibit various system facilities, or require alternative short-term action until they are cleared from the system. There needs to be a mechanism for reporting defects to the user community, together with the alternative action and some statement of intent for its correction. This usually takes the form of a software restriction notice issued through the HelpDesk. When the defect is corrected, this is similarly announced by a software release notice:

1060.50 Define/review system delivery procedures. Remedial software will usually be applied at predetermined intervals in all but catastrophic circumstances. These may include 'fixes' of any defects, enhancements or new facilities. The procedure will involve the running of a complete system test or simulation on a test database, prior to release to the operational system. This is particularly important for online systems, to ensure that operational parameters are not violated by any spurious side effects for a given fix.

1060.60 There must be a rigorous testing regime established by the maintenance team, which should reflect all stages of code development and testing as outlined in Stages 8–10. It should conform to systems delivery procedures as defined by Task 1070.50.

1060.70 Allocate responsibility for the maintenance of the various documents — user community for the desktop instructions/clerical procedures, operations team for the operations manual and the maintenance team for program specifications. Procedures for production, amendments and QA of the documents also need to be defined.

1060.80 Procedures need to be defined for the maintenance of any test or training databases. After each delivery the system should be examined to see if it has caused any major functionality changes that affect future system tests and testing and training databases. Where this is the case, amendments to the tests, supporting databases and documentation need to be updated.

1060.90 All the foregoing need to be integrated into a single statement to detail the total maintenance strategy. This will result in the production of the MSA.

1060.100 The MSA will include provision for the acceptance and sign-off of the various suppliers of the service to the users.

STEP 1070: DELIVER/PREPARE SYSTEM MAINTENANCE DOCUMENTATION (Fig. 8.47)

Tasks

Steps 1060 and 1070 assume the concept of a separate maintenance team/capability. In some instances this may not exist, and maintenance is provided by retaining appropriate members of the development team. This may result in some of the handover activities being curtailed; none the less all the tasks identified in 1060 and 1070 should be conducted to ensure that everything required for successful maintenance is in place.

1070.10 Identify where all systems documentation definitions and components are held, and the relationship between them. Most modern systems will employ a number of tools and aids to produce various aspects of the system. This may include 4GL and AGs tools, systems methodology workbenches and analyst/programmer workbenches. The concept of a central dictionary or data repository should have been established, the data of which may be held on an automated tool(s). There would be a considerable amount of paper-based documentation, for example, program specifications, coding, test scripts and results, and user manuals. Many of these may, in fact, be held on, or supported by, tools on magnetic media. Finally, all the supporting administrative filing is held in the project library.

1070.20 Documentation should be reviewed with the maintenance agency to determine which elements are required for future maintenance. There will in most cases be duplication of documentation, due to the proliferation and use of different automated tools. For those needing maintenance, certain elements may be selected for specific quality assurance prior to handover/acceptance. The most common elements selected would be program specifications, code, test histories and operation instructions.

1070.30 Paper-based documentation needs to be assembled, integrated and, in some cases, rationalized. This can be a significant task.

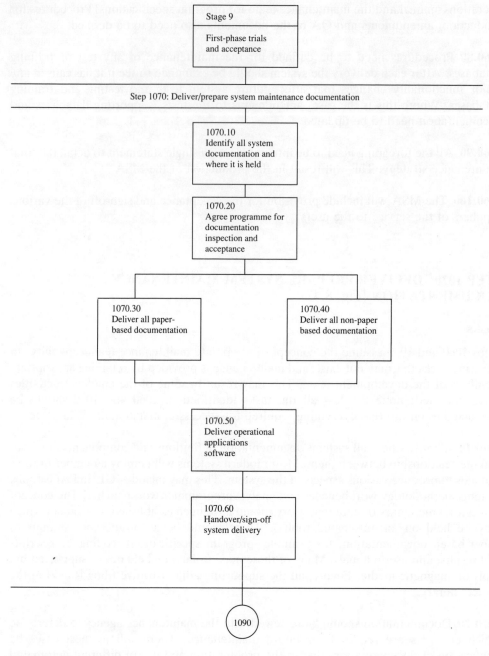

Figure 8.47 Step 1070.

1070.40 Appropriate dumps of non-paper-based data should be taken. This implies that the maintenance environment has copies of all the various tools and workbenches, with the appropriate versions of the software needed.

1070.50 The final versions of the applications software, source and object code, program libraries and control environment will then be delivered to the maintenance teams and/or operations. The operations environment assumes that all the required versions of hardware and software products, operations, etc., are available. The maintenance team must have the capability of replicating any terminal equipment LANs, WANs and gateways: this may require part of the network, hardware, software and connections to be replicated.

1070.60 The maintenance agency must sign off the system and be ready to support it fully before 'go live' is declared.

STEP 1080: REVIEW ALL TESTS AND TRIALS AND COMPILE SIS
(Fig. 8.48)

Tasks

1080.10 Determine the precise content and format of SIS. The draft SIS produced by Step 870 will be reviewed and the proposed content and format of the final SIS produced. Although guidelines are provided for the SIS, each project will be unique in terms of the project itself, the users and other participants, and the environment within which it is being implemented. This may require some amendment or addition to the 'standard' SIS, which will evolve during Stages 9 and 10 but will not be finally determined until the concluding steps of Stage 10.

1080.20 When the provisional content of the SIS is determined, a production schedule is drawn up. Unlike the SRS and SDS which can be finalized/refined after its publication, there is little scope for this with the SIS as it is an integral part of the delivery process.

1080.30 Project productivity and performance metrics should be drawn up, showing actual and estimated resource usage. Some will already be available as a by-product of other processes such as Winway Inspections. These should provide information for producing revised costings for various units of work, such as program specifications, code production or unit testing, for corporate feedback for future use and, hopefully, more accurate estimation. Other metrics such as function point counts may need to be produced, but could wait until after the project is completed.

1080.40 All the various documents referred to throughout the production stage — program documentation, operations manuals, user manuals, etc. — need to be finally reviewed and checked, to ensure that all final amendments have been incorporated. The SIS will not usually contain copies of all these documents, but it should indicate the philosophy behind their production, how they were produced, the final status/sign-off, and where they can be found.

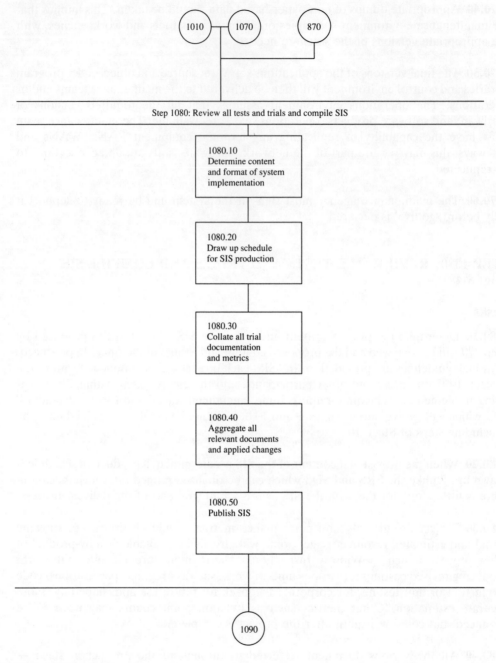

Figure 8.48 Step 1080.

1080.50 When all this is assembled, the SIS should be published and issued to all members of the project board, the user community and representatives of the operational system service suppliers.

STEP 1090: SEEK APPROVAL TO GO LIVE (Fig. 8.49)

Tasks

1090.10 The final meeting of the project board will review the SIS.

1090.20 The project board will sign off and accept the SIS, and in doing so, authorize that the system should become operational.

1090.30 On receiving authorization, operations, users and all service suppliers will commence operational running of the system at the due time and date. GO LIVE!

8.6 STAGE 11: SUPPORT AND MAINTENANCE (Fig. 8.50)

8.6.1 Objective

To provide the infrastructure for the operation and maintenance of the system.

8.6.2 Description

This stage ensures that errors discovered will be promptly dealt with, and that enhancements to the system will be implemented in a controlled fashion. These activities are performed within the framework of the corporate IT strategy, which will also provide for the production of a system post-implementation review (SPIR).

A post-implementation review considers the performance of the new system. Its objectives are to compare the costs and benefits of the system with what was expected, to assess whether expectations have been met, and to identify problem areas in development procedures which have had a detrimental effect on system performance.

STEPS

1110 Invoke operational management and control procedures

.10 Establish management board
.20 Determine management control procedures
.30 Confirm that all system administration procedures are in place and activated
.40 Authorize any final counts and other productivity metrics evaluations

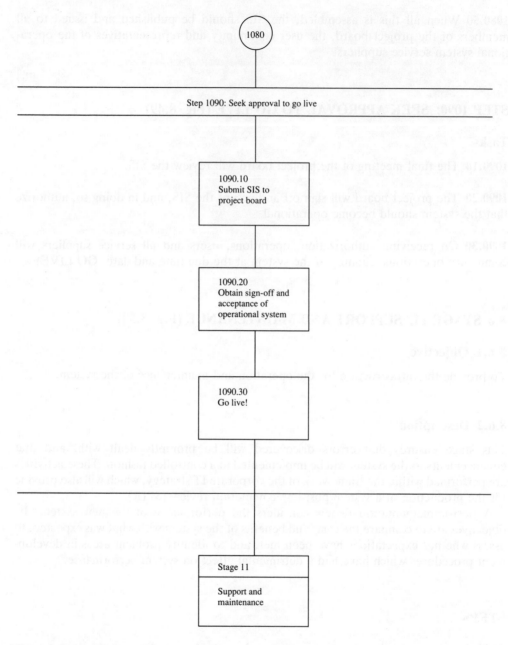

Figure 8.49 Step 1090.

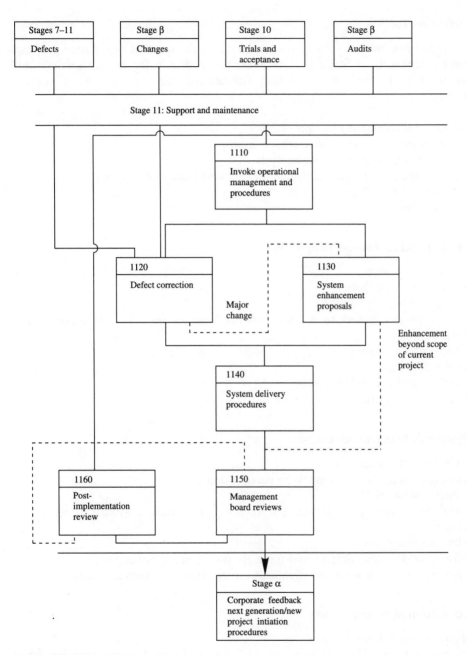

Figure 8.50 Stage 11.

1120 Defect correction

Any defects (and/or enhancements) must conform to the spirit of the change proposal procedures established in Stage β. However, the audience for impact analysis will probably need to be redrawn to reflect operational user and computer support populations.

.10 Review/revise change control procedures
.20 Issue software restriction notice where appropriate
.30 Conduct change control impact analysis
.40 Determine local or project management required (scope of change)
.50 Discharge and test change
.60 Submit for delivery

1130 System enhancements proposals

.10 Review enhancement
.20 Conduct impact analysis
.30 Produce cost/benefit analysis
.40 Refer to project board to assess corporate impact on other developments if appropriate
.50 Produce enhancement plans
.60 Assign resources
.70 Implement and test enhancement
.80 Submit to delivery process

1140 System delivery procedures

.10 Review delivery schedules
.20 Coordinate change/enhancements in current delivery
.30 Conduct system trials
.40 Review all system performance parameters and reiterate system trials where necessary
.50 Update documentation
.60 Publish next delivery contents and issue software release notice(s)
.70 Deliver amended software to operations for incorporation into live system

1150 Management board reviews

.10 Approve revised delivery schedules
.20 Review totality of CP's enhancements, etc., received since last management board review
.30 Review revised system performance parameters
.40 Make recommendations for any configuration enhancements
.50 Make recommendations for longer term existing project developments or new projects
.60 Produce report and submit for corporate strategy consideration

1160 Conduct post-implementation review

.10 Initiate post-implementation review
.20 Draw up objectives and review production plan
.30 Allocate resources and commission review report
.40 Review report and submit to management review

Stage 11 inputs

- SIS
- Requests for change/change proposals
- Enhancement proposals
- Corporate strategy policy

Stage 11 outputs

- Changes/enhancements impact analysis
- Project delivery schedules
- Software restriction and release notices
- Revised system performance parameters
- Relevant amended project operational/working documentation
- Management board reports for corporate strategy policy

STEP 1110: INVOKE OPERATIONAL MANAGEMENT AND PROCEDURES (Fig. 8.51)

Tasks

1110.10 Establish management board for managing the project during its operational life — the development board's terms of reference can be revised and its membership reconstituted. A separate management board can be set up for the specific project, or the management subsumed into a corporate operational systems management body that often exists for that specific purpose. In all cases, the participants in the operational management are likely to be different from those involved in development. Operational users will take a more prominent role in the running of the system, and the board will need representation of the actual computer operations and support staff.

1110.20 Whatever management structure is determined to be appropriate, the mechanisms for effecting control over the running of the operational system will need to be reviewed. This will determine how and what reports are to be submitted to the board, how it will achieve its management directives, how frequently it will meet with what agenda, and so on.

1110.30 All administration processes and procedures will need to be reviewed and the board reassured that they are in place. These will be detailed in the SIS.

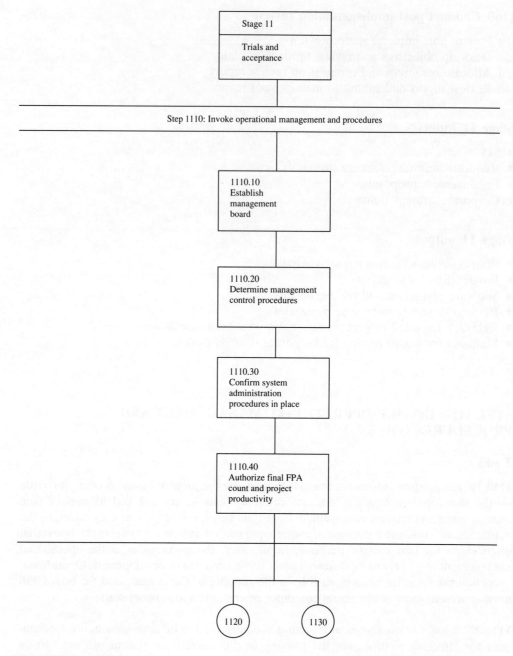

Figure 8.51 Step 1110.

1110.40 Authorize the final function point analysis count — or whatever productivity mechanism is felt appropriate — to assess the real performance of all the project-related resources, man, machine and material.

STEP 1120: DEFECT CORRECTION (Fig. 8.52)

Tasks

1120.10 Review/revise defect correction procedures. At this stage these will have either already been well established by the project, or any corporate procedures adopted, but they will need to be reviewed both in the light of the participants and of the information flow. Again the operational users and computer (and network where appropriate) operations and support staff will have an important role to play. The review needs to be carried out at the outset of operational running, but it is advisable to conduct periodic (say 6-monthly) reviews because the operational players will inevitably change over the life of the system.

1120.20 When defects are reported in the system they are examined by the maintenance team for their immediate impact. Where they require any changes to the system's operation, these should be detailed in a software restriction notice and distributed to all operational users.

1120.30 The change/defect/bug is then sent to all interested parties, as determined by the procedures in Stage β, for a more detailed impact analysis.

1120.40 On its return, the maintenance team will assess the impact analysis to determine whether any corrective action required can be discharged within the scope of the maintenance team's declared responsibilities and resources. If it cannot, further consideration will be required, as described in Step 1130.

1120.50 All tasks falling within the scope of the maintenance team are discharged and tested. The control of the production and testing will conform to the philosophies underlying Stages 7, 8, 9 and 10, but will be abbreviated to that which the management board consider necessary and appropriate.

1120.60 On satisfactory completion by the maintenance team the component will be submitted for consideration for the delivery process (Step 1140).

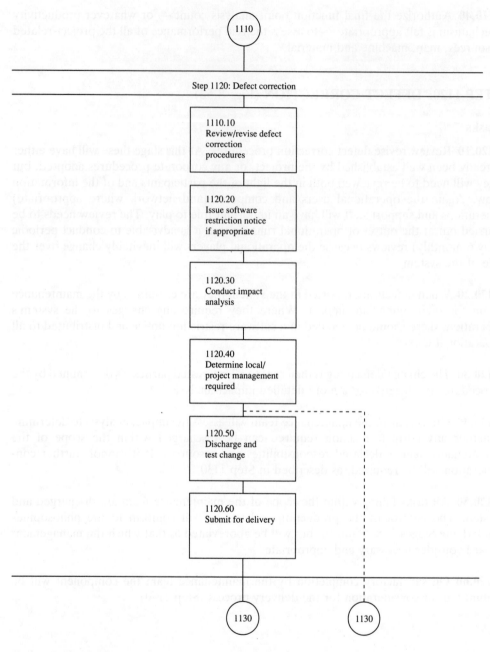

Figure 8.52 Step 1120.

STEP 1130: SYSTEM ENHANCEMENT PROPOSALS (Fig. 8.53)

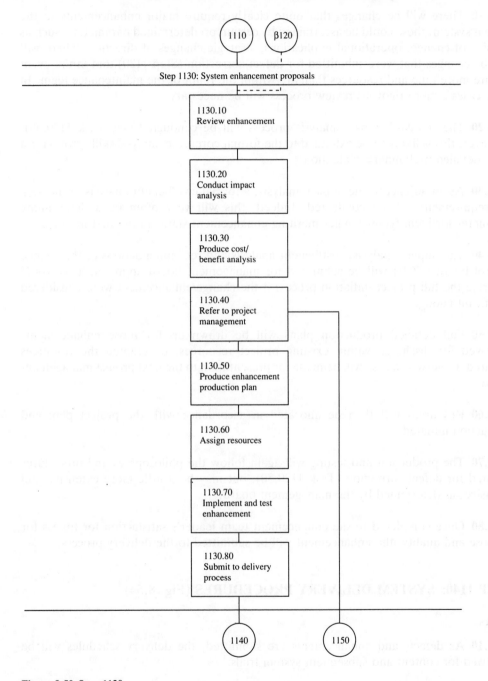

Figure 8.53 Step 1130.

Tasks

1130.10 There will be changes that quite clearly require major enhancements to the current system: these could be ascertained by certain predetermined parameters, such as the size of change, operational implications, strategic changes of direction. There will also be changes that were submitted for defect correction (Step 1120) that in the event require more time and resources than are within the remit of the maintenance team. In these cases a more rigorous review process will be necessary.

1130.20 The standard impact analysis process will be conducted (see Task 1120.30). However, this is likely to be extended to the formal corporate analysis skills group for a more detailed preliminary evaluation.

1130.30 As an adjunct to the impact analysis, a formal cost/benefit analysis of meeting the requirement will be conducted. Indeed, this will very often be a determining parameter for identifying changes meriting enhancement status in the first instance.

1130.40 The impact analysis, cost/benefit analysis and recommendations of the change control board (CCB) will be submitted for management board approval. This would generate the full project initiation process if the change/enhancement were considered significant enough.

1130.50 Full detailed production plans will be drawn up for those enhancements approved for discharge within existing project resources, or granted the resources required. Otherwise a case will be made for presentation to the next project management board.

1130.60 Resources will then be allocated in accordance with the project plan and production initiated.

1130.70 The production and testing will again follow the philosophies and procedures adopted for defect correction (Task 1120.50), but may be a little more extensive and intensive, as determined by the management board.

1130.80 Once completed to the enhancement team leader's satisfaction for fitness for purpose and quality, the enhancement will be submitted to the delivery process.

STEP 1140: SYSTEM DELIVERY PROCEDURES (Fig. 8.54)

Tasks

1140.10 As defects and enhancements are submitted, the delivery schedules will be reviewed for content and subsequent system trials.

1140.20 At a predetermined time before a scheduled delivery date, or as the scope of the delivery dictates, the delivery content will be approved and the systems trials plans promulgated.

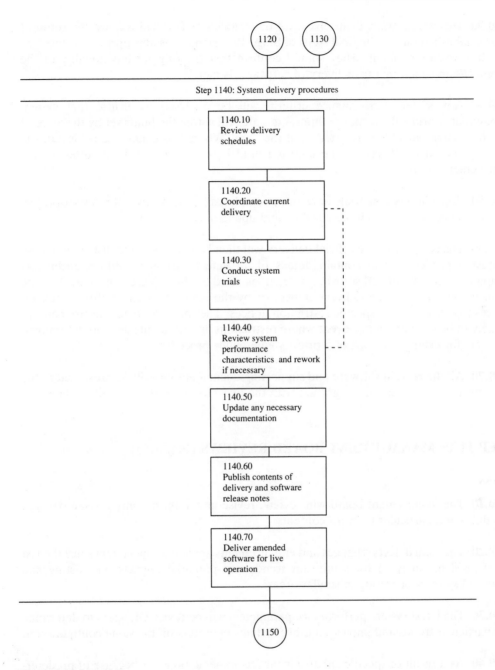

Figure 8.54 Step 1140.

1140.30 The system trials themselves will be conducted. This will require the rerun of trials established during the final steps of Stage 10, amended as appropriate, dictated by the changes/enhancement. They should confirm that the original functionality of the system, as amended by this delivery of software, is met.

1140.40 Any system performance criteria will be analysed to ensure that system throughput, workloads, response times, etc., are still within the limits set by the SLA. If not, the system should be retuned until they are. Where this cannot be achieved, the delivery contents will have to be adjusted until it is, and a report submitted to the management board.

1140.50 When all systems trials have been completed satisfactorily, all relevant project and user documentation will be checked and updated as necessary.

1140.60 The contents of the official delivery will then be published and distributed to all interested parties. It will contain details of all defects, changes and enhancements completed, and identify all software restrictions lifted by this release. This may be done as an integral part of the delivery notice, or by the issue of specific software release notices that relate to the specific restriction notices. The software release notice concept is likely to be required in any event where restrictions are lifted outside a predetermined delivery, for example as part of a priority/emergency procedure.

1140.70 All the revised software and supporting documentation will be presented to the appropriate authorities for integration with the live service on the prescribed date.

STEP 1150: MANAGEMENT BOARD REVIEWS (Fig. 8.55)

Tasks

1150.10 The management board will review, revise and authorize any revised delivery schedules and particular delivery contents.

1150.20 The total defects, changes and enhancements applied to the system since the last review will be analysed for significant trends and potential impacts on existing and proposed systems operating in similar areas.

1150.30 The latest system performance parameters will be reviewed, again to determine any particular trends and impact on other systems operating on the same configuration.

1150.40 As a result of specific enhancement recommendations, or because of predetermined limits being approached, the hardware, software and network configurations should be reviewed and any perceived required enhancements identified.

1150.50 The project board will then make recommendations on any configurations enhancement, or any new projects or major enhancements.

1150.60 The recommendations for developments and general feedback on the operational system will be compiled in a report and released for wider corporate strategic consideration.

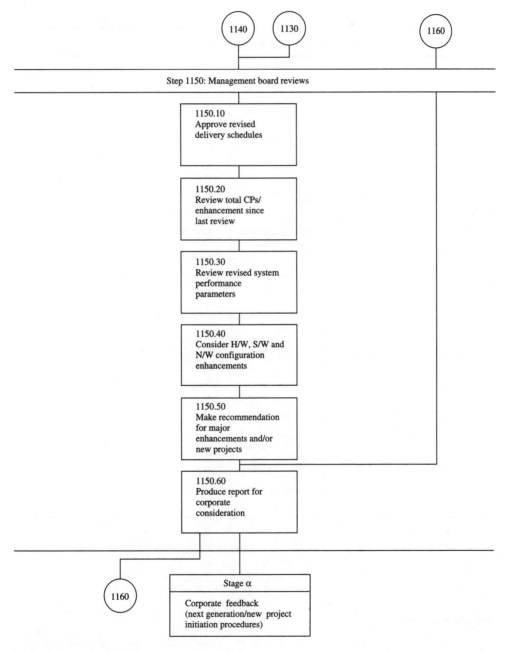

Figure 8.55 Step 1150.

STEP 1160: CONDUCT POST-IMPLEMENTATION REVIEW (Fig. 8.56)

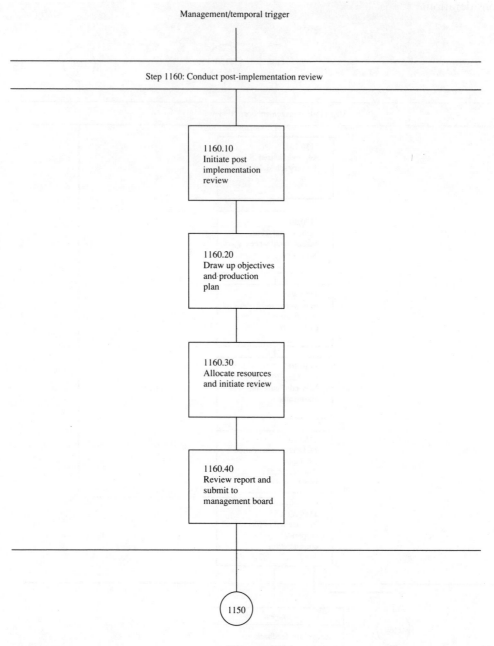

Figure 8.56 Step 1160.

Tasks

1160.10 A post-implementation review study will be initiated, usually after 6–12 months of operational running. The proposed contents of the study's report are detailed in Chapter 12.

1160.20 The objectives of the study should be drawn up by the management board, together with the plan/schedule for the report's production.

1160.30 Resources required for the study will be identified and allocated, and the study commissioned.

1160.40 The review report will be published on completion and submitted for management board consideration.

9

QUALITY AND DOCUMENTATION CONTINUUM

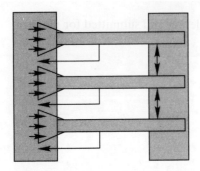

This chapter describes the Winway approach to quality management — this is intended to be BS5750-compliant. It places strong emphasis on the documentation and deliverables produced throughout the method, and the control procedures applied to their production. The concept of quality gates is introduced and a number of different types of QA review described.

9.1 THE WINWAY QUALITY APPROACH

The all-embracing ethos is that quality is dynamic. Quality should be built into the infrastructure, both for development and for the end product. This ensures that the application of quality assurance and control techniques is not perceived as an overhead, but as an integral part of the development process.

The dynamic application of quality assurance should be conducive rather than obtrusive. To achieve this, it should consume only the resources necessary to prove the production of the product at the earliest possible stage and by the most appropriate mechanism.

Quality assurance in the Winway approach features at the beginning of every project, forming part of the agreement on the level of quality to be agreed and achieved for the individual project. To achieve this, the activities and products the project will produce, together with the type of quality assurance to be applied, are agreed at the beginning of the project.

Agreement is also reached on the degree of quality control by the use of quality gates. A quality gate is a control point that identifies a critical decision point or baseline, or both. It signifies that progression from the point reached is subject to the quality control technique defined for that quality gate. The gate can be depicted as open or closed: open gates indicate that work may proceed beyond the gate; a closed gate indicates that the control point must be successfully executed before work can proceed. A special 'policy' closed gate is provided for critical documents/components: this indicates that project board, and/or the project managers', express approval must be obtained before proceeding further. Such documents might include detailed project plans, business options and technical options as well as the more obvious SRS, SDS and SIS.

Another reassurance factor is that critical baselines in the project life cycle, such as the production of the SRS, will be the culmination of a number of quality gates. This means that in order to reach the point of production of the SRS, a number of open and closed gates will have been successfully negotiated.

The dynamic application of quality and a 'divide and conquer' application of control through the quality gates means that there are no hidden obstacles or surprises at critical milestones.

9.2 OVERVIEW

9.2.1 Quality/documentation

A project will invest considerable effort in ensuring not only that the project has been developed on time and to budget, but also to a consistent and predefined level of quality.

Quality is achieved by adopting a number of practices and procedures, applied throughout the project life cycle. This is reinforced by a similar approach in ensuring consistency and continuity in the documentation produced. The overall strategy results in what is termed the 'quality and documentation continuum'.

The first element, and one of the most significant, in quality management is to ensure that the appropriate numbers of staff with the necessary skills and expertise are available at the right time. This in itself requires extensive planning. Initial overall plans are produced, which are progressively refined to produce detailed plans for the discharge of each major phase of the project. In the case of the particularly long phases such as implementation, detailed plans are produced at sensible and manageable intervals (usually every three months).

The production of realistic plans demands the existence of proven estimating algorithms. These do exist in some areas to a degree, for example, SSADM-related activities; however, these will be superseded by the proposed CCTA Guidelines publication. Details of how these might be applied using the Winway approach to the whole life cycle development are in Sec. 11.2

The estimates applied, together with the justification for them, should be detailed in the various project documents, viz. SRS, SDS and SIS, and any mid-phase statements that may be required by PRINCE for example.

When the plans have been produced and the necessary resources and skills determined, appropriate personnel should be recruited if not already in place. The strategy should be to produce a well balanced, productive and dedicated development team which can react flexibly to the changing demands placed upon them by project management.

The subsequent organization of the staff is not only determined by the numbers and skills required, but also reflects the level of quality to be integrated into the quality continuum and the quantity gate diagram(s).

The resources identified are organized into development team managers, analysts, programmers and so on, to reflect the hierarchy of responsibility and accountability and to enable the quality gates described in Secs. 9.1 and 9.4 to be implemented. This identifies some of the quality control mechanisms integrated into the project management and organizations; these are then augmented by quality assurance mechanisms.

The quality assurance mechanism can include conventional PRINCE and SSAD quality assurance reviews (QAs) and walkthroughs, in addition to Winway inspections. Whatever QA mechanisms are adopted, one of the most significant aspects in their use is the continuity of their application.

Normally, PRINCE/SSAD QAs are applied to the end product at the conclusion of a major phase of activity. This can give rise to many problems, both in organizing the QAs themselves and in rectifying any errors identified. The latter, in particular, can have a considerable impact on the scheduling of subsequent activities which depend on the end product under review. All these issues are addressed by the philosophy of the review methods applied, in particular, the enhanced Winway inspection techniques.

Enhanced Winway inspection procedures   The enhanced inspection procedures make a very significant contribution not only to the overall quality achieved, but also to the metrics against which the quality and productivity can be assessed. Full details of the technique are contained in Chapter 11.

Standards to be applied to each of the documents inspected and the detailed procedures to be followed should be drawn up before the inspections commence. One of the strengths of the process is that it does allow for revision of the standards and procedures themselves. Examples of standards, entrance and exit criteria, and the procedures are contained in Chapter 11.

The general philosophy to be employed is that a random selection of each of the documents to be inspected is produced. The resulting list provides a statistically acceptable cross-section based on a set of parameters agreed by the users and the project team. This ensures, for example, that individual authors working in different functional areas are present in the samples, and in the same proportion as they exist in the total population.

Inspections are scheduled throughout the production phase of a particular type of end product, and feedback from the inspection process is injected immediately to make any necessary refinements to standards and procedures.

Inspections continue until such time as the predetermined list is exhausted (initially this should represent some 10 per cent of the population), or until a consistently low level of errors, both in terms of their number and severity, is achieved. The eventual system users should be confident that the overall quality achieved was truly reflected. This confidence is achieved in most cases with something like 5–7 per cent of the documents being inspected.

The inspections are scheduled at regular intervals, say weekly, and are targeted to last around two hours, with as many documents as the time allows being inspected. The documents, together with the standards, the entrance and exit criteria and the error checklist, are distributed to the relevant inspectors, ideally at least ten days prior to the inspection. Each inspector is expected to spend up to two hours reviewing the document prior to the inspection.

The moderator (chairman) should be provided by an independent quality management group (QMG) if possible, to ensure the integrity of the exercise. Independent QMGs also fulfil several other important functions:

- They provide administrative support for the exercise, calling and conducting inspections, and distributing documentation.
- They hold the random selection lists, so that the project team had no prior knowledge of what was to be inspected before the relevant documentation was issued.
- They select (in conjunction with the project team) the most appropriate inspectors for a particular document.
- They complete the final inspection report.
- They maintain the metrics database of the inspections.

Several specific roles for inspectors are identified:

- *Peer group*: a team member with the skills required to produce the document under inspection. Ideally, this member would be drawn from the project but from a different team or functional area. This achieves consistency across the project.
- *Donor:* a team member, preferably the author of the document upon which the end product under inspection is based or derived. This provides consistency throughout the development life cycle and is an important aspect of the quality continuum.
- *Recipient:* a member of the team who will have to act upon or progress the end product into the next stage of development. This ensures fitness for purpose of the end product, and its contribution to the life-cycle consistency and quality continuum.
- *User:* a member of the user community who could validate the accuracy of the functional processes covered by the end product. With some of the more technical documents this is sometimes difficult to achieve, since lack of detailed knowledge of the techniques could inhibit the interpretation of the underlying functions (for example, when inspecting program code).
- *Specialist:* for certain documents, the technical elements require specific expertise to be available; this applies for example, to those end products involving aspects of database design, transaction processing design, 4GL coding, use of application generators, etc.
- All inspectors should be 'contemporaries' of the author of the end product being inspected. They are therefore of equal status in terms of position and standing in the relevant skills required. In addition, there should be no implications that the process is being used for any kind of direct management control or assessment, although the more impartial metrics provide an invaluable indication of project progress.
- A number of end products should be subjected to the Winway inspection process: program specifications, program code, SCL, test scripts and results, and user manuals. The method allows any end product a project manager may feel needs more intensive scrutiny, to be subject to inspection.

For each end product being inspected, the following are issued: the standards to be applied for the end product, the entrance and exit criteria, the error checklist and the inspector's observation report; examples of these can be found in Chapter 11.

All additional documents required for each inspection should be detailed in the project standards manual. However, a very important part of the Winway inspection process is that the auxiliary documents themselves are checked and refined as an integral part of the process.

In some projects, the lack of definition or even total absence of standards themselves, may result in the first few inspections being almost entirely dedicated to proving the standards, the supporting documentation and the fitness of the procedures for the purpose. Even if relatively stable standard documentation existed, there would probably still be a need to re-establish their fitness for purpose, as each project is unique in its own right. In any event, it is extremely important that the inspection process is set up early in the production cycle. This ensures that any problems are identified and rectified early, and ambient levels of error detection are achieved before the end of the production cycle. This enables the necessary confidence in the overall quality of all end products of a particular type to be achieved.

9.2.2 System documentation

The SRS, SDS and SIS form the backbone of the documentation element of the quality continuum. They serve a number of purposes, but particularly they provide for the collection of all the documentation produced during the most crucial phase of the project life cycle, namely analysis, design and implementation. The need for comprehensive, high quality standards should be accepted for all documentation produced throughout the whole life cycle of any project.

The 'draft' SIS is produced as a precursor to the later stages of user acceptance testing and system simulation. It is termed 'draft' to reflect that the SIS will be subject to refinement and embellishment as a result of those elements deemed necessary to support the demands of the more intensive later testing. The most significant elements in the draft SIS are the user manuals, desktop instructions, the job procedure manual, the network design and the initial service level agreement.

Each of the main system specification documents provides:

- A statement of all the activities conducted during a phase, including its signing off, as being acceptable to all the appropriate parties.
- Documentation of any changes applied to the previous documentation as a result of activities conducted during the current phase.
- The authority to proceed to the next phase of development.
- Detailed plans of how activities in the next phase are to be discharged.

The same philosophy of continuity is applied to the subelements of documentation during each of the major phases. This is achieved by ensuring the consistency and the integrity of the preceding and succeeding subelements for all end products.

9.2.3 Quality gate diagrams

Diagrams should be drawn up to indicate what quality assurance mechanisms are to be applied to what documents. Full details of the annotation to be applied, how they should be drawn up, and the supporting procedures, together with a specimen diagram are contained in Sec. 9.4.

It should be stressed that the specimen diagrams are exactly that. Each project should determine the precise quality assurance mechanisms they will adopt, what documents will be subject to them, and in what quantities. This is the baseline for the project's quality plan.

9.2.4 Inspection resource matrix

Having determined what documents will be subject to Winway inspections, it is very useful to produce a matrix of inspection (or roles) for each of the documents to be inspected in chronological sequence. This can be further enhanced by indicating the relative 'importance' of the various inspectors. For example, users would be most prominent for any document that had heavy requirement definition/specification. The matrix would indicate not only the profile of inspection required for each document, but the overall profile of the respective inspector's skills/resources required over the whole project life cycle. An example of such a matrix used in association with the quality matrix can be found in Sec. 9.4 (Fig. 9.2).

9.3 TYPES OF QUALITY ASSURANCE

9.3.1 Why have types of quality assurance?

While for many people QA may conjure up the use of formal inspection techniques, there are many ways that quality can be assured. Inspections have particular strengths which suit them to certain circumstances, but which are real weaknesses in others. The Winway system therefore identifies a number of different approaches which can be used; these are:

- Desktop reviews or examination reviews
- Manager checks or supervisory reviews
- Walkthroughs or confirmatory reviews
- Facilitated meetings or catalytic reviews
- Product or requirements reviews
- Inspections or compliance reviews

These are described in the following paragraphs. The applications of the different types of review are shown in Sec. 9.4.

Desktop reviews (examination) These are informal reviews of a document task to obtain feedback, guidance and advice on progress, and are generally conducted by one or two individuals. They can be viewed as 'operational'-level checks in that they are part of normal day-to-day working and probably require little advance planning or supervision. They are called 'examination' reviews because of this focus on reviewing and seeking guidance.

Manager check review (supervisory) These can be conducted by the appropriate levels of line manager for the author of the work or task, and may be informal or formal reviews as required. They are called 'supervisory' because they perform one or both of:

- Checks on the content of what is being/has been produced.
- Sign-off of the document or task to indicate that it is complete and acceptable.

At higher levels of management, the tendency will be towards the purely sign-off role.

Walkthrough review (confirmatory) These are peer-group reviews to examine a draft document in order to confirm that it is complete and correct — hence the term 'confirmatory' reviews. The peer group may be a mixture of technical project and business staff, depending on the document being reviewed. The reviews require some organization and planning, and are run by the author of the document. They can be seen as a very informal version of the inspection technique described in Sec. 11.1.

Facilitated meeting review (catalytic) These are formal meetings attended by a mixed group of individuals at various levels. The meeting is organized and controlled by the person responsible for producing a document/conducting a task. The purpose is to canvass the views of the attendees, to discuss options and details, and to reach a consensus on what is required. For this reason the term 'catalytic' review is used. The author will provide some draft input to stimulate discussion, and the result will be a reasonable foundation from which he can proceed. Catalytic reviews are described in Sec. 11.3.

Product review (requirement) This is a formal review of a completed document against a set of defined criteria. The purpose is mainly to determine that the contents are an acceptable reflection of the requirements the document is designed to satisfy. For this reason, they are also called 'requirements' reviews. The criteria must be defined in advance, and the reviews should be directed and involve a peer group of both technical and business staff.

Inspection (compliance) These are the formal inspections of a completed document or task. They are well planned, carefully prepared and closely managed, two- to three-hour reviews. They involve a rigorous examination of the document to identify errors, and are also called 'compliance' reviews. They involve a small number of carefully selected individuals with precise roles. The Winway inspection technique is described in Sec. 11.1.

9.4 QUALITY GATES

9.4.1 The concept

Throughout the development life cycle there are various documents and tasks which need to be reviewed. Such reviews are conducted using one of a number of approaches, as described in Sec. 9.3. Each review is known as a quality gate, i.e. a gate which must be passed through before progressing down the development life-cycle path.

9.4.2 Closed and open quality gates

Some reviews must be successfully completed before progression to the next task is allowed. These are called closed gates, in that they prevent progress until successful review allows them to be opened. Typically, product reviews are closed gates.

When a closed gate requires senior management or project board approval before progress can continue, these are known as policy closed gates and would typically be required for a major project deliverable, such as SRS, SDS, SIS, project plans or consideration of technical or business options.

Other reviews do not prevent progress but are important in helping to achieve and check progress. These are called open gates, and are typically desktop reviews and walkthroughs.

9.4.3 Quality gates notation

The notation used is of a barred gate, superimposed by a 'Q', and the gates are shown as open or closed as appropriate. Within each diagram, gates are serially numbered. The volume of source documents submitted to the review is shown as a percentage figure to the left of the gate. For closed gates, the following task, which cannot start until the review is completed successfully, is identified by writing its name underneath the gate. Several examples of these quality gate matrices appear in Figs 9.1a–c.

9.4.4 Signing off quality gates

All closed gates, and selected open gates (sufficient to provide an audit trail for each document) must be formally signed off. These forms will be used in senior-level manager checks, where the focus is sign-off rather than checking.

9.5 PERFORMANCE METRICS

The verification of the application of the quality assurance framework will demand metrics to be derived. These are important for two reasons: firstly, to demonstrate to the IT unit that quality is no longer an elusive concept, but a reality. Secondly, it demonstrates to the customer or sponsor that an ambient level of quality is being achieved. The ambient level of errors determining the overall quality of the document

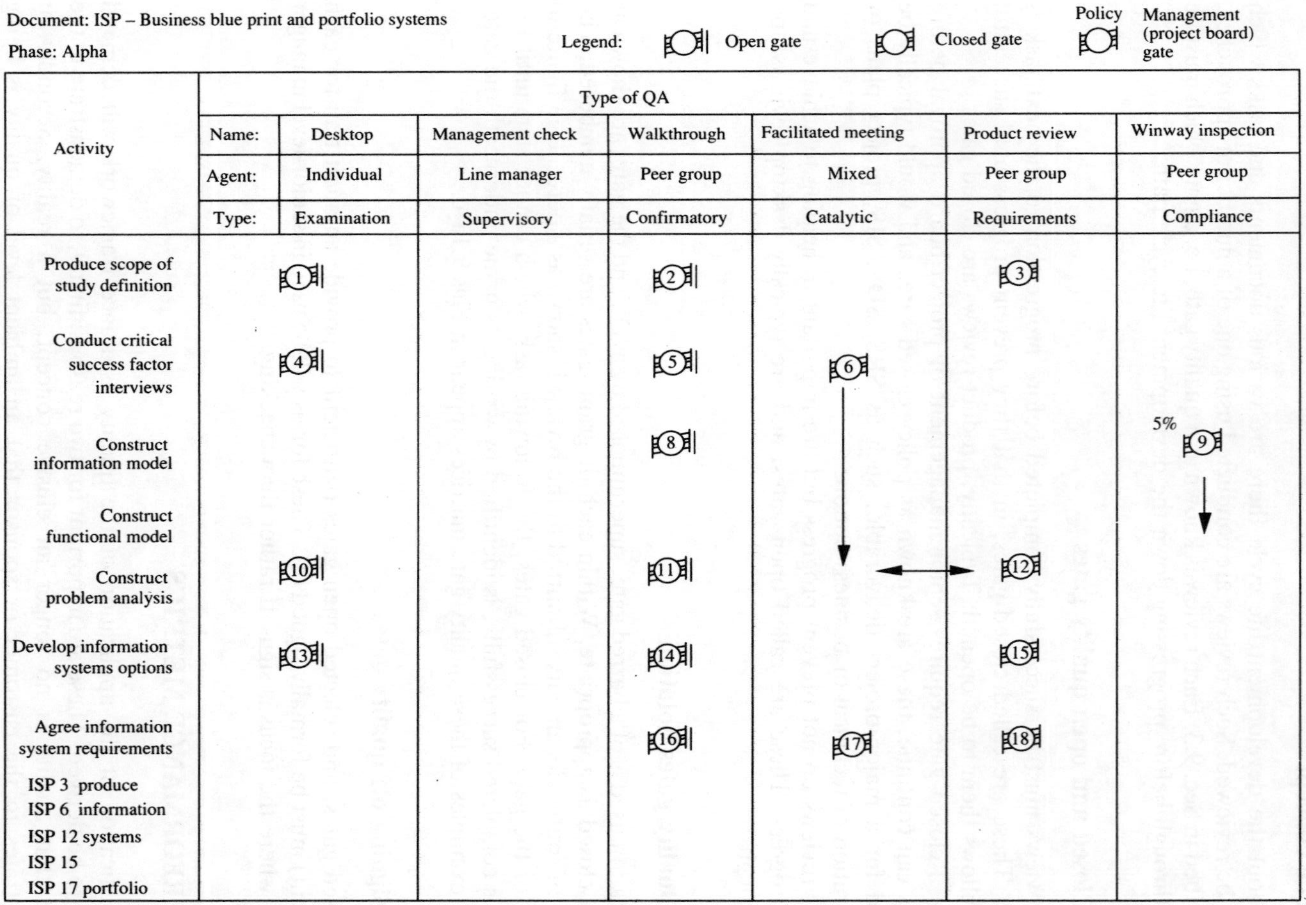

Document: ISP – Business blue print and portfolio systems
Phase: Alpha

Legend: Open gate   Closed gate   Policy   Management (project board) gate

Type of QA

Activity	Desktop / Individual / Examination	Management check / Line manager / Supervisory	Walkthrough / Peer group / Confirmatory	Facilitated meeting / Mixed / Catalytic	Product review / Peer group / Requirements	Winway inspection / Peer group / Compliance
Produce scope of study definition	1					
Conduct critical success factor interviews	4					
Construct information model			2		3	
Construct functional model			5	6 →		
Construct problem analysis			8			9 (5%)
Develop information systems options	10		11		12	
Agree information system requirements	13		14	17	15	
			16		18	

ISP 3 produce
ISP 6 information
ISP 12 systems
ISP 15
ISP 17 portfolio

Figure 9.1a Example of a quality gate matrix.

Document: ISP – Business blue print and portfolio systems
Phase: Alpha

Legend: Open gate | Closed gate | Policy | Management (project board) gate

Activity	Type of QA						
Name:	Desktop	Management check	Walkthrough	Facilitated meeting	Product review	Winway inspection
Agent:	Individual	Line manager	Peer group	Mixed	Peer group	Peer group
Type:	Examination	Supervisory	Confirmatory	Catalytic	Requirements	Compliance
Classify information system	[19]		[20]			
Define technical environment	[21]		[22]			
Define infrastructure	[23]		[24]			
Produce capacity plans	[25]		[26]		[27]	
					[28]	
Isp20 produce						
Isp22 technical						
Isp26 architecture						
Isp27 definition						

Notes

① This phase is undertaken by senior, experienced specialists. The emphasis is therefore on individual and peer group checks rather than supervisory.

② Emphasis is placed on the use of facilitated meetings and product review peer groups.

Figure 9.1b Example of a quality gate matrix.

Document: Draft SRS
Phase: Requirements analysis

Legend: Open gate | Closed gate | Policy | Management (project board) gate

Ra		Type of QA					
	Name:	Desktop	Management check	Walkthrough	Facilitated meeting	Product review	Winway inspection
	Agent:	Individual	Line manager	Peer group	Mixed	Peer group	Peer group
Activity	Type:	Examination	Supervisory	Confirmatory	Catalytic	Requirements	Compliance
Produce context diagram		1	2			3 Draft SRS	
Produce DFDS		4	5	10% 6		7 Draft SRS	
Produce LDS		9	10	11		12 Draft SRS	
Produce requirements catalogue		13			14	15 Draft SRS	8 Draft SRS
Produce elementary processes descriptions		16	17	10% 18		19 Draft SRS	10% 20 Draft SRS
Produce draft SRS						21 Policy SRS	

RA3
RA7
RA8
RA12
RA15
RA19
RA20

Figure 9.1c Example of a quality gate matrix.

Document	Inspection type				Resource type				
	Peer	Donor	Recipient	Specialist (specify)	User	Analyst	Designer	Programmer	Other (specify)
Data flow diagrams	Analyst	Analyst	Analyst/designer user*	User from specific user area	✓	✓			Functional area user
Elementary process diagrams	Analyst	Analyst	Analyst/designer user* Prog spec † Team leader	Functional area user specialist	✓	✓			Functional area user Program & team leader

Notes

* Member of the user group who is integral part of the development team

† Member of the team who will be required to produce programme specifications from these documents if available

Figure 9.2 Inspection resource matrix.

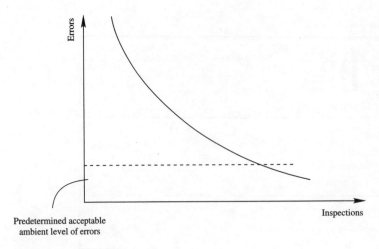

Predetermined acceptable
ambient level of errors

Figure 9.3 Quality metrics curve.

should be decided in advance. It can vary from document to document, depending on the level of quality required, which reflects the importance of the document. Once the actual level of errors is consistently lower than the predetermined ambient level, then inspections of the particular document may cease. The metrics should be maintained as a corporate database which shows individual project and overall IT performance trends, published and distributed to all people who have a vested interest.

The faults identified during inspections will provide useful information about progress against that planned, a clear statement on the effectiveness of the inspection procedures, and the inherent quality of evolving deliverables. The results should be plotted as a graph and should produce a negative exponential curve, as shown in Fig. 9.3. Any significant variations must be investigated and accounted for, and the metrics should form part of project reporting.

PART 3

TECHNIQUES AND DOCUMENTATION

This part describes the formal techniques referenced or recommended by the method. It also defines the documentation required.

10

COMMON TECHNIQUES

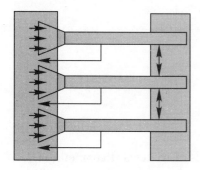

This chapter provides an overview of a number of new techniques referred to in this book which are in common use. It is intended as an introductory insight, not a technical description; it provides sufficient information in each case to enable the reader to understand how the technique works, and where possible, there are references to more detailed descriptions.

10.1 BOSTON MATRIX

This is a technique which originated from the Boston Consulting Group of America.[23] It is used to classify the organization units, usually defined in terms of products and services offered, in a growth–share matrix. The vertical axis is the market growth rate and predicts the annual growth rate of the market or market niche into which the product or service is sold. The horizontal axis shows the relative market share of the product or service, as compared to that of its keenest competitor. The market growth rate goes from a low of 0 per cent to a high of 20 per cent, as shown in Fig. 10.1, although the ranges will obviously depend on the actual market growth rate for the individual product or service (or related product/service). A decision also has to be made in determining what is 'high' and what is 'low'. In the example, it has been divided at 10 per cent intervals although again this will depend on the actual market analysis.

The relative market share is an indication of competitiveness against the keenest competition, and is used as a yardstick in determining the strategic positioning relative to the competition. These yardsticks are:

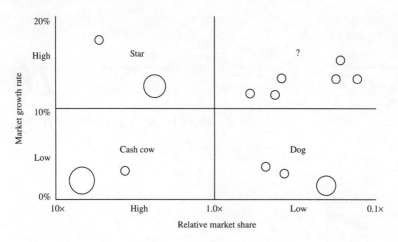

Figure 10.1 Boston matrix.

- 0.1 indicates 10 per cent of the market share.
- 10 indicates leadership, i.e. it has ten times the sales of its keenest competition.

The relative market share is divided at 1.0 into high and low market share. The positioning of the products or services, or even related products or services, in the matrix allows them to be classified into one of four types:

1. *Cash Cows*. These are low-growth, high-share organization units. They are cash-rich in that they generate wealth for the company. The company may use this wealth in many ways, but it is usually used to pay overheads and fund other organization units that wish to develop, but who are at present cash users.
2. *Dogs*. These are low-growth, low-share organization units, usually generating sufficient wealth to maintain themselves but not a source of company wealth.
3. *Stars*. These are high-growth, high-share units; however, since they have rapid growth they also require cash to finance that growth. The investment will level off and it is envisaged that they will become cash cows for the company.
4. *?(Question marks)*. These are low-share units in high-growth markets. They require considerable investment to maintain their share and could require even higher investment to increase their share. These are the real business problems: they are the biggest risk in terms of investment to turn them into stars, but they require the initial investment and the 'star' investment to make them wealth earners.

The circles in the matrix (Fig. 10.1) represent the results of the analysis, and show the company's current organization units and their wealth contribution. Typically this represents the way the organization has formulated its resources to support its products and services. In this example, the company has two stars, two cash cows, three dogs and six question marks. The size of the circle is relative to the wealth contribution of the unit — not just its sales but the bottom line contribution of that unit.

From the example, it can be seen that the company has some real problems. It has a number of dogs, but more importantly it has a significant number (50 per cent) of question marks which are drawing on the reserves created by its cash cows. However it has two growing stars to finance. What should it do? There are four plans of action it can follow:

1. **Build.** This strategy calls for an increase in market share and may even require a longer term view at the cost of short-term income. This is an appropriate strategy for question marks who are to be grown into stars.
2. **Hold.** This strategy is to preserve the market share. This is appropriate for strong cash cows, to both protect and preserve the wealth it generates.
3. **Harvest.** This strategy sets to increase the short-term cash flow regardless of the long term. This strategy is most appropriate where the long-term future of the product or service is bleak and it cannot or should not be turned into a wealth earner. Therefore it is appropriate to weak cash cows, question marks and dogs.
4. **Divest.** The strategy is to sell or liquidate the business because its resources can be put to better use in other areas. This is particularly relevant to dogs and question marks that the company cannot finance, or which cannot be harvested.

The matrix will change as products/services are added or as change occurs. Typically each product/service and its associated organization unit has a life cycle, which is depicted in Fig. 10.2.

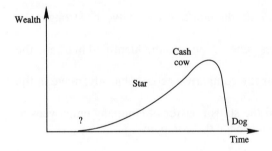

Figure 10.2 Product/service life cycle.

Decisions can be made on the best use of resources — hence some question marks never make it to stars, some stars never make it to cash cows and some dogs never happen, or are divested as soon as they become apparent.

10.2 SWOT (STRENGTHS, WEAKNESSES, OPPORTUNITIES AND THREATS) ANALYSIS

10.2.1 Strengths and weaknesses

This technique is complementary to the Boston matrix, and indeed draws upon the technique when assessing business or organization strengths and weaknesses.

This technique is an analysis of the business or organization in terms of its strengths, weaknesses, opportunities and threats. The analysis can be conducted overall for the entire business, or at lower levels, say a department or division. If the latter, it is almost always in terms of products/services and their positioning. It is best applied at the business level, with relevant information being supplied from business functions and abstracted to give an overall picture of the company's relative positioning.

Business strengths should be assessed from a number of points: these should be market- and customer-driven, not product- or service-driven. The reason for this is quite simple: products/services and technologies are subject to obsolescence, whereas the market and the customer are often in perpetuity. The following are good pointers to a company's strengths:

- Relative market share (Boston matrix) — the higher the share the stronger the company.
- Price competitiveness — the higher the competitiveness the stronger the company.
- Value for money — the better value or added value offered to a customer, the stronger the company.
- Product quality — the higher the quality, i.e. meeting customer requirement first time, the stronger the company.
- Knowledge of customer — the more information intelligence on customers' requirements now and in the future, the stronger the company.
- Knowledge of the market — the more information intelligence on markets, now and future, the stronger the company.
- Marketing effectiveness — the more accurate the marketing activity, the stronger the company.
- Sales effectiveness — the greater the sales penetration into the identified markets, the stronger the company.
- Geographical effectiveness — the greater the company's geographic advantage in the market, the stronger the company.
- Resource skills — the more finely tuned the skills register of company employees to the market, customer and products, the stronger the company.

Strengths can initially be classified as strong, average or weak, although this should be refined to produce a scale of effectiveness from one to ten. Conversely, weaknesses are identified from the strengths — if it is not a strength then it is a weakness! This is a useful exercise in pointing out the key strengths and weaknesses of the company.

10.2.2 Opportunities

Opportunities are assessments of potential 'opportunity routes' for the organization. These are investigated on three levels:

- *Level 1 opportunities*. These are opportunities available to the company within its present scope of products, services, financing and resources.
- *Level 2 opportunities*. These are opportunities to integrate with other parts of the marketing system within the industry, and usually involves acquisition or control within the supply, distribution and competitor chain.

- *Level 3 opportunities*. These are opportunities that lie outside the industry and involve diversification for growth.

Level 1 opportunities There are two streams of opportunity to be categorized:

1. Market penetration and development
2. Product/service development

Increased market penetration is an attractive route, as it utilizes existing marketing and sales resources to try to win a larger share of existing markets. Again this links with the Boston matrix in determining what is and is not feasible. Market development is the cultivation of new markets or niches for existing products/services. This links with the strengths of knowledge of the market and of the customer, and may also link with geographical effectiveness and resource skills.

Product/service development is in response to an opportunity — not for any prevailing technological reasons. The products and services are either evolved or improved to present new and better products/services to the market. This may well link with knowledge of the market and customer, and will certainly utilize the skills register.

Level 2 opportunities This involves opportunities for acquisition or control across the supplier–distribution channels and competitor chain. This is primarily for the following reasons:

- Increased control over supplier or distribution chain.
- Cost containment, reduction or displacement.
- Increased or complete control over competitors by acquisition or share capital.

Level 3 opportunities This is often used where the company sees itself moving away from its traditional industry and diversifying into other, perhaps related, industries that suit its strengths or help eradicate its weaknesses. This can be achieved by:

1. Adding new products/services that have synergy with the existing products/services.
2. Adding new products/services that the current market and customers need and will buy.
3. Adding new products/services that are totally unrelated to the current ones but which the market and customer base require.

10.2.3 Threats

Threats must be viewed at the product or service level. A threat is something that could, if left unchallenged, adversely affect the product or service and eventually lead to its death. A threat should be assessed against its potential severity and the probability of its ever occurring. In statistical terms it is best to classify threats as high/low severity and high/low probability, and attention should be focused on high-severity, high-probability threats. Counter-measures should be developed to deal with the threat: this will call upon the information supplied by the earlier SWOT analysis and also from the Boston matrix.

10.3 CRITICAL SUCCESS FACTORS

10.3.1 Background

The critical success factor (CSF) interview is used to understand the business infrastructure. It has proved an invaluable technique in determining and expressing the business as a set of objectives, goals and information, and takes away the subjectivity of individual personalities and provides an enduring statement of the business. A full description of the technique is to be found in *A Primer on Critical Success Factors* by Bullen and Rockart.[5]

The following offers some guidance on the preparation, structuring and questions of CSF interviews. It is important that a standard approach is adopted for quality control and preceding/succeeding continuum control.

What is a CSF?   A CSF is a management technique used to establish the few areas where things *must* go right to guarantee success in the business.

Why do we need them?   To assist the business managers in concentrating on the critical factors of the business. This allows the technical staff, together with the managers, to identify what information is needed and what systems are required to achieve business goals.

What is a business goal?   This is a specific target to be met by a business area over a period of time.

What must you bring with you to the interview?   A clear understanding of your job and what it is you are trying to achieve, i.e. what are your goals and in what timescales? It is particularly useful if you have prepared some notes.

Some questions that will help you

- What areas of the business do you think about most during both your business and your leisure hours?
- When you are preparing to go on, or come back from a holiday, what few things do you focus your attention on?
- Which areas, if they went wrong, would cause you and/or the company significant trouble — not simply problems, but failure?

Finally . . . Please try to think of the ways you measure achievement now. What problems do you meet internally and externally in achieving goals? A diagram of the procedure is in Fig. 10.3.

10.3.2 Types of CSF and their significance

Industry   Factors determined by the industry you are in and their influence upon each organization in that industry.

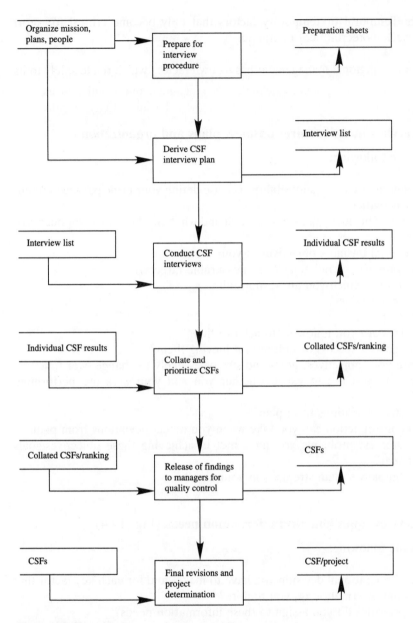

Figure 10.3 The critical success factor procedure.

Competitive strategy The organization's competitive strategy, often visualized as business and marketing strategies, will dictate some factors.

Environmental factors Events outside the control of the organization but which dictate some factors, for example, government legislation.

Temporal factors Temporal or temporary factors that only become critical for short periods of time, such as recruitment or training.

Managerial factors Functional management has its own factors which relate solely to its function.

10.3.3 CSF interview questionnaire: business plans and organization

Tozer[6] proposes the following:

- What is your general area of responsibility? (please define your principal accountabilities and major activities).
- What is the status of business plans in your area and what are the main components of those plans?
- What are the overall business objectives in your area?
- What are your primary overall goals (i.e. measurable targets)?
- For each function for which you are responsible:
  - What are your objectives?
  - What are your goals?
  - Which strategies are you following to achieve them?
  - What factors govern success or failure in achieving them?
- In what way are your objectives, goals and strategies likely to change over time?
- What measures do you use to gauge whether you and your area are performing successfully?
- How do you detect deviations from plan?
- What types of control action can you take when you detect deviations from plan?
- What are the greatest problems you have met in achieving these objectives/goals within the last year?
- What are the company's main strengths in your area?

10.3.4 CSF interview questionnaire: information needs (Fig. 10.4)

Tozer[6] proposes the following:

- For each type of operational decision you have to make, and for each key factor that you monitor, what information do you require?
- What relative priorities do you assign to these information needs?
- How up to date does this information need to be? — up to the minute, daily, weekly, etc.?
- For each piece of information currently received, how good is it in terms of completeness, accuracy and timeliness?
- What are the most important sources of current information?
- In what areas do you most urgently need better information than at present?
- Which information sources lie within your direct control as opposed to outside?

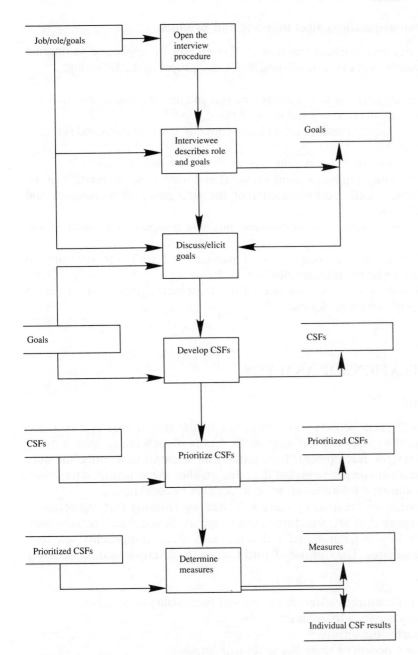

Figure 10.4 CSF interview structure and objectives.

10.3.5 CSF interview questionnaire: markets and products

This is aimed at externally oriented functions, although equally applicable to internal 'service' managers such as systems development. Tozer[6] proposes the following:

- What are the primary needs of your market sector(s) and how did you establish them?
- How are products or services directed to meet these needs?
- In what way do you expect the market, and consequently your products and services, to change with time?
- Are current volumes of business in your area likely to increase or decrease?
- What do you see as the company's main strengths and weaknesses in relation to the competition? Please specify sectors, nature of the strengths and weaknesses and source(s) of information.
- What factors do you monitor to assess your business position in relation to the competition?
- What information do customers/agents/third parties need from the company to monitor performance of the relationships?
- What information does the company need from customers/agents/third parties to monitor the level of service performance?

10.4 ENTITY RELATIONSHIP ANALYSIS

10.4.1 Background

An entity model is the generic data structure of the system that is used as a basis for developing the system to support processing needs. Entity models are created at many different points in system development, from initial trial attempts to describe the data relationship to a detailed composite logical data design, showing structure, data fields, access paths and volumetric information, prior to detailed physical design.

When entity models are created, they are validated by ensuring that the required functions can be supported: if data structures cannot support the required functions, they are modified. This is a diagram-based technique with three components: entities, relationships and attributes. The Concise Oxford Dictionary descriptions of these terms is:

'*Entity:*   a thing with distinct existence, as opposed to a quality or relation'
'*Attribute* 1 a quality ascribed to a thing;
              2 a characteristic quality'
'*Relation* 1 what one person or thing has to do with another;
              2 the existence or effect of a connection, correspondence or contrast prevailing between things'

Entities are often described as 'anything of significance to an organization, about which data needs to be held'. Examples might be Person, Order or Account. These are examples of types of entity and it is important to differentiate between a type, e.g. Person, and the actual occurrences of that entity, e.g. John Smith, Fred Bloggs etc.

'Relationship' describes an interdependency between two entities, for example the relationship between Person and Company entities could be described as 'employed in'.

'Attributes' are details which help to define, classify, identify or quantify an entity, for example attributes of Company might be Name, VAT number, Address.

There are various notations for drawing the diagrams (often called logical data structures) which all include most of the following:

10.4.2 Entities

Each entity is shown in a box:

Figure 10.5 Entity notation.

The size of boxes is not significant, different shapes being used simply to facilitate, vertical and horizontal relationship lines. Entity names are always singular. Symbols on the line describe the nature of the relationship.

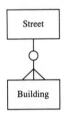

Figure 10.6 Relationship notation.

10.4.3 Relationships

Relationships are shown as lines joining two entities, thus:

A *crows foot* at one end of a line indicates that one or more of the linked entities are involved in the relationship, e.g. in Fig. 10.6 one (or more) building(s) is involved in a street. If there is no crows foot on a line this indicates that only one of the linked entities is involved, e.g. one street is involved with a building. It is not permissible to have crows feet at both ends of a relationship line, this usually means that further analysis is required. A circle at one end of a line means that the entity does not have to be related to the other, i.e. it may *participate* in the relationship. For example, a street does not have to have buildings. If there is no circle on the line then the entity cannot exist unless it is cross referenced to the other entity, i.e. it *must* be linked – a building must be on a street. Some notations use hatched lines rather than circles.

Relationship names must describe the nature of the cross-reference from one entity to the other. It is normal for relationships to be named at each end of the line, so that the precise purpose of the cross reference from each entity to the other can be clearly defined. The names must include a verb to describe the activity causing the link. When used with the other symbols, this gives a syntax to the diagram so it can be read, as in the example in Fig. 10.6.

- *One* Street *may* be the location of *one* or *more* Buildings.
- *One* Building *must* be located in *one* Street.

In some cases, two relationships cannot exist at the same time. These alternatives are called exclusive relationships and are shown by curving lines (see Fig. 10.7). A person must be an employee or an applicant.

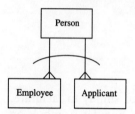

Figure 10.7 Optional relationship.

A simplified example of a data model is in Fig. 10.8.

Exclusivity of the relationship can be expressed from parent to child, or from child to parent.

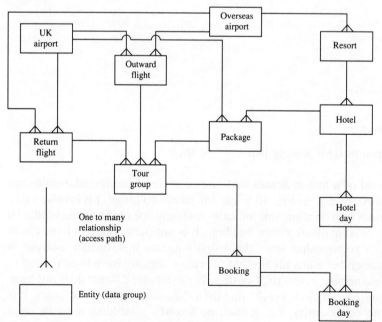

Figure 10.8 Simple example of an entity model.

10.5 DATA FLOW DIAGRAMMING

Data flow diagrams are operational pictures of how data moves around an information system, and between the system and the external world. They are used to represent existing physical systems, to abstract from these the information flows which support user needs, and to define a logical picture of the required system. During physical design, the operations schedule is built around the required system's data flow diagrams, using the following notation:

processes are described in boxes, with serial numbers in the top left-hand corner and responsibilities in the top right (Fig. 10.9):

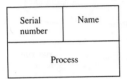

Figure 10.9 DFD process notation.

Information used by the processes is called data stores, and is shown thus:

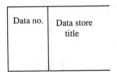

Figure 10.10 DFD data store notation.

The flow of information between data stores and processes is shown as a line joining two boxes, with the name of the information being passed added, thus:

Figure 10.11 DFD data flow notation.

Information (inputs) coming into and (outputs) going out of the process all have some person/group as their source or destination. These are called external entities as shown:

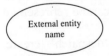

Figure 10.12 DFD external entity notation.

It is also usual for a dotted line to be drawn around the processing, data stores and data flows to show the scope of the process. This means that external entities appear outside the line, as shown in Fig. 10.13.

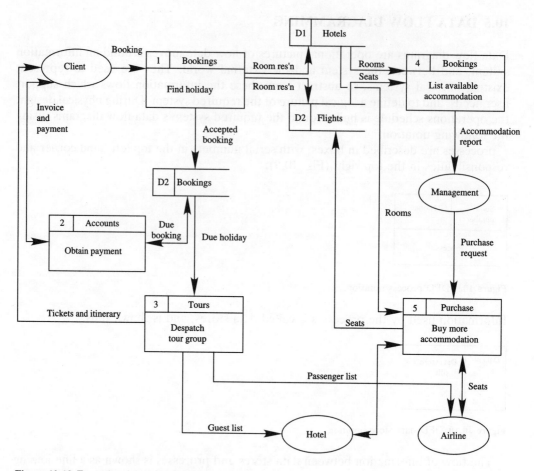

Figure 10.13 Example of a data flow diagram.

10.6 FUNCTIONAL DECOMPOSITION (FD)

This is a diagram-based technique for recording logical processing requirements, as shown in Fig. 10.14. The box at the top of the page represents a main process, and the indented boxes below identify its component activities or tasks. Each indented box can then be placed on a new sheet at the top of the page and expanded into its compound tasks. Seven or eight indented boxes should be sufficient to describe even the most complex process. At the very top level therefore, the whole system can be represented on one page.

Processes at all levels are always described by active words such as 'despatch', 'create' or 'allocate', and the individual levels of decomposition can be combined onto one large page for clarity, as shown in Fig. 10.15. This also shows the strict hierarchical numbering convention which means that any single process box can be readily identified for its place in the system and its relative level of detail. Some processes may be optional — only being performed under certain circumstances, for example: Allow discount to order price when customer has credit rating of 'A'. This option is shown by dotted lines on the

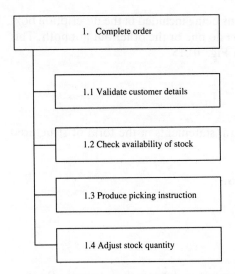

Figure 10.14 Example of a functional decomposition diagram.

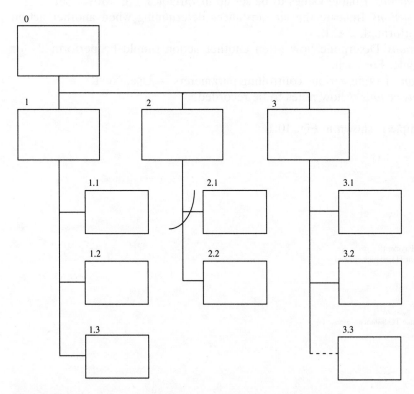

Figure 10.15 Example of alternative layout of functional decomposition.

diagrams (see 3.3 in Fig. 10.15) with the conditions being included in the description box. Some processes may be mutually exclusive — you do one or the other but not both. This is shown by a curving line, as for 2.1 and 2.2 in Fig. 10.15.

10.7 ACTION DIAGRAMS

These are a means of defining detailed procedural statements in the form of structured narratives, which use a formal syntax:

- Upper case letters are used for KEYWORDS.
- Options are enclosed in square [brackets].
- Alternatives are shown within larger brackets.

There are seven different action types:

1. *Entity actions* These cover the options for accessing data, such as Create, Read.
2. *Relationship actions* Show how relationships between entities can be established, transferred or broken, for example Associate, Transfer.
3. *Assignment actions* Enable values to be set up in variables, e.g. Move, Set.
4. *Conditional actions* Indicate the circumstances determining when another action should be performed, e.g. If.
5. *Repeated actions* Determine how often another action should be performed, for example, While, For each.
6. *Control actions* Define various controlling parameters — Use, Next.
7. *Miscellaneous actions* Allow notes to be recorded.

A simple example is shown in Fig. 10.16:

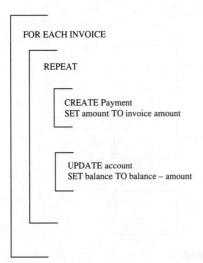

Figure 10.16 Example of an action diagram.

10.8 ENTITY LIFE HISTORY (ELH)

Entity life history (ELH) diagrams provide a dynamic view of the data in order to show the effects of time on the system. A chart is drawn for each of the entities represented in the system, showing all the events which affect the entity during its life. Events include those which create or delete it, and those which change the state of the data items associated with it. When defining ELHs, the origin of each event must be identified, and the processing of each transaction defined. Further detail, such as error recognition and processing and dealing with unexpected events, is then added. Each event is shown in a box (Fig. 10.17).

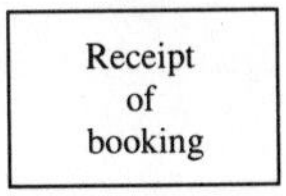

Receipt of booking

Figure 10.17 ELH event notation.

The naming must show the effect of the event, that is, what has happened to the entity as a result of the event.

Events do not happen in isolation. They relate to each other in one of three ways — sequence, selection and iteration.

Sequence One event follows another in strict sequence. This is shown by the order of events across the page (Fig. 10.18):

Booking
Receipt of booking
Invoice despatch date
Receipt of payment
Holiday despatch date
Holiday completion

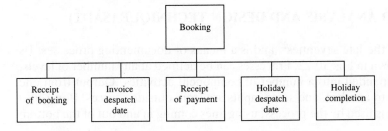

Figure 10.18 ELH event notation.

The sequence is left to right, and applies to all the events linked together at the same level. Thus the left-hand box represents creation of the affected entity, and the right-hand box its deletion.

Selection In some cases it is possible to choose between two or more events. These are shown by small circles drawn in the top right-hand corner of the box (Fig. 10.19):

Iteration Iteration means that the event may happen once, many times, or not at all. This is shown by an asterisk in the top right-hand corner of the box (Fig. 10.20):

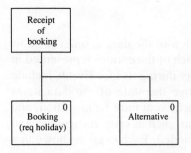

Figure 10.19 ELH selection of events.

Figure 10.20 ELH iteration of events.

Further refinements allow for events which may happen in a random order, and also points where the flow stops and resumes at some unconnected point in the structure. An example of part of an ELH is seen in Fig. 10.21.

10.9 STRUCTURED ANALYSIS AND DESIGN TECHNIQUE (SADT)

SADT was defined in the late seventies[22] and is a means of documenting processes. Its components are as shown in Fig. 10.22. Processes can be defined at any number of levels, so each box can be expanded into a number of component activities. Output from one process may be inputs to another, and some inputs are from outside sources. Boxes also show how information is used by the process, using lines coming in and out of the bottom of the box.

Finally, special controls over the activity are shown as lines entering the top of the box.

While this diagramming technique has not been widely adopted in its own right, it is used in information engineering and a variation on the theme has been adopted in Version 4 of SSADM, in the reference manual to document the method.

10.10 RELATIONAL DATA ANALYSIS (RDA)

10.10.1 Introduction

Relational data analysis was defined by Codd. It is often called third normal form analysis (TNF), or normalization. Codd describes normalization as:

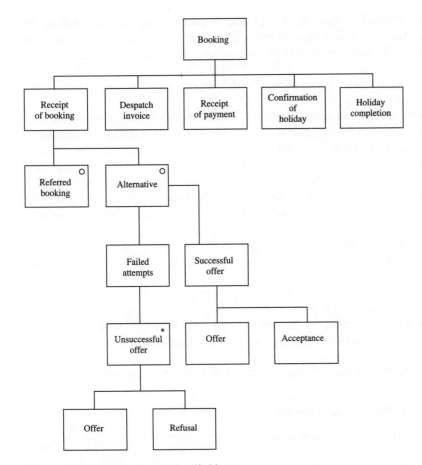

Figure 10.21 Example of an entity life history.

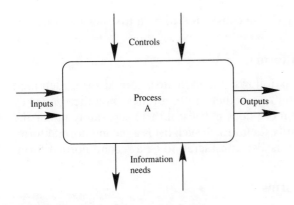

Figure 10.22 Example of an SADT diagram.

'A step-by-step reversible process of replacing a given collection of relations by successive collections in which the relations have a progressively simpler and more regular structure. The simplifying process is based on non-statistical criteria.'

Codd has specified a terminology to be used with normalization, but in this book more familiar terms are used.

Use of normalization has been the subject of some discussion, because it structures data in a simple form which is very useful in a relational database design environment. However, it can help in data analysis with the problem of entity identification, because the results of normalization are simple, clearly defined data structures called third normal forms (TNFs) which can be used as entities. This approach will result in a low-level definition of entities, a requirement for additional relationships and more complex data models, but the benefits resulting during analysis and design can justify the extra workload.

Normalization identifies three types of error which can occur in a data structure (hereafter called an entity); if these three are corrected then an ideal TNF will result. These error types are that:

1. The entity contains repeating groups of data.
2. Not all data in the entity relies on the whole key for its unique identification.
3. Some data depends on non-key fields for its identification.

Normalization is therefore carried out in three stages as described below.

10.10.2 Creation of first normal forms

For each entity, isolate repeating groups as follows:

- Identify the key attributes by underlining, and identify any groups of attributes which occur more than once.
- Separate each such group of attributes as a unique first normal form, and identify its key attributes by underlining.
- The remainder of the original entity is also considered to be a first normal form.

10.10.3 Creation of second normal forms

Isolate data dependent on part keys as follows: for each first normal form identified above, examine each attribute to determine whether or not it relies upon the *whole* key for its unique identification. If one or more does not, list it/them separately under the part of the key that does uniquely identify them. Each such list is a second normal form. The remainder of the first normal form is also considered to be a second normal form.

10.10.4 Creation of third normal forms

Isolate derivable data by examining the attributes of each second normal form, to determine whether they rely upon the key attribute or some other attribute for their unique identification. Each attribute/group of attributes identified by other than the key attribute should be removed from the second normal form and listed separately under the attribute that does uniquely identify it/them. Each such case is a third normal form; the remainder of the second normal form is now also a third normal form.

10.11 FAGAN INSPECTIONS

10.11.1 Introduction

Fagan inspections are named after the IBM employee who developed them. He specified a very controlled approach for reviewing documents to ensure that they could be fully checked for completeness and accuracy, and that people other than the author could make targeted and constructive comments to improve them. They have been widely used since, but have some drawbacks: they can involve a lot of people, can go on for too long, need to be repeated too often if there are errors, involve reading the document out aloud, are generally applied to all documents, and so on. The Winway inspection method uses a tailored version of Fagan which avoids all these problems and makes them much more (cost)-effective. This is detailed in Sec. 11.1.

10.12 DEPENDENCY DIAGRAMS

These represent the interaction of process models, showing a static hierarchical view of processing needs. They show the sequence of activity and are very useful for proving the other models to identify inaccuracies and omissions. They can be used for high-level functions or detailed processes.

The technique is diagram-based and its components are:

• Individual processes or functions, shown as:

• A source of destination for information, shown as:

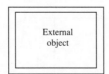

• Any occurrence or moment in time which activates a process, shown as:

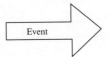

• A flow of information from one process to another, shown as:

Request for insurance →

where the words on the line describe the information passed.

An example of a dependency diagram is shown in Fig. 10.23. There are detailed conventions for naming process and information flows so that they can be related to the process and data models. It is also possible to model exclusive and optional dependencies, as in the FD techniques.

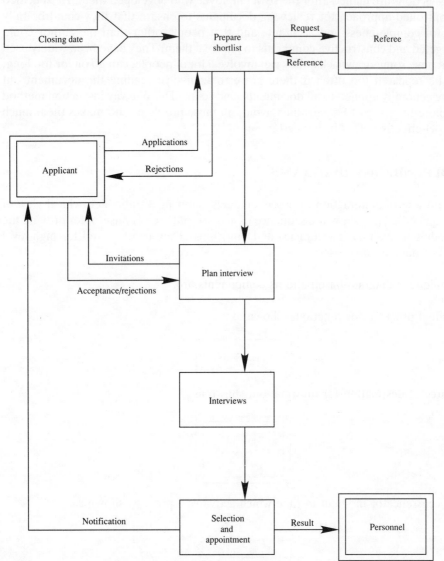

Figure 10.23 Example of a process dependency diagram.

11

WINWAY TECHNIQUES

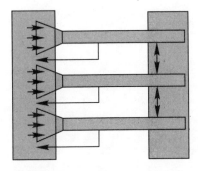

This chapter provides an overview of the techniques referred to in this book which are specific to Winway. There is sufficient detail to allow the reader to understand how the techniques work and how to put them into practice.

11.1 WINWAY INSPECTIONS

11.1.1 Introduction

Winway inspections are a tailored version of Fagan's method which avoids all the problems mentioned in Sec. 10.11.1, and makes them much more (cost)-effective.

11.1.2 Roles and responsibilities

There are a number of defined roles associated with the inspection procedure and each has defined responsibilities. These roles are:

- Moderator
- Inspector
- Author
- Scribe

The following describes each of these roles and their corresponding responsibilities, then places each in context by describing how the responsibilities are discharged within the inspection procedure.

Moderator The moderator's role is primarily to ensure that inspections are carried out and brought to a successful conclusion. The responsibilities associated with this role are as follows:

- Notifies participants on the Forthcoming Inspection form
- Ensures document is available for review
- Review document against entry criteria
- Appoints inspectors and allocates reader responsibility
- Circulates documents to inspectors
- Arranges overview meetings as required
- Chairs overview meetings
- Chairs inspections
- Summarizes and agrees consensus views
- Categorizes error types with the inspectors
- Maintains objectivity of inspectors and author
- Determines outcome of inspection with the inspectors
- Provides defect list to author
- Checks changes/corrections made by the author in response to defect list
- Signs off the inspection
- Gathers statistics

Inspector The inspector is drawn from the same peer group as the author of the document to be inspected. Inspectors are primarily responsible for providing constructive comments on the document inspected. This is further subdivided by the user or donor and recipient inspectors. A donor inspector is the person who produced the document from which the current document is derived. This ensures consistency of the evolution of the document.

Recipient inspectors are representatives of the people who will actually receive the document as input to their tasks, and will be required to action or progress the document to its succeeding phase. Overall, the inspectors' responsibilities are to:

- Scrutinize the document from their viewpoint, for example business user, recipient, etc.
- Prepare notes on errors, defects, observations.
- Attend overview meeting as required.
- Provide constructive feedback in the inspection of the document.
- Consider all the error types and subtypes.
- Agree error type severity.

Author The author is the person who produced the document. His primary responsibility is to produce clarification on any issue raised, and to carry out any remedial work required. His responsibilities are to:

- Make the document available to the moderator.
- Attend overview meetings to explain work to inspectors and moderator.
- Provide clarification on points raised in the inspection by moderator or inspector.
- Undertake rework as defined by the defect list.

Scribe This is simply the person who is charged with taking notes during the inspection. Their responsibility is to take notes as required, to document the inspection meeting and record the outcome. This role is usually undertaken by the moderator.

11.1.3 Inspection procedure

Each of the subsequent sections describes the key processes included in the inspection procedure — planning, overview, preparation, inspection meeting and post-inspection.

11.1.4 Planning

The planning is carried out by the moderator, who chooses and notifies the participants of the inspection, using the Forthcoming Inspection form (see Chapter 12). The moderator selects the inspectors, distributes the documentation to be read and commented on, and books the services required to carry out the inspection meeting. The author should assemble the document, and the moderator is responsible for ensuring that the document is ready for review. The moderator uses the following checklist to determine readiness:

- Has the document been proofread?
- Has the document been checked and authorized by the author's team leader?
- Is the document laid out in accordance with house style standards?
- Does the document appear to meet the entry requirements for the type of document?

Unless the answer to all the above is 'yes', then the inspection review should be deferred. This may appear 'mechanized' but it is a valid part of the procedure. Inspections which were deferred because the initial work has not been done have resulted in a tightening of procedures and actual discipline. In some circumstances the document may not be completed, but provided the moderator is satisfied that it will be completed by a given date, and will be fit to inspect, then they proceed to the next stage. In the case of larger documents, it is not possible to review them all at one sitting. In such circumstances the moderator either organizes a series of inspections to review the document a part at a time, or takes an extract from the document and confines the review to that part only.

The moderator aims to appoint three or four inspectors, who are chosen to ensure that the work is scrutinized from different viewpoints. For example, to review analysis work the moderator appoints both analysts and users as inspectors. The moderator should avoid overusing certain members of staff: all staff at the same level should be encouraged to be inspectors. This also prevents a jaundiced view developing. When asked to perform inspections, staff can assume that the request has come from senior management and so do not need to seek agreement from their immediate superior prior to accepting the role.

Donor and recipient inspectors are appointed, as they are key to the success of the inspection.

The moderator issues a checklist and the Inspection Recording Form to each inspector. If the material is such that it can be presented by reading, the moderator nominates one of the inspectors to be the reader. If the material includes diagrams, the author should walkthrough the diagrams.

The checklist for inspectors provides specific guidance, viz:

- Aim to understand the materials and assess their suitability.
- Record errors, inconsistencies, ambiguities, omissions, standards violations and queries for notification at the inspection.
- Do not spend time redesigning the product.
- Deal with minor typographical and grammatical errors outside the inspection.
- Limit total preparation time to two hours, but do not expect members to be effective at the inspection if they are inadequately prepared. Log time spent and advise the moderator so they can update statistical records.

The inspection recording form is part of the overall documentation and is in Chapter 12 for reference.

The documentation is distributed to inspectors (electronically when this is practical), and the moderator attaches any notes considered necessary/helpful to the inspectors. Distribution should take place at least one week prior to the inspection meeting.

11.1.5 Overview meeting

The overview is a preliminary meeting lasting approximately 30 minutes, in which the author may provide background and/or a description of the document to be inspected. This is not a mandatory meeting — it is called at the request of the inspectors, and is arranged by the moderator. The purpose of the overview is to allow the author to present the material for inspection and to explain and clarify as required — the author's objective is to educate the inspectors, who must all attend. The inspectors do not publicly detect errors and omissions at this time. Others may attend for educational purposes.

11.1.6 Preparation

The preparation period is spent away from the inspection meeting place. Each inspector individually studies the document to ensure a complete understanding. They record any ambiguities, errors and perhaps more importantly, any omissions. Any typographical or minor grammatical errors should be noted and drawn to the attention of the moderator who deals with them *outside* the meeting. The inspectors are guided by the entry and exit criteria for the particular document type, that is, the standards for that document.

All errors and omissions are recorded by the inspectors on the inspection recording form, which they bring with them to the meeting. An important feature of the preparation is that each inspector reviews the document in the light of their particular role. This enables different views of the document to be considered.

11.1.7 Inspection meeting

The inspection meeting takes place only with a complete inspection team in attendance. A meeting may go ahead with an inspector not present, provided that the moderator has received written confirmation that the absentee has undertaken their duties and has nothing to report or provides written comments. In exceptional circumstances an inspector may appoint a colleague to attend the inspection meeting in their place in order to present their findings.

Meeting format The reader reads the document aloud, or the author walks through any diagrams. The other inspectors (and the moderator and author) listen and interrupt whenever they wish to raise a query or note an error. Most of the observations will be made on the basis of the inspectors' prepared notes. However, more points usually come to light as the team interacts. It is important that the document is read verbatim to prevent misunderstanding — paraphrasing is not advisable.

The moderator encourages discussion, summarizes the views on the errors, and notes the consensus regarding the need for changes. When all errors have been identified, a severity classification is allocated to each. The severity classification definitions are:

- High — a serious error, which could have a knock-on effect on other documents/ products and could lead to corruption of data and/or program failure (a 'show-stopper').
- Medium — errors not covered by High or Low definitions.
- Low — errors that are unlikely to affect the interpretation of the document.

Where there is not a consensus view on the severity of the error, the most severe is assumed.

Roles of team members at the meeting The effect of the inspection is to improve the quality of the author's work and thereby the quality of the project as a whole. However, its purpose is to identify defects, not to provide remedies: that is the task of the author after the inspection. The moderator keeps this prime objective to the fore, and encourages inspectors to take a constructive attitude and not to 'maul' the document or its author. The moderator performs the general duties of meeting chairman, ensuring that the meeting is timely, does not run for longer than two hours, and that time is not wasted pursuing irrelevancies.

The authors realize the prime objective and that criticism is not to be taken personally. The authors should remember that they produced the document on behalf of the project, and that it is not 'owned' by them exclusively. The author should avoid becoming defensive, but at the same time should not be bulldozed by criticism when clarification might result in its being withdrawn.

Exit criteria The inspectors consider all aspects of the error types and subtypes for the type of document. The outcome is determined by the inspectors in association with the moderator, and takes account of the objectives as set out in the relevant entry criteria. There are three possible outcomes to the inspection:

1. Passed — the document is accepted without change.
2. Passed — the document is accepted without reinspection, subject to change(s) being made, and an appropriate person is designated by the moderator to check the changes when completed.
3. Failed — the end product is not accepted. The identified errors are to be corrected and the document subjected to another inspection. The date of this further inspection is determined before the meeting closes.

11.1.8 Post inspection

Rework by the author No later than one working day after the meeting, the moderator provides the author with the list of defects, clearly set out on an inspection recording form. Without delay, the author works through the form amending the document. The author must avoid making any changes other than those required by the inspection; an exception to this is that the author may make corrections to typographical and minor grammatical errors which have been identified by inspectors outside the meeting. The aim is to complete the rework while the outcome of the inspection is still fresh in people's minds. Every effort is made to complete the rework within one week of the inspection meeting.

Checking by moderator The moderator (or appropriate person) checks that the changes and corrections required are fully complied with and that no other changes (except as permitted above) have been introduced.

Sign-off Documents which pass the inspection are signed off by the moderator, and a hard copy of the inspection report (see Chapter 12) is held as a master. The moderator signs and dates the box provided on the authorizations page. If only part of the document was inspected, the details are provided.

11.1.9 The inspection schedule

Every month, a schedule will be agreed by the project and stage managers. As a general rule, inspections will be held on the same day each week (although they can be held on alternative days subject to prior arrangement). Two weeks before the inspection, product(s) will be selected by the moderator from a predetermined random selection of planned end products. The inspection team will be selected and notified (using the Forthcoming Inspection Form) immediately afterwards. During the following two days the appropriate materials will be distributed to all members of the inspection team.

11.1.10 Inspection standards

For each document to be inspected, standards must be created to define:

- Preceding documents identifying the document upon which the inspected document is based or derived.

- Reference documents. Any other documents referenced during the production of the inspection.
- Entry criteria. Those which must be complied with before the inspection can commence.
- Exit criteria. These determine the status of the document on completion of the inspection. These are:
  - Accepted without change.
  - Accepted subject to changes being made (to be verified by the author's line manager).
  - Not accepted, to be revised and reinspected.
- Error checklist. A list of standard error types and/or of particular significance to the inspection document.
- Inspection team composition. Details the roles involved in the inspection.

An example of the standards used for user manual inspections:

Preceding documents Program specification (and the EPDs and DFDs from which they are derived).

Project standards The user manual should comply with the project documentation standards.

Entry criteria

User manual objectives The purpose of an inspection for the user manual is to ensure that it is deemed fit for purpose by its potential users. The information should be presented in a comprehensive and intelligible form which adheres to the documentation standards. Although the relevant document is for use within the user community, it should be noted that the acceptance of the format of the document by the inspectors will not preclude the content itself being liable to change.

Users will have the opportunity to check and comment on the user manual with regard to its function content outside the inspection process.

Documents for inspection To qualify for inspection, the user manual completion record should have been signed off and dated by the stage manager.

Reference documents not to be inspected Although the program specifications (EPDs and DFDs) are not to be inspected, errors in these documents should be reported if they affect the user manual.

Attendance An inspection will not take place without either the attendance of a complete inspection team or written confirmation that any absent participant has undertaken his/her duties outside the meeting, and has nothing to report.

Exit criteria The inspectors must have considered all aspects of the error types and subtypes. The outcome of a particular inspection will be determined by the inspectors in association with the moderator, and will take account of the objectives (as defined in the entry criteria) which apply to the end product being inspected. There are three possible outcomes of the inspection:

1. The end product is accepted without change.
2. The end product is accepted subject to change(s) being made, and the stage manager is authorized to check the changes when completed. This outcome applies when the end product has to be amended before its objectives can be met.
3. The end product is not accepted. The identified errors are to be corrected and the end product subjected to another inspection. The date of this second inspection should be determined before the first inspection closes.

Error types and subtypes

FUNC function Have all functions in the program specification been included in the user manual?

EXTE external Will the user manual be able to coexist with other end products?

USER user interface Is the interface (screens and error messages) suitable (i.e. intelligible) for the target user(s)? Do all screens conform to human–computer interface (HCI) standards?

AMBI ambiguity Are all descriptions comprehensible and easy to follow? Does the document include any grammatical ambiguities?

INCO inconsistency Is the user manual consistent with the program specification?

SUPP support Will the user manual be maintainable and enhanceable?

TYPO typographic Does the document contain a spelling or grammatical error which does not produce any other type of error?

STAN standards Does the user manual conform to the project standards? Is it comprehensive and easy to understand?

Inspection team composition

Moderator The moderator chairs the inspection meeting, collates the errors, records the outcome and later distributes the error list to the other participants.

Author The author of the user manual explains the content of the end products as required by the inspectors.

Inspectors The inspectors should examine the end products using the list of error types and subtypes as defined earlier.

Mandatory Inspectors Inspectors without whom the inspection cannot take place:

- Donor analyst — analyst responsible for program specification(s) on which the manual is based.
- Peer analyst — an analyst to inspect the technical content of the user manual.
- Users — user community member(s) who will be prime users of the document.

Other inspectors These are inspectors who will normally be invited to each inspection but will decide individually whether or not to attend — probably none in this case.

Standards for other inspections Winway Systems Ltd can provide a full set of inspection standards for all inspections. Training courses for the Analyst Quality Framework and the Programmers Quality Framework are also available.

11.2 ESTIMATING

The algorithms recommended for estimating overall IT resource required to support various phases of project development, based on function point analysis (FPA) MKII as published by the CCTA, should be used. Figure 11.1 shows overall life-cycle profile of

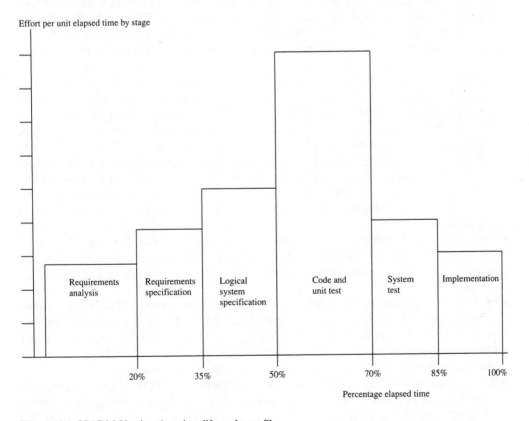

Figure 11.1 SSADM Version 4 project life-cycle profile.

the relative IT resource required per unit of elapsed time, for each of the stages in SSADM Version 4.

At the time of writing the model has yet to be calibrated using actual experience gained discharging projects under Version 4; however, there are some observations to be taken into account and certain specific elements that must be explicitly allowed for:

- A slight overhead (say 5 per cent throughout the whole life cycle, although there may be slight variations for the different phases) should be added to take into account any overheads of the value-added features inherent in the Winway approach:
  - Winway QA inspections
  - Production of SRS, SDS, Draft SIS and SIS
  - Additional project management controls, feedback and PAL
  - Use of strategic planning, but this will precede the normal project development and should be allowed for separately
- Must be explicit about skill mix required of IT staff during the latter stages of the project life cycle. (During the analyst and design stages, conventional analysis and design skills will be required.)
  - Code and unit test (mapping on to Winway Stages 7 and 8). Analyst resources will need to be retained to support a number of activities, but this support should expedite considerably the code production itself, effectively reducing the number of programmers that would be required more conventionally. The analyst tasks would include the direct support of programmers; the production of test scripts and results; and the conducting of the independent tests themselves; production of the first-draft user manuals and operational procedures, the latter in conjunction with programmers. The ratio of programmer-to-analyst skill resources will be between 2:1 and 3:2 and may result in a slight overall increase in resource required for this stage.
  - System test (mapping on to Winway Stage 8). Some programming staff will be required to support analyst staff, as they move into full systems testing. They will be required for 'bug fixing'. Typically this may be of the order of 50/50 during very early stages, reducing rapidly to the core required to support the system during user acceptance testing (Stages 9 and 10) and into live running. This of course will be dependent on the 'stability' and quality of the system, but if the techniques inherent in Winway are adopted then any overall increasing resource support will be minimal.
- That which is identified as 'Implementation' maps on to Winway Stages 9 and 10, Trials and delivery, which although it utilizes relatively small amounts of project IT resources, mainly in a support capacity, will require substantial user and operations support.
- Mark II FPA counts should be taken at various points in the project's life, particularly on publication of the final versions of the FSR, SRS, SDS and SIS. This will enable a profile of any changes in FPA at clearly defined points in a project's life cycle, which can be analysed to give a typical development profile. The FSR and SIS counts will also be used to calibrate and refine the estimating model itself.
- The profile only reflects traditional IT-skilled resources. There will be considerable need for non-IT resources, primarily users, at various stages of the project. This is reflected diagrammatically in Fig. 11.2.

Effort per unit elapsed time by stage

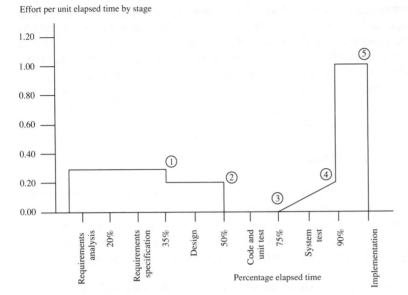

Figure 11.2 User resources required through project life cycle.

1 Ratio of user staff to project staff higher than 1:2, i.e. up to 50 per cent of IT staff.
2 User staff involvement can be reduced by up to half that used in the analysis stage, depending on the development environment and use of prototyping. The participation will be reduced depending on the technical nature of the development environment, but will be increased if prototyping is being used. Typically it will require two thirds of staff numbers involved in analysis. They will be needed to confirm user aspects of program specification, HCI and TP and database design.
3 Very limited participation, as users are not usually able to provide much input to code 'authentication', but will begin to get involved in the later stages to accept user documentation and confirm acceptability of unit and link testing.
4 User participation builds up rapidly during system testing to:
   – Confirm acceptability of systems testing strategy and to inspect tests themselves.
   – Determine the approach strategy to be adopted for user acceptance testing.
   – Validate actual usability of user documentation, rather than conformance to documentation standards.
   – Gain knowledge of and confidence in system.
   – Begin to train trainers, determine user training strategy, and produce training material.
5 Most intensive phase for user participation to prove all aspects of system functionality, conformance to requirements, adequacy of documentation, to provide system administration and security procedures, and to prove service levels, system recovery and resilience from user perspective, etc.

The use of the estimating guidelines and packages should in no way affect the need to produce detailed stage plans for the next phase, at the end of each major phase's activity, that is, as part of the production of the FSR, SRS and SDS. These will be drawn up to cover the detailed requirement of the immediate next activities, and will reflect the experience/knowledge of the project staff and/or vendor/supplier regarding specific development environments.

11.3 FACILITATED MEETINGS

This technique is used when a peer-group level of agreement is required — when people who have the same job titles or similar roles, or will share the same procedures, need to agree on operational issues. The meeting is held away from the job or office and is chaired by a session leader who prepares and circulates an agenda and any background reading material. The participants read and make comments and come to the meeting prepared to participate.

The agenda is set out as a number of objectives. At the meeting the session leader addresses each of these objectives and each participant is asked to comment in open forum. Problems are solved and decisions made during the meeting. Anything that cannot be resolved immediately is listed as an Action and one or more of the participants are allocated to resolve it by a given date. At the end of the meeting, the session leader summarizes the results and indicates the likely effect of the decisions taken. The session leader includes the Actions in the project action list, then personally follows this up and circulates the attendees with the results.

This technique is particularly useful where a consensus of opinion is required and/or there are too many people to interview and follow up individually.

11.4 PROJECT MANAGEMENT MEETINGS AND PROJECT ACTION LIST (PAL)

The interface between the de facto structured methods and project management standards viz SSADM and PROMPT/PRINCE are well documented and understood. These interfaces can be carried over into the extended life-cycle stages as far as the general philosophy is concerned, but with the additional interfaces and feedback loops as indicated in the detail of the method. There are however some specific additional mechanisms/facilities provided by the Winway method, designed to aid general management and information dissemination. The latter point recognizes that one of the biggest problems facing any project is communication, both within the project team itself and from the project to all the agencies it has to deal with.

In all projects of any reasonable size it is advisable to have regular management meetings to discuss general progress, and to ensure that duplication of work — or worse the omission of work — is minimized.

These meetings should follow the PRINCE standards — each team leader/area will report on activities completed during the previous week/fortnight, depending on the reporting period, the activities to be embarked upon in the current period, and any particular problems that might have a significant impact. Progress must be reported against the formally lodged project plans as they appear in the FRS, SRS or SDS, amended as appropriate. Almost all but the smallest projects will be aided in this respect by some sort of automated project managers' workbench or package.

The meetings should be conducted under the chairmanship of the project manager against a published agenda, which will change as the project progresses, to reflect changing project team composition/organization and interfaces with different external bodies and agencies. An example of the structure for such meetings appears below.

Project Management Review (PMR) meetings agenda

1. Minutes of last meeting
2. Matters arising (these will normally be addressed under the appropriate agenda item)
3. Review of each area
    3.1. Team 1
        3.1.1 Last week's activities
        3.1.2 Current week's activities
        3.1.3 Potential problems
    3.n Team n
        3.n.1 Last week's activities
        3.n.2 Current week's activities
        3.n.3 Potential problems
4. Input/output to/from highlight reports
5. Input to/from project board
6. Input to/from any other significant bodies/committees/meetings
7. Any other business
8. Date of next meeting

These should be minuted and distributed before the next meeting, so that any action points will be continuously progressed. In addition these actions will be recorded in the project action list (PAL), which will be described in full later. In addition a copy of the minutes will be put on the 'float file'. This is a fairly well known concept, but it is worth expanding a little because it can be an extremely powerful and useful mechanism for information dissemination. In PRINCE terms, the facility will be controlled by the project control office (PCO), who will be responsible for the maintenance of the plans used in the project management meetings. All members of the project team will supply a copy of any correspondence, papers and minutes of meetings that they receive/generate, and which they consider may be of wider interest to the project members as a whole. The PCO will assemble all such papers on a regular basis (say weekly); these will then be inserted into the float file and circulated to the whole project team. Several copies of each float file may be required, depending on size of the project, the objective being that the circulation list should be sufficiently small to ensure that the float file can be circulated to all individuals in a reasonably short period (not more than two weeks). The float file must not be held up because of any individual's absence — it must be passed by hand and any absences reported to the PCO, who will bring that particular file to the individual's attention on his return.

The purpose of the PAL is to provide a single central repository of all actions that affect the progress of the project. This will be maintained, distributed and regularly reviewed by senior project management. The distribution of the list will be determined by the project manager, but it will be dictated by the members attending the regular reviews, in that they will be required to update the project manager not only on actions they are directly assigned, but also any that fall within their control. The distribution of the PAL also makes a significant contribution to information dissemination and inter- and intra-project communication.

The information to be captured for submission to the PAL must include:

- The tasks/actions themselves.
- Their interdependencies, where appropriate.
- The 'prime' action officer, and any others involved.
- What groups/agencies have an interest in the actions.
- Critical date for completion.

An example of the pro-forma that may be used for capturing this information can be found in Chapter 12.

The most obvious source of information for the PAL are formally minuted meetings. However, there will be many occasions when meetings take place on a more informal, ad hoc basis, which are not minuted but none the less result in actions and/or tasks and activities which must be recorded. All too often these are not, and potentially very important information is lost to management.

A great deal depends on individual officers recording information and submitting it to some central repository. To encourage this the procedure must be simple, with the minimum of bureaucracy. This is the whole objective of the PAL submission form, in that for the less formal meetings its completion should be a relatively simple and negligible time-consuming activity. There does, however, need to be a mechanism for controlling this — the PCO. The PCO will maintain a diary of all meetings, which will be presented to the project management weekly; they will determine which meetings will be minuted. Formal minutes must be lodged with the PCO within five working days of the meeting, for distribution, inclusion in the float file, etc. All meetings will require a PAL to be submitted to the PCO within two working days of the meeting. The PCO will maintain the full PAL documentation. A full list will be published, at a period to be determined by the project manager, coincidental with the senior project managers' PAL review meeting. An example of the pro-forma for the full PAL contents can be found in Chapter 12.

It is relatively simple to maintain the list on computer and, with word processing/ spreadsheet facilities, many extremely useful reports can be produced. The most obvious example is the lists with tasks appearing in criticality-date order. Extracts can also be produced by individual acting officers, and/or by agencies involved, enabling only those specific tasks to be pursued, thus eliminating time that might otherwise be spent pursuing irrelevant actions. Action lists of related or dependent tasks can be produced, as can actions deriving from a single source such as a specific meeting.

Once the information is captured, it clearly provides a very powerful management tool. Production and mangement of the information that is the key, and the PAL and the attendant procedures outlined indicate how this problem can be solved.

11.5 STRUCTURED PROTOTYPING

11.5.1 Why prototype?

The single deciding factor affecting the delivery of quality systems is getting the requirements right. A number of tools and techniques exist that allow those require-ments to be modelled, but very few exist that facilitate requirements acquisition and expression.

Prototyping is used firstly as a communication medium through which the analyst and the sponsor can begin to visualize what the requirement could/should be, that is, the acquisition and expression of that requirement. This is a dynamic view of the system requirements; it is an opportunity to transform a static, documented approach to analysis and design into something that the sponsor can perceive as tangible.

Adopting a structured approach to prototyping allows both the analyst and the sponsor to confirm or refute the content of the deliverables produced so far. This in itself allows plans to be reappraised, and strategies for later steps and tasks to be reviewed in the light of the findings. Above all, the prototype can become the first solid brick in the production of the system house.

The project sponsors' problems, requirements and solutions are often captured in static form as a list or catalogue. Often, because of the textual nature and unstructured expression, much is lost in the translation. The requirements captured in a static form are then expressed in a static form, in data flow diagrams, entity models and so on. Modelling is undertaken in a set of diagrammatic and textual techniques which at worst is one step removed from how the requirement will be modelled later — screens, transactions, etc.

Sponsors have difficulty in expressing and visualizing exactly what their true business needs really are; typically this manifests itself as fuzzy logic, where the sponsor only has a vague idea of what they may require. Also, it may well be that the business functions to be supported are highly volatile or immature, and susceptible to (unpredictable) changes. The only predictable thing is that unpredictable changes will occur! There is a need for a dynamic, real-world view of the requirements: this is achieved through prototyping.

The analyst can devise a strategy through prototyping which can define the information and the logic — users often confuse the 'how things are done' with the 'what must be done', that is, the procedures with the process. The analyst can also devise a strategy that concentrates on the enduring business functionality, even in volatile environments. Indeed, if the environment is volatile, rapid, prototyping and/or package-based or constrained solutions may be a valid development strategy. Here, prototyping is used primarily to investigate the required functionality and to consider design alternatives. A more stable environment will obviously be easier! Mature business functions and clear goals are an ideal basis for the capture and expression of business requirements.

11.5.2 Exploratory prototypes

A combination of inexperienced computer users, no existing systems or too many existing systems, and fuzzy or complex logic, conspire against both sponsor and analyst. An exploratory prototype concentrates on building logical models and defining standards to add to the development procedure. It provides both analyst and sponsor with a number of possibilities, and provides an insight into the real requirement.

11.5.3 Functional prototypes

A functional prototype is used to model a discrete part of the overall business functionality, which can be one or more detailed business algorithms and the information they use. The prototype investigates all aspects of the algorithm's implementation: data, processes and procedures — the How and What aspects.

11.5.4 Scope

The scope of a prototype depends entirely on what is to be proved and the factors that affect this ability. In general terms, a prototype will be built for an individual business algorithm or aspect of the design, but, through incremental prototyping, larger logical units of the systems can be prototyped. In principle, the complete system could be prototyped over a period of time.

Factors affecting the decision-making process are: system criticality and complexity, user commitment, business volatility, resource availability and timescales. The practical application of the scope can be found in Sec. 11.5.6.

11.5.5 Usage in analysis and design

There are two clear alternatives: either the prototype is used to explore requirements, and once established is disregarded, or it is actively used as the basis of the design-and-build strategy. Depending on the system and its environment, either approach is valid. Often what starts as an exploratory prototype becomes the first stage in a design, prototype and build strategy, the exploratory prototype being used to confirm the requirements. This is particularly applicable to 4GL environments.

11.5.6 Prototyping guide

Prototyping is a method within a method — a way of capturing and expressing requirements, used within the overall methodology framework. As such, all infrastructure activities are appropriate:

- Quality assurance
- Planning
- Control
- Deliverable(s)
- Tasks
- Estimates

The following guide provides a framework in which successful prototyping can be achieved.

Agree the scope and objectives The scope can be from either the entire system or down to individual business algorithms. The first task is to agree the business functionality, and from this determine the composition of the prototype. The relationship between functionality and the system level support is summarized in Fig. 11.3.

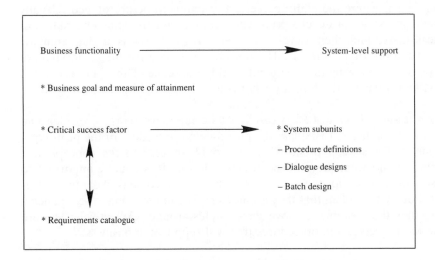

Figure 11.3 Business functionality and system level support.

First, assess which business goals and which critical success factors are to be supported. Agree the requirements catalogue entries supporting the goal or critical success factor; it is now possible to identify the system subunits, which are wholly defined by the procedure definitions that support that aspect of the business under study. Hence the scope is determined by the business functionality, and not by technical issues. In parallel to this it is possible to consider a system as being a number of levels for prototyping. Each level is equivalent to a discrete element of business functionality.

Level 1: procedure definition This is the lowest level for prototyping and involves one procedure definition only. This is prototyped for all its constituent parts — primary input and output, secondary input and output, primary processes, secondary processes, events, data access and procedure usage.

Level 2: design area (subset of related procedures) A group of related procedure definitions from one of the system design areas is prototyped. The dependency of the procedures is an important part of the prototype evaluation.

Level 3: design area (of related procedures) A complete design area of the system is prototyped. The construction and constituents of this design area are an important part of the prototype evaluation.

Level 4: critical mass system The critical mass system is to be prototyped. This is defined as 'The design areas that contribute to success or failure of the system and within those design areas only the procedure definitions that contribute to the success or failure of the system.' This means that some design areas may be totally excluded, and some procedure definitions within included areas may themselves be excluded. Some mandatory requirements can still be categorized in terms of critical mass success or failure.

Level 5: system This is where the entire perceived system is to be prototyped. Usually this is undertaken as a series of Level 3 prototypes, culminating in the determination of Level 4: critical mass, and then Level 5: system. Figure 11.4 is a diagrammatic representation of the prototyping levels. The objective is to confine the prototyping to the agreed scope only, reviewing the documents within the scope. This is a useful aid to focusing analyst and sponsor attentions on what is to be achieved by the prototyping.

Organize briefing sessions In almost every case it will be necessary to organize at least an informal session with the users, to explain the purpose and procedure of the prototype. They must come to the session prepared, and should understand the concept of a procedure definition and what they will be responsible for. It is equally important to stress to the users the reasons for the activity and what the outcome is likely to be. It is always difficult, but try to explain that they are not simply coming along to see 'dancing screens' nor are they there simply to move screen fields around. Collectively, you are trying to define the processes and procedures that will support the business.

Project planning Prototyping has two problem areas: the first is lack of planning. Symptomatic of this is no real beginning and no real end to the prototype. The second is creeping functionality — the prototype's scope and inclusion list seem to grow and grow. The net result of these two problems is uncontrolled, expanding prototypes. To control this there must be a project plan for each series of prototype sessions: the scope is defined in terms of system deliverables, such as procedure definitions in analysis, dialogue designs in the design phase, and so on.

The quality continuum provides the continuity between prototypes in the analysis and design phases. The plan should work from deliverables — if the scope is a design area consisting of ten procedure definitions, then these, together with the supporting documentation, are the deliverables for planning sessions.

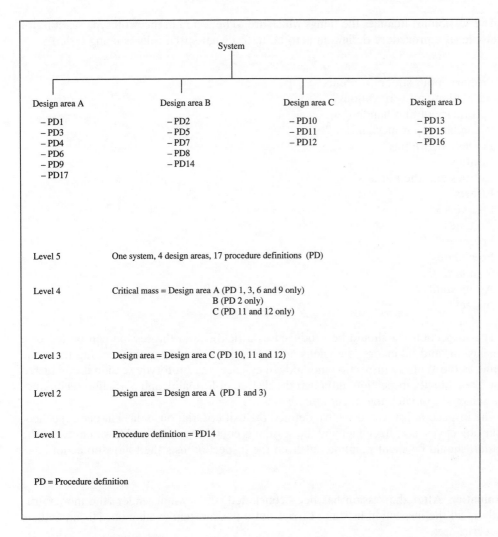

Figure 11.4 Prototyping levels.

The prototyping inspection (standards and session execution) provides the method of quality assurance and control of the session deliverables. It provides entry and exit criteria, attendance and evaluation.

The procedure definitions and the dialogue design provide the input to the inspection procedure for prototypes. No creeping functionality can be introduced to a procedure definition — it is a definitive.

Session execution Each session is executed according to the agreed scope and objectives, and the session is not begun unless all the entry criteria are satisfied — are the objectives agreed; are all the documents to be inspected and documents to be used for reference available? has the attendance specification been met?

The session list itemizes the things which are to be tested in the prototype session: for example, if a procedure definition is to be tested what specifically is being tested?

- Primary input stream contents?
- Validation and verifications?
- Secondary output handling?
- Secondary input mechanisms?
- Process algorithms?
- Entities?
- Entities and their access?
- Effects?
- Frequencies?
- Volumes?
- Processes?
- Procedures?
- Standards?
- Applicability?
- Impact?

The inspection list should be produced as a tick list, so the session can be led to a conclusion, and all errors, omissions and exceptions should be noted, using the same forms as the Winway inspection method. In essence, the prototype session is conducted just like a quality inspection, although the degree of formality and particular techniques are selected to match the target attendees.

The inspection list will also have defined the exit criteria: once this has been reached, your objectives have been met and the session is concluded. The final few minutes of the session should be spent pointing out from the inspection lists the follow-up action.

Evaluation After the session has been concluded, the session leader (the moderator) gathers all the inspection lists and carries out a postmortem evaluation. His immediate concerns are:

- Effect on prototyping plan
- Effect on preceding or succeeding deliverables
- Likely impact of the errors, omissions and exceptions
- The best way forward from here.

The evaluation will result in the inspection list being analysed and a follow-up action list produced, which in turn will contribute to the project action list (PAL).

Follow-up action The follow-up action list details specific actions against session attendees, with target dates for completion. It also includes a summary of the findings.

11.5.7 Functional prototype checklist

General

Have all the deliverables needed been assembled?
Have all participants been briefed as to their role and responsibility?
Has pre-prototype session documentation been circulated, e.g. procedure definitions, screens, etc.
Have adequate resources been set aside for the session?

Procedure definition

Have you agreed the content for the input stream(s) being handled?
Validation of secondary input/output agreed?
Events valid
Process logic correctly interpreted
Access path validated
Entities correctly defined
Volumes and frequency of execution agreed

Business needs

Can the user relate the prototype directly to a business need in support of a goal or critical success factor?
Can you pinpoint all the requirements this prototype will meet?

Procedures

Have you pointed out the changes in existing user roles in terms of tasks and responsibilities?
Is the user satisfied as to how they will use it in their environment? (as well as to what it will do?)

Acceptance

Has the prototype been accepted?
Have you documented the follow-up action?
Have you explained the impact of changes/acceptance on other deliverables?

Fuzzy logic, complex logic

Have all the problem areas been investigated?
Have results been recorded?
Have genuine problems and their solution(s) been investigated?

11.5.8 Prototyping inspection (Standards and session execution)

A copy of this inspection form is in Chapter 12.

Preceding documents These are all the documents that provide continuity with the documents under review during the prototyping session; for example, if a procedure definition is being reviewed, then its preceding documents are the data flow diagram and the entity model.

Standards compliance This section lists any agreed standards that must be complied with: for example, the procedure definitions must be prepared to template standards. The inspection checklist may be set to certain standards, such as what to inspect, in what order, and on what priority. The session itself may be executed to a certain standard, for example, the process narrative is always walked through on a whiteboard, and any terminals must be switched off when this takes place.

Entry criteria (objectives, documents, reference documents) This lists the objectives set for standard prototyping sessions, and specific objectives for the session to be executed. It also lists the documents that may be needed during the session, for example, the procedure definition template will be needed, and the data flow diagrams may be needed for reference purposes.

Attendance This specifies who is to attend and in what capacity — moderators, categories of business user, inspectors, scribe, etc.

Exit criteria This is used to determine when the inspection prototype has successfully met its objectives. Typically this is the completion of the error list or the end products acceptance. The error list should be attached to the inspection checklist.

Evaluation/follow-up action This records any immediate recommendations noted during the session execution, by whom, and in what timescale. This activity should also include statistical analysis, similar to the standard Winway inspection method.

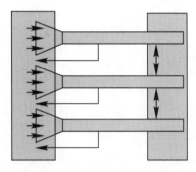

12

DOCUMENTATION

This chapter contains examples of the forms recommended for use in the preceding chapter, and contents lists for each of the recommended study reports.

12.1 ISP — BUSINESS BLUEPRINT

The following contents list is proposed:

0. Document control

    0.1 Header page
    0.2 Contents list
    0.3 Change history
    0.4 Document references
    0.5 Terms, abbreviations and conventions

1. Introduction

    1.1 Purpose
    1.2 Scope

2. Strategic study overview

    2.1 Introduction
    2.2 Constraints

Annexe 10: Information systems options
Annexe 11: Information systems portfolio
Annexe 12: Technical architecture
Annexe 13: Capacity plans

12.2 ISP — PORTFOLIO SYSTEM

The following contents list is proposed:

0. Document control

0.1 Header page
0.2 Contents list
0.3 Change history
0.4 Document references
0.5 Terms, abbreviations and conventions

1. Introduction

1.1 Purpose
1.2 Scope

2. System overview

2.1 Introduction
2.2 Constraints
2.3 Objectives, goals and priorities
2.4 Information requirements
2.5 Functions supported
2.6 System classification (type and environment)

3. System objectives

3.1 Scope of the system
3.2 Priorities and schedules
3.3 Objectives, goals and priorities
3.4 Goal attainment
3.5 Critical success factors
3.6 Relationship to existing investment

4. Information requirement

4.1 Information subject areas
4.2 Subject area/function

5. Functional requirement

5.1 Functions

Annexe 1: Scope definition
Annexe 2: Objectives and goals definition
Annexe 3: Critical success factors
Annexe 4: Information model
Annexe 5: Function model
Annexe 6: Subject area/function matrix
Annexe 7: Capacity planning
Annexe 8: Project plans and schedules

12.3 FEASIBILITY STUDY REPORT (FSR)

The following contents are proposed:

0. Document control

0.1 Header page
0.2 Contents list
0.3 Change history
0.4 Document references
0.5 Terms, abbreviations and conventions

1. Introduction detailing

1.1 Reason for the study
1.2 Terms of reference
1.3 Study objectives
1.4 Scope of the study
1.5 Constraints
1.6 Completion date
1.7 Consultation
1.8 Management of the study

2. Management/executive summary

2.1 The recommended solution
2.2 The options considered but rejected
2.3 The plans for the full study stage
2.4 The preferred procurement path
2.5 The plans for the implementation of the system

3. Study approach

4. Existing business and IS support to the business

4.1 The business objectives
4.2 The functions and processes currently undertaken
4.3 The organization of the business area, and the various roles and responsibilities
4.4 The current and potential areas of strength and weakness
4.5 Any relationships with other business areas and organizations
4.6 Any existing IS support, detailing the functions supported or not; strengths and weaknesses; the technological opportunities and constraints

5. Future IS support

5.1 A description of the system's place in the IS strategy
5.2 An overview of the scope of the required system and its functionality
5.3 Details expressed in measurable terms for the requirements
5.4 The implications of any geographic distribution of IS support
5.5 Details of the service performance required of the proposed system

6. Proposed system

6.1 A narrative overview of the logical system, based on the selected business option(s)
6.2 An outline of the alternative technological options, together with a summary of the necessary technical framework
6.3 The advantages and disadvantages of the team's proposals

12.4 DRAFT SYSTEM REQUIREMENT SPECIFICATION (SRS)

The contents of this report are as for the SRS. Annexes 19–22 will not be completed at all; the remaining contents will be in draft form only for expansion and/or refinement in Stage 3.

12.5 THE SYSTEM REQUIREMENT SPECIFICATION (SRS)

The following contents list is proposed:

0. DOCUMENT CONTROL

0.1 Header page
0.2 Contents list
0.3 Change history

0.4 Document references
0.5 Terms, abbreviations and conventions

1. Introduction

1.1 Purpose
1.2 Scope

2. System overview

2.1   Introduction
2.2   Constraints
2.3   Current problems and requirements
2.4   Processing overview
2.5   Information requirements
2.6   Inputs
2.7   Outputs
2.8   Data conversion
2.9   User and access control
2.10 Impact

3. System functions

3.1 Batch functions
3.2 Online functions
3.3 Housekeeping

4. Man–machine interface design

5. Audit, security and control

6. Service level requirement

Annexe 1: Problems and requirements list
Annexe 2: Data flow diagrams
Annexe 3: Data flow descriptions
Annexe 4: Elementary function descriptions
Annexe 5: Common function descriptions
Annexe 6: Event catalogue
Annexe 7: Retrievals catalogue
Annexe 8: Composite logical data diagram
Annexe 9: Entity descriptions
Annexe 10: Attribute inventory
Annexe 11: Relationships inventory
Annexe 12: Data store/entity cross-reference
Annexe 13: Entity life histories

Annexe 14: Logical dialogue controls
Annexe 15: Logical dialogue outlines
Annexe 16: Screen standards
Annexe 17: Code lists
Annexe 18: Audit security and control
Annexe 19: Business systems options
Annexe 20: Technical systems options
Annexe 21: Draft service level agreement
Annexe 22: Design stage plans

12.6 THE SYSTEM DESIGN SPECIFICATION (SDS)

The following contents are proposed:

0. DOCUMENT CONTROL

0.1 Header page
0.2 Contents list
0.3 Change history
0.4 Document references
0.5 Terms, abbreviations and conventions

1. Introduction

1.1 Purpose
1.2 Scope
1.3 Change management
    1.3.1 Change control requests
    1.3.2 Impact of changes

2. System overview

2.1 Introduction
2.2 Current problems and requirements
2.3 Processing overview
2.4 Information requirements

3. System design overview

3.1 Database design
3.2 Process design
3.3 Program specifications
3.4 System testing
3.5 Data conversion
3.6 Manuals

    3.7   User involvement
    3.8   QA procedures
    3.9   User training
    3.10 Hardware installation

4. Man–machine interface design

5. Audit, security and control

6. Service level requirement

Annexe 1: Problems and requirements list
Annexe 2: Data flow diagrams
Annexe 3: Data flow descriptions
Annexe 4: Elementary function descriptions
Annexe 5: Common function descriptions
Annexe 6: Event catalogue
Annexe 7: Retrievals catalogue
Annexe 8: Composite logical data diagram
Annexe 9: Entity descriptions
Annexe 10: Attribute inventory
Annexe 11: Relationships inventory
Annexe 12: Data store/entity cross-reference
Annexe 13: Entity life histories
Annexe 14: Logical dialogue controls
Annexe 15: Logical dialogue outlines
Annexe 16: Screen standards
Annexe 17: Code lists
Annexe 18: Audit security and control
Annexe 19: Business systems options
Annexe 20: Technical systems options
Annexe 21: Draft service level agreement
Annexe 22: Database design
Annexe 23: Program specifications
Annexe 24: System testing strategy
Annexe 25: Data conversion requirement
Annexe 26: Data take-on strategy
Annexe 27: Supporting manuals and operational documentation
Annexe 28: Implementation stage plans
Annexe 29: Project standards manual

Annexe 29 contains only deviations from or additions to site/project standards used during this phase, and the justification for them. Otherwise it will merely be a reference to the appropriate standards/methodologies used, such as SSADM.

12.7 DRAFT SYSTEM INFORMATION SPECIFICATION (SIS)

This is very often a conceptual, as well as a draft, document, in that it will not usually be published as a discrete document, being composed of various elements of the SIS in various stages of production. It is draft in that its components will be subject to revision and expansion, and that some elements of the SIS will not exist at all at this stage. The objective is to provide all the documentation necessary to ensure that user testing and system acceptance trials can be conducted in a comprehensive and meaningful way. In this respect the conceptual document will comprise of all the documentation produced for the SDS, updated to reflect any significant changes incorporated, and the following SIS annexes:

Annexe 30: System testing details and acceptance report
Annexe 31: Interim findings of data conversion/database loading programmers
Annexe 32: Draft user manuals
Annexe 33: Draft job procedure (operations) manuals
Annexe 34: Draft desktop procedures

12.8 THE SYSTEM IMPLEMENTATION SPECIFICATION (SIS)

The following contents are proposed:

0. Document control

    0.1 Header page
    0.2 Contents list
    0.3 Change history
    0.4 Document references
    0.5 Terms, abbreviations and conventions

1. Introduction

    1.1 Purpose
    1.2 Scope
    1.3 Approving authority

2. System overview

    2.1 Introduction
    2.2 Current problems and requirements
    2.3 Processing overview
    2.4 Information requirements

3. System implementation overview

3.1 History
3.2 Change management
3.3 Quality/documentation
3.4 Standards
3.5 Training
3.6 Initial database status
3.7 Initial TP design status
3.8 Project productivity
3.9 Development/maintenance strategy
3.10 Post-implementation review

4. Human–computer interface

5. Audit, security and control

6. Service level requirement

Annexe 1: **Problems and requirements list**
Annexe 2: **Data flow diagrams**
Annexe 3: **Data flow descriptions**
Annexe 4: **Elementary function descriptions**
Annexe 5: **Common function descriptions**
Annexe 6: **Event catalogue**
Annexe 7: **Retrievals catalogue**
Annexe 8: **Composite logical data diagram**
Annexe 9: **Entity descriptions**
Annexe 10: **Attribute inventory**
Annexe 11: **Relationships inventory**
Annexe 12: **Data store/entity cross-reference**
Annexe 13: **Entity life histories**
Annexe 14: **Logical dialogue controls**
Annexe 15: **Logical dialogue outlines**
Annexe 16: **Screen standards**
Annexe 17: **Code lists systems tables**
Annexe 18: **Audit security and control**
Annexe 19: **Business systems options**
Annexe 20: **Technical systems options**
Annexe 21: **Service level agreement**
Annexe 22: **Database design**
Annexe 23: **TPMS design**
Annexe 24: **Network design**
Annexe 25: **Program specifications**
Annexe 26: **Program code**

Annexe 27: **Job control procedures**
Annexe 28: **Unit and system test strategy and metrics**
Annexe 29: **User acceptance test strategy and metrics**
Annexe 30: **Installation plan and narrative**
Annexe 31: **Project infrastructure proving strategy**
Annexe 32: **Data centre acceptance/sign-off**
Annexe 33: **File conversion strategy**
Annexe 34: **Database load strategy**
Annexe 35: **User manuals**
Annexe 36: **Job procedure manual**
Annexe 37: **System maintenance guide**
Annexe 38: **Desktop procedures**
Annexe 39: **System maintenance strategy**
Annexe 40: **Project standards manual**
Annexe 41: **Project performance and productivity metrics**
Annexe 42: **Network configuration control and management**
Annexe 43: **Proposals for post-implementation review**
Annexe 44: **Financial plan and performance comparison**

Note: a number of annexes will include copies of the various sign-off certificates, as required by the project owner. The most common elements requiring some sort of formal acceptance, and the various agencies involved are:

Annexe 45: User confirmation of problems/requirements addressed by the delivered system and identification of those not addressed for feedback into corporate strategies loop.

Annexe 46: Identification of state of any code lists and/or systems tables current at the time of delivery, and acceptance of responsibility for their subsequent maintenance.

Annexe 47: Statement of all aspects of security applied, to be confirmed by the security branch as conforming to any corporate security requirements and data integrity/recovery mechanism accepted by technical support group(s).

Annexe 48: Copy of signed off agreement (SLA) between service supplied and owner (chief user) of system is essential.

Annexe 49: Database and transaction processing design, signed off as technically sound and conforming to any corporate standards, by appropriate central technical support group. Network design to be similarly endorsed by central communications group.

Annexe 50: All aspects of program specifications and code to be signed off as acceptable for maintenance/development purposes, by central maintenance team. This may be provided by retaining appropriate members of the development team, but none the less this documentation must be critically examined for fitness for purpose.

Annexe 51: Certification that systems testing was completed to all interested parties' satisfaction, and that the system was acceptable for embarking on user acceptance tests.

Annexe 52: User acceptance certificate to confirm that the system had met all tests determined for user acceptance.

Annexe 53: Statement of all infrastructure trials conducted, and confirmation that any specific performance criteria (as determined by the SLA) have been met.

Annexe 54: Copy of 'handover' certificate confirming that system is adequately documented and performs satisfactorily to various operations and software support group(s)' requirements.

Annexe 55: Confirmation that the data conversion was carried out satisfactorily, and initial database contents as defined are acceptable.

Annexe 56: All aspects of user documentation are suitable, acceptable and adequate for the user community to use the system effectively and efficiently.

Annexe 57: All aspects of operational documentation are suitable, acceptable and adequate for operations staff to run the system effectively and efficiently.

Annexe 58: All bug-reporting, HelpDesk, software restriction, release, and delivery procedures are understood and acceptable to both the user community and the agents responsible for discharging the various activities.

Annexe 59: Whereas various elements of the areas covered by these documents may be subject to some sort of sign-off procedures, their prime purpose is to provide feedback to corporate strategies for their review and refinement.

12.9 SYSTEM POST-IMPLEMENTATION REVIEW (SPIR)

The following contents are proposed:

0. DOCUMENT CONTROL

    0.1 Header page
    0.2 Contents list
    0.3 Change history
    0.4 Document references
    0.5 Terms, abbreviations and conventions

1. Introduction

    1.1 Purpose
    1.2 Scope
    1.3 Approving authority

2. System overview

    2.1 Introduction
    2.2 Current problems and requirements

2.3 Processing overview
2.4 Information requirements

3. User requirements

3.1 Resolution of problems and requirements
3.2 Provision of required functions
3.3 Provision of required data
3.4 System changes

4. Cost/benefit analysis

4.1 System development costs, actual vs. planned
4.2 Future operational costs, actual vs. planned
4.3 Realization of financial benefits
4.4 Realization of other tangible benefits
4.5 Realization of non-tangible benefits
4.6 Timescales
4.7 Effect on other systems (including superseded)

5. System operation

5.1 Human–computer interface
5.2 User views of the system
5.3 Resource requirements
5.4 Service level performance
5.5 Audit control and security
5.6 User documentation
5.7 System support

6. System sizing and performance

6.1 Database sizing and growth
6.2 Transaction volumes and growth
6.3 Hardware requirements (planned vs. current vs. future)
6.4 Software requirements (planned vs. current vs. future)
6.5 Response times
6.6 Input volumes and error rates
6.7 Output volumes and error rates

7. System development

7.1 Requirements analysis stages
7.2 Logical design
7.3 Technical design
7.4 Development and testing
7.5 Delivery and support

8. System maintenance

8.1 Maintenance team responsibilities
8.2 Technical documentation
8.3 Operating documentation

9. Data Protection Act

9.1 The need to comply
9.2 Actual performance

12.10 FORTHCOMING INSPECTION FORM

Project:	Index no:
Sub system:	Page:
Stage:	Version:
Author:	Date produced:
Remarks:	Checked by:
	Date checked:

Forthcoming inspection — Inspection serial no. [   ]

1. Inspection administration

Inspection date:

Inspection time:

Location:

Documentation availability date:

2. Inspection type (tick one box)

☐ Program specification   ☐ Analyst test

☐ Program code   ☐ Link test

☐ Test script   ☐ User manual

☐ Test results   ☐ Other

3. Distribution details (tick relevant boxes)

☐ Moderator:
☐ Author:
☐ Inspector 1:
☐ Inspector 2:
☐ Inspector 3:
☐ Inspector 4:
☐ Project manager:
☐ Stage manager:

12.11 INSPECTION RECORDING FORM

Project:	Index no:
Sub system:	Page:
Stage:	Version:
Author:	Date produced:
Remarks:	Checked by:
	Date checked:

Inspection recording form   Inspection serial no. ☐

1. Inspection administration

Inspection name:

Inspection date:

Inspection time:

Location:

Amt. of time (hrs):

No.	Location	Sev.	Type	Subtype	Description	Action

Note: All inspectors are to complete this form, bring it to the inspection and hand it to the moderator on completion of the inspection.

12.12 INSPECTION REPORT FORM

Project:	Index no:
Sub system:	Page:
Stage:	Version:
Author:	Date produced:
Remarks:	Checked by:
	Date checked:

Inspection report form   Inspection serial no. ☐

1. Inspection administration

Inspection date:

Inspection time:

Duration:

Duration of inspection: No. of pages:

2. Participants

Moderator:

Author:

Inspector 1:   Inspector 3:

Inspector 2:   Inspector 4:

3. Inspection outcome ☐ Accepted no changes   ☐ Accepted with changes   ☐ Unacceptable

Error type	HIGH	SEVERITY MEDIUM	LOW
LOGI	–	–	–
FUNC	–	–	–
EXTE	–	–	–
USER	–	–	–
TYPO	–	–	–
AMBI	–	–	–
INCO	–	–	–
PERF	–	–	–
SUPP	–	–	–
STAN	–	–	–
TOTAL			

4. Moderator's/sign-off

Confirmed that the inspection has been completed.

Signed: Name: Date:

12.13 PROJECT ACTION LIST (PAL)

Item serial number	Task number	Task/action	Related task	Source/ originating meeting	Action officer	Other agencies involved	Critical date

12.14 PROJECT ACTION LIST REPORT (PALR)

Meeting _____

Source code _____

Date _____

Venue _____

Attendees _____
_____
_____
_____

Task	Rel tasks	Action officer	Agencies involved	Critical date

304

12.15 PROTOTYPING INSPECTION FORM

Prototyping inspection (Standards and session execution)	1/2

System: design area:

Preceding documents

Standards compliance

Entry criteria

    * Objectives

    * Documents

    * Reference documents

   Attendance

(cont)

PROTOTYPING INSPECTION FORM (Cont)

Prototyping inspection (Standards and session execution)
Exit criteria   * Errors   * End product acceptance   Evaluation/follow up action

REFERENCES

1. Jackson, M.: "System Development", Prentice-Hall Inc., 1983.
2. British Standards Institute: BS 5750.
3. British Computer Society: "Guide to Software Quality Management System Construction and Certification Using EN 29001," British Computer Society, 1990.
4. Rockart, J. F.: Chief Executives Define Their Own Data Needs, *Harvard Business Review*, p. 81, March-April 1979.
5. Bullen, C. V. and J. F. Rockart: "A Primer of Critical Success Factors," Center For Information Systems Research, Massachusetts Institute of Technology, CISR 69, June 1981.
6. Tozer, E. E.: "Planning For Effective Business Information Systems," Pergamon Press, 1988.
7. National Computing Centre: "Strategic Information Technology Planning", Art Benjamin Seminar, National Computing Centre, 1988.
8. Martin J.: "Strategic Data Planning Methodologies", Savant Institute, 1980.
9. Boehm, B.: Software Engineering, *IEE Trans. Comput*, vol. C-25,12, 1976.
10. Stanway, J. and A. Windsor: "A Methodology For Data Analysis Leading To Database Design". Published privately, 1976.
11. Gane, C. and J. Sarson: "Structures Systems Analysis: Tools and Techniques", IST Databooks, 1977.
12. National Computing Centre: "SSADM Version 3 Reference Manual", National Computing Centre, 1986.
13. National Computing Centre: "SSADM Version 4 Reference Manual", NCC Blackwell Ltd, 1990.
14. PA Computers, "Benefits of Software Engineering Methods and Tools", study for the OTI, 1979.
15. Price Waterhouse Consultants Ltd: "Software Quality Standards: The Costs and Benefits", Price Waterhouse Ltd, 1988.
16. de Marco, T.: "Software Quality Standards", Yourdon, 1982.
17. Crosby, P.: "Quality is Free", McGraw-Hill, 1979.
18. Smith, Dr. J. "How To Take Part in The Quality Revolution", PA Management Consultants, 1985.
19. National Computing Centre: "PRINCE: Structured Project Management", Blackwell, 1990.
20. Chambers, A.: "Computer Auditing", Pitman Press, 1985.
21. Ashworth, C. and M. Goodland: "SSADM: A Practical Approach", McGraw-Hill, 1989.
22. Ross, D. and K. Schumann; "Structured Analysis for Requirements Definition", *IEEE Trans. on Software Engineering*, vol. SE–3, 1, 1977.
23. Cotler, P.: "Marketing Management", Prentice Hall International, 1983.

GLOSSARY OF TERMS

3GL	Third-generation language
4GL	Fourth-generation language
ACS	Audit, control and security
AG	Application generator
BAA	Business area analysis
BS	British Standards
BSD	Business system design
BSI	British Standards Institute
BSO	Business systems options
CASE	Computer-aided software engineering
CCB	Change control board
CCTA	Central Computer and Telecommunications Agency
CLDD	Composite logical data design
CP	Change proposal
CSF	Critical success factor
DB	Database
DBA	Database administrator
DBMS	Database management system
DDS	Data dictionary system
DFD	Data flow diagram
DTI	Desktop instructions
EFD	Elementary function description
ELH	Entity life history
EN	European norm
ERA	Entity relational analysis
FD	Functional decomposition
FEP	Front end processor
FPA	Functional point analysis
FS	Feasibility study
FSR	Feasibility study report
HCI	Human–computer interface
H/W	Hardware

IE	Information engineering
I/O	Input/output
IOT	Infrastructure operational trials
ISO	International Standard Organisation
IS	Information system
ISP	Information system planning
JCL	Job control language
JPM	Job procedure manual
LAN	Local area network
LDS	Logical data structure
LPS	Logical process specification
LSDM	Learmonth Structured Design Method
LSS	Logical structured specification
N/W	Network
MIS	Management information systems
MSA	Maintenance strategy agreement
OEM	Original equipment manufacturer
PAL	Project action list
PCO	Project control office
PD	Physical design
PDC	Physical design control
PMS	Performance measure
PMC	Project management checkpoint
PRINCE	Projects in controlled environments
PRL	Problems and requirements list
QA	Quality assurance
QC	Quality control
QMG	Quality management group
QMS	Quality management system
RA	Requirement analysis
RDA	Relational data analysis
RDB	Relational database
RFC	Request for change
RS	Requirement specification
SADT	Structured Analysis and Design Technique
SCL	System control language
SDM	Structured design method
SDS	System design specification
SIS	System implementation specification
SLA	Service level agreement
SMG	System maintenance guide
SPIR	System post-implementation review
SQL	Structured query language
SRS	System requirements specification
SSAD	Structured systems analysis and design
SSADM	Structured Systems Analysis and Design Method
S/W	Software
SWOT	Strength, weaknesses, opportunities, threats
TD	Technical design
TNF	Third normal form
TP	Transaction processing
TQMS	Total quality management system
TSO	Technical systems options
UAT	User acceptance tests
WAN	Wide area network

INDEX